The Last Neanderthal

The Last

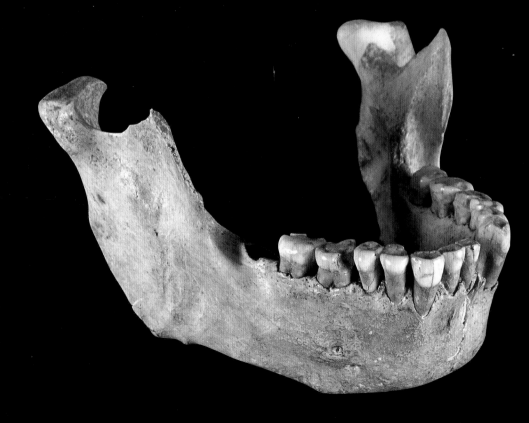

1

The Last Neanderthal?

Lower jaw of a Neanderthal from
Zafarraya, Spain, where
Neanderthals lingered until
27 thousand years ago.
*Courtesy of Celilio Barroso Ruiz and
Fernando Ramirez Rozzi.*

Ian Tattersall

Curator and Chairman
Department of Anthropology
American Museum of Natural History

Neanderthal

The Rise, Success, and Mysterious Extinction of Our Closest Human Relatives

A Peter N. Nevraumont Book

MACMILLAN · USA

for

Gisela and Andrea

Macmillan
A Simon & Schuster Macmillan Company
1633 Broadway
New York, New York 10019

MACMILLAN is a registered trademark of Macmillan, Inc.

Library of Congress Cataloging-in-Publication Data

Tattersall, Ian
      The last Neanderthal : the rise, success, and mysterious
    extinction of our closest human relatives / by Ian Tattersall.
          p. cm.
      "A Peter N. Nevraumont book."
      Includes bibliographical references and index.
      ISBN 0-02-860813-5
      1. Neanderthal man.   I. Title.
    GN285.T37   1995   95-16621
    573.3—dc20   CIP

10 9 8 7 6 5 4 3 2 1

Printed in Hong Kong by Everbest Printing Company
through Four Colour Imports.

This book was created and produced by
Nevraumont Publishing Company
New York, New York
President: Ann J. Perrini

Illustrations: Diana M. Salles, American Museum of Natural History
Book design: José Conde, Studio Pepin, Tokyo, Japan

Contents

Preface

Human beings have always been fascinated by their place in nature. As Malcolm W. Browne of *The New York Times* wrote not long ago, "Conscious that we must have sprung from somewhere, we are lured to the riddle of our origins." Perhaps no extinct species in the entire human fossil record is as germane to the understanding of those origins as is *Homo neanderthalensis*. There is certainly no better way in which we *Homo sapiens* can judge our own uniqueness in the living world than by measuring ourselves against the Neanderthals and their achievements.

Yet in the public mind the Neanderthals remain mired in the quicksands of mythology: bywords for benightedness, and the butt of more cartoons even than the dinosaurs. Pity the poor Neanderthals, for their public image problem is no more than an artifact of history. Neanderthals were the first kind of extinct human to be discovered, and the nineteenth-century savants who labored to explain this strange new discovery had no perspective to help them understand it. In pre-evolutionary times, the choice was stark: if the Neanderthals weren't fully modern humans, they must have been brutes or oddities. So, brutes and oddities they became.

Today we know a lot more about the Neanderthals, and we have a larger perspective for evaluating them. Many scientists now prefer to minimize the differences between us and the Neanderthals, and clearly the dismal public image of Neanderthals demands rehabilitation. But has the pendulum swung too far? The aim of this book is to paint as full a portrait as possible of these capable and fascinating human precursors and of the world they lived in, so that you can decide for yourself if we are justified in construing the Neanderthals in our own image, in the image of the brute—or of neither.

. . .

Any book such as this one necessarily draws on the work of many people, far too numerous to name here, but to all of whom I am grateful. I would particularly like to mention the influence over the years of my American Museum of Natural History colleagues Niles Eldredge, Eric Delson, and John van Couvering—none of whom will necessarily agree with everything I have written here. Thanks are also due to Jaymie Brauer for her help in chasing down bibliographic references, to Stephanie Hiebert for her sensitive copyediting, and to Joanna Grand for preparing the index. The book's elegant design is the work of José Conde. Finally, my appreciation goes to Peter N. Nevraumont and Ann J. Perrini of the Nevraumont Publishing Company, to Natalie P. Chapman of Macmillan Books, and to all of the gifted photographers, artists, and other colleagues, separately acknowledged (though Diana M. Salles deserves special mention), who have contributed the splendid illustrations.

Prologue

■

The Last Neanderthal sat in the lee of the rock shelter wall, watching the sun dip toward the snow-flecked western horizon and absorbing its dying warmth. Behind her, her grandson kindled a fire from embers that had been kept alive ever since her group had reached this place. She was old now, very old— over 40, in fact. The sight of the youngster, less beetle-browed than she but bearing in his heavy face the traces of his grandmother's lineage, drew her thoughts back to those long-ago events that had brought her here. She had been barely 12 when rumors had reached her family of the tall, slender, and odd-looking strangers who had arrived in the next valley—strangers who had effortlessly taken over the landscape, cutting down the reindeer herds on which her cousins' lives had depended. Some of those cousins had come over the mountain to join her group, unwilling to be absorbed into the invaders' unfamiliar society, but it was not long before the strangers themselves had appeared. By guile they had persuaded her family to part with her and her older sister, that they should become wives for two of the low-ranking young men in the group. Those early years had been hard for her, seeing the rest of her family gradually edged out of their home territory toward the sea, and battling an unfamiliar language and strange new lifeways. It had been a long time, too, before she had ceased to be the object of ridicule in her new family for her coarse features, and after her sister died she had felt intensely alone. But her son was an adept learner, and his great strength had lent him prowess as a hunter. As she glimpsed him returning in the gathering dusk with his companions, laden with fresh meat, she suddenly felt that her life had not been without its rewards.

His heart pounding in his chest, the Last Neanderthal collapsed behind a screen of low bushes. As his tortured breathing subsided he was dimly aware that he had lost his pursuers, at least temporarily. When those tall, odd-looking strangers had come over the hills that marked the boundary of his group's range in its isolated Iberian outpost, instinctive fear had spread among its members. They had seen no other humans, even of their own kind, in several months. For reasons they didn't comprehend, their Neanderthal neighbors no longer appeared at the pass through the mountains where the two groups had met and exchanged members since time immemorial. What did these strange new people represent? The Last Neanderthal and his companions were soon to learn. The strangers had immediately spotted the Neanderthals at their campsite below the rock ledge, and the men had spread out and melted into the low, bushy vegetation that dotted the landscape. The Neanderthals sensed danger but could not understand exactly why. The males had gathered their hunting equipment and were huddled together, uncertain what to do. Suddenly they found themselves surrounded by the strangers, who leapt into their midst with fearsome yells, spears jabbing. The surprised Neanderthals responded vigorously but had clearly been outwitted by the agile newcomers. As his companions fell around him, the Last Neanderthal crept away from the fray. A yell told him that he had been spotted, and he sprinted for the nearest cover. After a long chase through country familiar to him but not to his pursuers, the unformed thought came to him that he might be safe. But for how long?

We will never know the exact story of the Last Neanderthal. These two brief scenarios cover the extremes of possibility, and although I am personally convinced that the second is closer to the truth than the first, there's no avoiding the fact that the event in question took place almost 30,000 years ago and is reflected in circumstantial evidence at best. Similarly, the archaeological record, which directly reflects only a narrow range of activities, gives us much less information than we would like to have in answering questions such as how intelligent these close relatives of *Homo sapiens* were, or whether they had language, or how they viewed the world. Nonetheless, as the following pages testify, we do know a great deal about the Neanderthals—enough, certainly, to make them a substantial yardstick by which to judge our own uniqueness.

Who Were the Neanderthals?

1 There is some confusion about the spelling of the word "Neanderthal." Many recent authors prefer the form "Neandertal" because the term derives from the German for "Neander Valley." Although the German word for valley at one time was spelled "Thal," early in the twentieth century a revision of German orthography dropped the "h." By that time, however, the original German spelling had become entrenched in English usage, and for that reason it is retained here.

2 The adjective "human" is extremely ill-defined, having entered the language long before anyone realized that we are connected by ancestry to the rest of the living world. As used here, "human" does not refer to beings possessing precisely those capacities that make modern *Homo sapiens* unique in nature; rather, it is more loosely employed to refer to all primates that share a common ancestry uniquely with us, from *Australopithecus* on. This interpretation makes "human" equivalent to the traditional term "hominid," deriving from the zoological name Hominidae for the family to which we and our fossil relatives belong. Recent usage of "Hominidae" has tended to be more inclusive, embracing certain of the great apes, as well as us and our immediate ancestors. For the sake of simplicity, however, the traditional usage of "Hominidae" is followed here.

NEANDERTHAL.[1] No noun in the entire lexicon of science is more evocative, but apart from vague imputations of primitive brutishness, how many of us can really specify what that term evokes—or should evoke? This book attempts to answer the questions we all have about the Neanderthals: *Who* were they? What *kind* of people were they? What sort of world did they live in, and how did they cope with it? And, of course, what became of them?

Let's start with the easy bit. At one level, who the Neanderthals were is a simple question to answer. When we use the word "Neanderthal" we are referring to a distinct (and now extinct) species of human, *Homo neanderthalensis*, that lived during the later part of the Pleistocene epoch, more familiarly known as the Ice Age. According to the latest dating techniques, this time span was in the range of 200,000 to 30,000 years ago. *Homo neanderthalensis* is closely related to us— indeed, is probably the closest relative we have in the entire known human fossil record—but Neanderthals were not simply a variant of our own species, *Homo sapiens.*

This last point is still disputed by many paleoanthropologists (students of the human[2] fossil record), who prefer to classify the Neanderthals in the subspecies *Homo sapiens neanderthalensis.* Views on this matter are important, for they have strongly affected the interpretation both of the Neanderthals' place in human evolution and of the nature of their extinction. Let me repeat, then, that

in my view and that of a growing number of colleagues, there is no good reason to doubt that the Neanderthals deserve recognition as a species of their own.

How do we know this? By examining morphology—what the fossil remains of Neanderthals look like. This approach, however, immediately raises a problem, for among sexually reproducing organisms, species are best viewed as the largest populations within which individuals can reproduce successfully. Members of such populations recognize each other on criteria such as behavioral signals and external appearance. Details of the skeleton that don't show up externally are irrelevant to the decision of whether it's appropriate to mate. Nonetheless, the unfortunate fact is that morphology of the bones and teeth is all we have to go on in allocating fossils to species, for it's vanishingly rare that anything beyond these "hard tissues" ever preserves in the fossil record.

Neanderthal fossils are highly distinctive in the build of their skeletons, and particularly in the shape of their skulls. If you look at the skeletons of two closely related living primate species (brown and black lemurs, for example), you invariably find that the differences between them are significantly smaller than those distinguishing the typical Neanderthal skeleton from our own. By all established standards of mammalian systematics it is clear that *Homo neanderthalensis* is a distinct species—despite the dead weight of paleoanthropological tradition.

Cro-Magnon

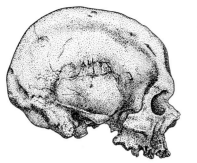 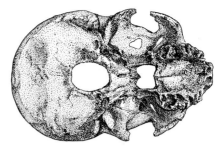 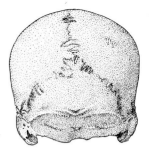

Neanderthal

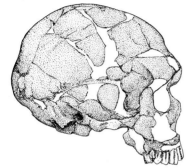 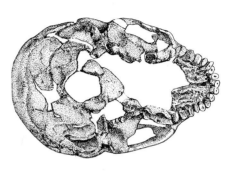 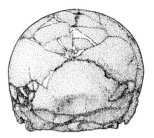

2

Comparison between the crania of a Neanderthal (La Ferrassie 1, France; on bottom) and of an early modern European (Cro-Magnon 1, France).

Side, front and rear views are shown. Note the capacious but long and low braincase of the Neanderthal, and the heavy, arching brow ridges above the squarish eye sockets. (see Plate 59) Compared to the modern human the Neanderthal has a large, "pulled-out," and forwardly-positioned face, with a broad nasal region and swept-back cheekbones. The Neanderthal cranial vault is rounded in rear view; maximum skull breadth is achieved much higher up in the modern human.
Illustration by Diana Salles.

Individuals of the same species naturally vary a little among themselves, so it's not worthwhile to try to demonstrate that two fossil skulls that show only minor differences belong to separate species, even when you think they might. With two forms as consistently distinctive as modern humans and Neanderthals, though, you can be highly confident of just that conclusion.

What Did the Neanderthals Look Like, and Where Did They Live?

The Neanderthals were different from us, but how different? Enough, certainly, that you don't have to resort to subtle aspects of morphology to demonstrate the difference. But there are some very significant similarities between us and them, too. Let's look briefly at a few of these similarities and differences.

One important similarity between the skull construction of Neanderthals and that of modern humans—which has profoundly affected their interpretation—is raw brain size. The volume of the brain is of almost iconic significance to paleoanthropologists, for increase in brain size has

been perhaps the most consistent theme to have characterized the evolution of the human family during its four-million-year-plus documented existence. The "classic" Neanderthals who inhabited Europe toward the end of the Ice Age had brains that were, on average, even larger than ours are today. Classic Neanderthal brains averaged about 1500 ml in volume, while the current worldwide average is less than 1400 ml. Clearly, we cannot discriminate against Neanderthals on brain size. But neither should we be mesmerized by this feature, for, it's only fair to point out, brain size is no criterion for including or excluding this form or that from membership in a particular species. Although *Homo sapiens* and *Homo neanderthalensis* had brains of similar size, so do virtually any other pair of closely related primate species (our black and brown lemurs, already quoted, spring to mind), not to mention some distantly related ones.

On the other hand, the large Neanderthal brain was enclosed in a skull of very different shape from that of our own. [Plates 2 and 3] The fossil cranial vaults that contained Neanderthal brains are

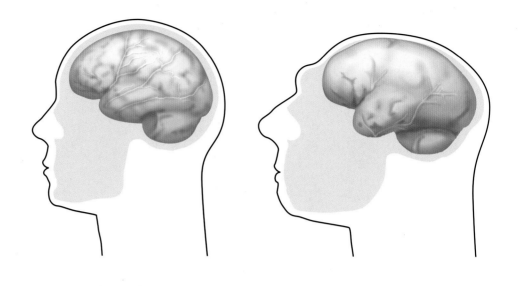

3

Diagram to illustrate the relation of cranial vault to brain shape in a modern human (left) and a Neanderthal.

The skull vault develops passively during growth in response to the enlarging brain inside it. The brain of Neanderthals was as capacious as those of modern people. However, it was longer and lower, and lay somewhat behind as well as above the face. The significance of the difference in brain shape is not well understood.
Illustration by Diana Salles.

long and low, and in rear view they curve inward and upward. This configuration contrasts strikingly with the high, rounded modern human skull, with its arching forehead and bulging sides. At the back of the Neanderthal skull is a characteristic protrusion, often called an "occipital bun," upon which certain neck muscles were anchored into pits (suprainiac fossae), rather than on to the bony projection (the occipital protuberance), sitting at the base of a smoothly rounded occiput, that is typical of our own crania. This specialized skull shape is particularly interesting because the skull vault is developmentally an unusual structure. In this region of the skull the bone is laid down in a soft membrane instead of being preformed in cartilage. The bones of the skull roof are thus carried passively outward by the expanding brain as the individual grows, so the shape of the braincase closely mirrors the form that the brain itself wants to assume. Given that the shape of the skull tells us a lot about the external appearance of the brain (although some thin membranes, and in places blood vessels and reservoirs, intervene between brain and bone), we might hope to learn something from the inside of the skull about the brain itself—as indeed we do. The problem, however, is that knowing the external shape of the brain doesn't tell us much about its internal organization, which is what counts most if we want to know about its capacities as a functioning organ. More about this later. The main point here in

deciding about the species status of the Neanderthals is that large brain size is overshadowed by the difference in braincase shape. And the cranial differences don't stop there.

Unlike that of modern humans, the Neanderthal skull is decorated in front with a pair of large, rounded, bony ridges above the eyes. These brow ridges appear to be linked functionally to the retreating Neanderthal forehead, in association with the peculiar condition of the Neanderthal face. In *Homo sapiens* the face is usually rather small, and it is tucked below the front of the braincase. Among the Neanderthals, on the other hand, the large face is more forwardly situated and projecting. It also appears pulled out in the midline, while the cheekbones are swept back behind a broad nasal aperture. In the absence of a more or less vertical forehead such as we have, this particular facial geometry made it necessary to have a structure—the brow ridges—at the top of the face to absorb the heavy stresses generated in the face during chewing. The powerful jaw musculature that achieved this may also be reflected in other unusual features of the Neanderthal skull, such as the "mastoid tuberosity" found on each side toward the rear of the braincase, at the lower back limit of the temporal muscles that attached to the side of the cranial vault. The posterior temporal muscles would have been of particular importance during use of the front teeth, which were employed extensively by the Neanderthals for purposes other than cutting food.

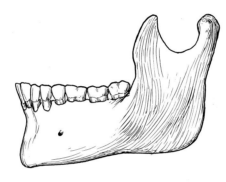

Comparison between a modern human lower jaw (left) and that of a Neanderthal (based on the specimen from Amud, Israel).

The Neanderthal mandible is long and robust, with insignificant development of a chin at the front, and typically has a space between the last tooth and the rising mandibular ramus.
Illustration by Diana Salles.

modern human   *Neanderthal*

There are other differences between the Neanderthal skull and modern human skulls. The lower jaws of the two species, for example, are altogether distinctive. [Plate 4 and see Plates 1, 81, 82, 106, and 114] Most significantly, perhaps, we modern humans possess a forwardly jutting chin at the front of the mandible. Like other extinct humans, Neanderthals generally lacked this structure, which acts as a buttress for the highly stressed front of the rather short modern jaw. In Neanderthals, whose faces project more, the buttress lies behind the front of the jaw. Rarely, a Neanderthal fossil will show some hint of a chin, but such features are expressed weakly at best. Neanderthal lower jaws reflected the prominence of the face in another characteristic way. The whole row of teeth is quite forward in the longer jaw, such that, seen from the side, there is a space between the last tooth in the row (the third molar) and the front of the vertical ramus of the mandible, which

rises up toward the jaw joint. In modern humans a distinct gap is very rare, and in side view the ramus often at least partly obscures the third molar.

On the inside of the ramus there is an additional distinction. In most Neanderthals, in contrast to nearly all other humans, living and extinct, there is a distinct bony prominence next to the hole (the mandibular foramen) that admits the mandibular nerve as it travels downward from the brain. This prominence is related to the attachment of the sphenomandibular ligament from which the lower jaw is suspended and around which it rotates. Again, we see a peculiarity that is presumably associated with the specialized chewing apparatus of the Neanderthals. Less likely to be associated with the face-chewing muscle complex are differences in the base of the skull, which we'll look at in detail later.

Distinctions between Neanderthals and modern humans are not confined to the

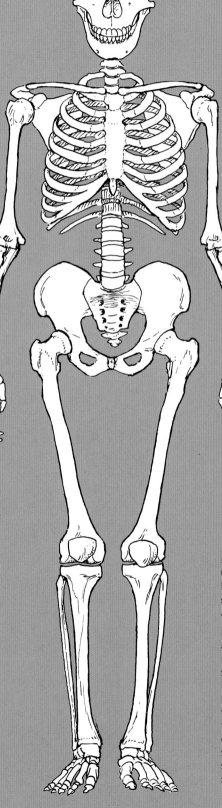

5

Comparison between a Neanderthal (left) and a modern skeleton.

The Neanderthal build was more robust than that of modern people, and generally shorter, with a broad rib cage, long collar bones, and wide shoulder blades. Forearms and lower legs were relatively short, and the limb bones heavily built with thick walls. Joint surfaces were large. In the pelvis the hip joint faced farther outward, and at the front the upper surface of the pubis was long and slender. The hands were especially strongly built, with broad fingertips. *Illustration by Diana Salles.*

Neanderthal

modern human

7

Diagram comparing the Kebara pelvic inlet with that of a modern human.

This view from above superimposes a modern human male pelvic inlet (black) on that of the Kebara pelvis (blue). Dimensions of the inlet are about the same in both, though its positioning is rather diffferent. Note the elongated pubic rami (bottom) in the Kebara specimen.
Illustration courtesy of Yoel Rak.

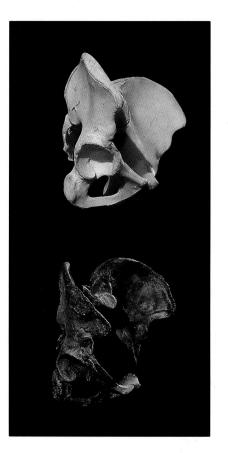

6

View of the Neanderthal pelvis from Kebara, Israel (below), compared to a modern human pelvis.

The Kebara skeleton includes the most complete Neanderthal pelvis known. Among other features it possesses broader iliac blades and longer, thinner superior pubic rami than those of modern people. The hip joint also faces more sideways: a dissimilarity apparently related to a minor difference in locomotion.
Photograph courtesy of Yoel Rak.

skull. There are plenty of differences in the body skeletons, too. [Plate 5] For a start, Neanderthals were a great deal more robustly built than we are. The main joints of the body in Neanderthal fossils are larger than ours tend to be, and the long bones have thick walls, with extensive surfaces for the attachment of well-developed muscles. The great strength of the arms is reflected in the shape of the shoulder blades, which had broad areas of attachment for powerful muscles running from the upper arm. Differences of this kind show up even in young children, arguing against the notion that the great muscular development of the Neanderthals was acquired as the result of a particularly strenuous lifestyle.

Especially interesting is the shape of the Neanderthal pelvis, recently analyzed by Tel Aviv University's Yoel Rak on the basis of a skeleton discovered at the Israeli site of Kebara. The pelvis of the Kebara individual, the first complete Neanderthal pelvis to be discovered, has in common with less well preserved Neanderthal specimens a morphology of its front upper part that is quite distinct from that of modern humans. [Plates 6 and 7] The structure, known as the superior pubic ramus, is elongated and slender with a distinctive cross section. It lies far forward; in a female it would have carried the birth canal forward with it. Such features had previously been speculated to be adaptations permitting the passage of a large-headed baby—even, possibly, after an extended gestation period. The Kebara specimen, though, like other less complete fossils that also show this condition, is male. Rak thus concluded that the peculiarities of the Neanderthal pelvis resulted from a difference in gait between *Homo neanderthalensis* and *Homo sapiens*, a conclusion reinforced by the fact that the hip socket faces more sideways in Neanderthals than it does in modern humans. I hasten to add, though, that the Neanderthals were fully adapted upright walkers, and that if you saw one walking along, you probably would not notice much difference from the way we move.

As distinctive as the Neanderthal pelvis are the body proportions of *Homo neanderthalensis*. Neanderthals tended to be quite short: in life, males from European sites probably averaged about five feet six inches in height, and females about five feet three inches. Neanderthals had relatively long thighs and upper arms, and the Kebara skeleton shows that their large, barrel-chested trunks were long and their legs short compared to those of modern humans.

This litany of the ways in which Neanderthal and modern skeletons differ is far from exhaustive, but it's sufficient to make the point that *Homo neanderthalensis* differs from *Homo sapiens* in more than enough features for us to conclude that they are separate species. I certainly cannot think of a pair of populations of living primates that differ to an equivalent degree in their skeletal structure and are not classified in separate species. As I've emphasized, species are a tricky thing to

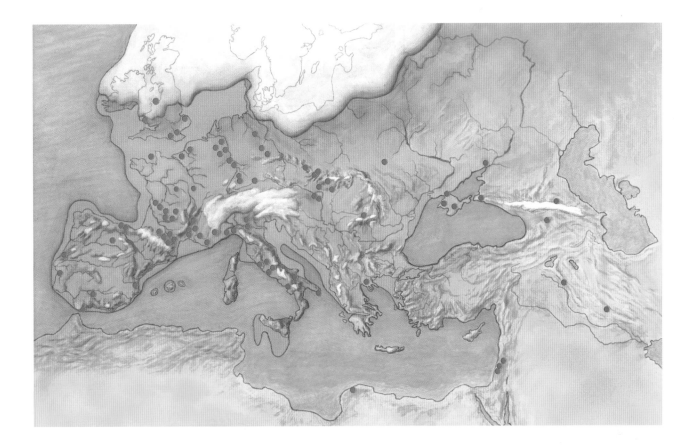

13

Map of Europe and western Asia, showing the most important sites from which Neanderthal remains have been recovered.

Ice cover and shorelines are shown as they were at the height of the last glacial period. Current shorelines are also indicated.
Illustration by Diana Salles.

8–12

Stages in the reconstruction of a Neanderthal face.

Based on the Shanidar 1 skull (see Plate 76), we see here the process by which deep and superficial layers of muscle are added sequentially to a skull reconstruction, with the final addition of the outer layers and external features. Such details as hair color, texture and distribution, form of ears and lips, and skin and eye colors, are of course conjectural.
Reconstructions by Vito Cannella and G. J. Sawyer; photographs by Vito Cannella.

define on the basis of skeletal morphology, but when two primates differ from each other as much as Neanderthals and modern humans do, you can conclude with confidence that they are not conspecific.

Of course, the fact that Neanderthals did not look exactly like us and do not belong to our species does not imply that they were by any means the sluggards of popular mythology. [Plates 8, 9, 10, 11, and 12] Quite the contrary. What the differences between us and them do mean, however, is that we cannot claim that the Neanderthals were simply a variation – by implication an inferior variation – of ourselves. The big-brained Neanderthals were highly successful, dominating Europe and western Asia for 150,000 years – or maybe considerably more – during a period of extremely tough climatic conditions. As far as we can tell, that's a good deal longer than our own species has been around. The Neanderthals coped, and coped well, in circumstances that would tax the ingenuity of any human species. We'll see how.

Meanwhile, to round out our introduc-

tory Neanderthal portrait, I must emphasize that Neanderthals were not a worldwide phenomenon, as we are today. Humans of one kind or another were widespread in the Old World during the Neanderthals' time, although they had not yet reached the Americas. The distinctive Neanderthal species, however, occupied only a part of this vast human range. [Plate 13] Sites at which Neanderthal fossils have been found are distributed – for the most part quite sparsely, except in western France – from the Atlantic in the west to Uzbekistan in the east, and from Wales in the north to Gibraltar and the Levant in the south. There is no biological evidence at present that they ever entered Africa or Arabia, or occupied any part of central or eastern Asia. As we will see in the next chapter, this relatively local distribution fits in well with what we know about how new species arise and spread. Keep in mind, though, that the Neanderthals form only part – albeit the best-documented part – of the human evolutionary picture during what was evidently a highly eventful period ∎

How Evolution Works

THE Neanderthals belong to a rather recent phase of a long human evolutionary history. In Chapter 4 we'll go back to the beginning and summarize that four-million-year-long story in order to understand the background from which the Neanderthals emerged. But first let's look at the evolutionary process itself, because knowing how evolution takes place and how our current comprehension of this process developed is essential to understanding many of the controversies that still surround the study of the Neanderthals. And it's also essential to understand that, however "special" we modern humans may think we are, we are not the result of a special process. Our species evolved through the same mechanisms that gave rise to all others.

 ### The Early Days
It's quite possible to argue that the elements of evolutionary thought were already in the air by the time Charles Darwin and his compatriot Alfred Russel Wallace had their historic presentations read to the Linnaean Society of London in 1858 and really started the evolutionary ball rolling. It was the particular genius of these two men, however, to see that there was only one rational explanation for the way in which the vast diversity of nature is organized, and to articulate a convincing mechanism by which this order had come about. The essence of that organization is that species cluster together into a series of steadily more inclusive groups, something that

had been acknowledged long before the mid-nineteenth century. We, for instance, belong to a group (the superfamily Hominoidea) that also includes the apes; hominoids all belong to a bigger group (the suborder Anthropoidea) that also includes the monkeys; all anthropoids belong to a larger group (the order Primates) that also includes the lemurs; primates belong to the larger group of mammals; and on and on until we reach a giant cluster that embraces all living things. [Plate 14] The process by which this regular ordering of nature has come about is evolution, succinctly defined by Darwin as "descent with modification." All the many millions of living species are descended from a single ancient common ancestor, via an immense array of intermediate ancestors. For example, we share an ancestor with the other hominoids that existed more recently than did our joint ancestor with monkeys, and so forth. To give rise to this diversity, physical—evolutionary—change occurred in the ancestral lineages. The driving force of this evolutionary change Darwin called "natural selection": essentially a process of natural winnowing from one generation to the next.

Darwin knew that no two individuals of any species are identical. He was also aware, as animal breeders had been since time immemorial, that variations among members of the same species are often inherited: offspring tend to resemble their parents. The fact that he didn't know how inheritance worked didn't matter; the basic realization was enough. Darwin

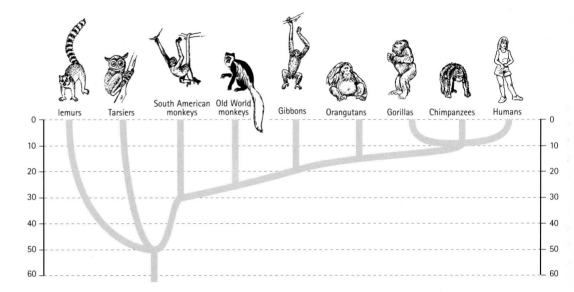

14
Diagram showing the evolutionary relationships of the major groups of modern primates.

The main uncertainty in this scheme is the place of the tarsier, grouped by some with the lemurs and lorises and by others with the monkeys and apes.
Illustration by Diana Salles; reproduced from The Human Odyssey *by Ian Tattersall (Prentice Hall, 1993).*

then paired this observation with another: in each generation of every species more offspring are produced than can possibly survive to produce the next generation. [Plates 15 and 16] After all, if every individual reproduced with equal success, the world would in short order contain standing room only. In his Linnaean Society paper, Wallace calculated that, even using conservative assumptions on rates of reproduction, a single pair of birds could potentially produce as many as 10 million descendants in a mere fifteen years. With typical caution, Darwin chose elephants—some of the slowest reproducers on the globe—to illustrate the same point. He figured that, starting with a single pair of elephants, and assuming one birth only every ten years over a sixty-year reproductive span, after only 750 years the

pair would have 19 million descendants. Yet the world is not overrun with birds or elephants, for, other things being equal, the populations of living things tend to remain relatively stable because excess individuals are weeded out of the reproductive pool by natural forces such as early death or lowered reproductive success of fertility.

Darwin's and Wallace's critical observations were that if some inherited variations enhance their possessors' survivability and reproductive success in any given environment while others decrease it, the more favorable of these characteristics will become more common with time in each species while those less favorable will tend to disappear. As the generations roll by, then, physical change will accumulate within species purely as a

result of differential reproductive success—which is really all that natural selection is. Because reproductive success is closely related to how well individual organisms make their living within their environments, with time natural selection tends to promote efficient adaptation of populations to those environments.

Working as he did in staunchly Christian Victorian England, Darwin was faced not simply with the task of providing a convincing mechanism for evolution. To establish his notion of evolutionary change, he also needed to demolish the prevailing idea, founded in religious dogma, of the unchangeability of species. Species are the basic *kinds* of organisms. Although we look upon them today as reproductive units—the largest populations within which successful interbreeding is possible—in Darwin's day they were viewed more or less as idealized types to which the individual organisms composing them had to conform, however imperfectly. Species had been placed on Earth by the Creator pretty much as they were, and that's how they were expected to

stay. Darwin had to concede, of course, that species had some type of reality in space—though he was keenly aware of the practical difficulties frequently encountered in defining them. The idea of natural selection, however, cleverly enabled Darwin to attack the notion of immutability by denying species reality in *time*. Through gradual generation-to-generation adaptive change, species became not discrete entities, but rather segments of steadily changing lineages: over time, they simply evolved themselves out of existence as changes accumulated within them.

Darwin called his great book *On the Origin of Species*, but he was pretty successful in avoiding the question implicit in his title. New species had to originate in the splitting of lineages, but Darwin concentrated his own attention—and that of other naturalists—on physical transformation *within* lineages. In this shuffle the rather basic matter of the origins of natural diversity tended to get lost, a lapse for which—in my view—paleoanthropology is still paying a hefty price a century and a half later. Yet technical problems with the classic Darwinian view did not go unnoticed, even at the time. Thus, only a year after the *Origin* appeared, Darwin's friend and defender Thomas Henry Huxley expressed strong reservations about the idea that natural selection could by itself produce new species, because he didn't know of a single case in which its analogue, artificial selection by animal breeders within an existing species, had produced "another group which was, even in the slightest degree, infertile with the first." This observation was the first substantive indication that the classic Darwinian formulation of the evolutionary process might be incomplete, but more than a century was to pass before its implications were fully understood.

 ### The Evolutionary Synthesis
The Darwin/Wallace discovery of natural selection and the associated notion of adaptation represented an extraordinary achievement, providing an elegantly simple explanation for what was at first glance a mind-bogglingly complex organization of nature. A fuller understanding of the mechanisms of evolution, however, had to await the elaboration of the principles of inheritance that took place largely in the first few decades of the twentieth century. The inheritance of physical traits, it turned out, does not consist of a "blending" of the characteristics of the parents, as had widely been believed. Instead, traits are transmitted to offspring by discrete entities—genes—which are passed along intact from generation to generation, even though they might not always find expression in the anatomy of their possessor. The genes remain intact, that is, except when mutations—essentially copying errors—spontaneously occur, giving natural selection new genetic variants to act upon. Further, because in sexually reproducing organisms each individual receives half of his or her genes from each parent, and many traits are controlled by numerous genes, the genetic reshuffling that takes place between generations provides an additional source of new variations for selection to promote or to eliminate.

Once the basic rules of inheritance had been formulated, the way was open for biologists of all kinds to explore how what was becoming known about genes fit in with the phenomena of physical evolution. As you might expect, the early years of this process were a time of great dissension—even confusion. All concerned were feeling their way in a new area of scientific investigation, and scientists' intuitions led in a lot of different directions. Some geneticists thought, for instance, that mutation pressure might push evolutionary change along by an inevitable accumulation of minor changes in genes. Others opted for the origin of new species in quantum leaps, taking their cue from the observation that "sports" (individuals exhibiting sudden deviations from the norm) occasionally crop up within species. Remarkably, natural selection was largely disregarded in the resulting many-sided debate. It took several decades for general agreement to be reached, and for natural selection to be seriously reincorporated into the discussion. But following the formulation of modern population genetics by R. A. Fisher and J. B. S. Haldane in England and Sewall Wright in America, after the mid-1930s, a consensus rapidly emerged to which—at least in the English-speaking world—almost all biologists found themselves able to subscribe. Relief at the final prospect of general agreement presumably accounts for why the new view caught on so quickly.

Grandly termed the "Evolutionary Synthesis," this exquisitely straightforward new model of the evolutionary process combined the notion of natural selection with shifts in gene frequencies within populations, thereby satisfying both the naturalists (who were the ones concerned with the diversity of living nature, and who were by now mostly calling themselves "systematists") and the geneticists. One of the most compelling images in tying these two themes together was proposed by the geneticist Sewall Wright, who came up with the metaphor of the "adaptive landscape": Each individual in any population possesses a unique combination of genes (genotype), and some of these combinations produce individuals more fit than others to survive and reproduce in a given environment. Wright constructed the equivalent of a topographic map in which the contour lines connected points not of equal elevation but of equal fitness (ability to survive and reproduce). On the hilltops were found the fitter genotypes, while those less fit occupied the valleys. As Wright saw it, the problem faced by each species was to maximize the number of individuals on the hilltops and to reduce as much as possible the number of those in the valleys, a result that should inevitably emerge from the operation of natural selection. (Wright realized, however, that chance factors, which he termed "genetic drift," might also affect the distribution of genotypes.)

Wright's metaphor, which neatly linked natural selection with the distributions of genotypes, proved extremely influential. Several important evolutionary thinkers picked it up and elaborated it in various ways, notably to explain how natural selection could, over the long haul, produce not just change in lineages but the discontinuities in which nature abounds. Among complex organisms, each species, as Darwin had had to admit, is a separate genetic package, unable to exchange genes with any others, no matter how closely related. The peaks in Wright's landscape came to be seen as ecological niches, to which the species occupying them were well adapted. Species would cling to these peaks, avoiding the hostile territory of the valleys. The landscape itself was not, however, static; in the words of the paleontologist George Gaylord Simpson, it was "more like a choppy sea." Natural selection had to work constantly to keep species balanced on peaks that shifted beneath them as environments changed; sometimes a peak would split in two, carrying different populations of the same species in different directions. With selection for different conditions operating on each new peak, the emergence of new species seemed inevitable.

In this way the architects of the Evolutionary Synthesis managed to reduce all the many levels of evolutionary change (modifications within species, the splitting of species, and the formation of larger groups) to the action of a single simple mechanism. Evolution was seen as a gradual and continuous process, unfolding over huge periods of time and consisting essentially of the accumulation within lineages of organisms of multiple tiny genetic mutations (and, in the case of sexually reproducing forms, recombinations). Given enough time, the accumulation of such small effects produces large evolutionary changes. These changes take place under the guiding hand of natural selection, as environmental factors promote certain variants and prune others. Finally (and perhaps most critically), this process of gradual accumulation of small genetic changes is also responsible for the origins of biotic diversity, as lineages diverge under environmental influence.

Even the paleontologists, who studied the fossil record and who were thus the guardians of the archive of evolutionary change, fell rapidly under the spell of the Synthesis. There were few holdouts after

Simpson, one of the leading vertebrate paleontologists of the day, argued brilliantly for the Synthesis in his book *Tempo and Mode in Evolution,* published in 1944, and in later works. Yet the Synthesis actually relegated paleontologists to a back seat in the development of evolutionary theory. Under its dictates the geneticists and to a lesser degree the systematists held the keys to the mechanisms of the evolutionary process; all that was left to the paleontologists was the essentially clerical business of documenting that life had indeed evolved as predicted by theory.

Students of the human fossil record were as bewitched as any other paleontologists by the magic of the Synthesis. As bystanders in the debate over evolutionary mechanisms they were probably even more deeply affected by the Synthesis once its ideas had sunk in. Certainly, they were more than ready to listen when two of the most prominent authors of the Synthesis, the geneticist Theodosius Dobzhansky and the systematist Ernst Mayr, saw fit to share the benefits of their insights with them. The Synthesis had developed largely out of what Mayr called "population thinking": the realization that species consist not of individuals that conform to a greater or lesser extent to a basic archetype, but rather of clusters of unique individuals and populations. There exists no ideal "type" against which any individual can be measured. Most species, indeed, are composed of distinctive but variable populations that are bound together not by what they look like but by the reproductive continuity among them. Dobzhansky used this observation in 1944 to propose that Peking Man and Java Man (extinct humans far more remotely related to us than the Neanderthals are) fell within the range of variation of *Homo sapiens.* Half a dozen years later Mayr, for his part, argued that the australopithecines (even more remotely related to us) deserved inclusion in our own genus, *Homo.*

The advent of population thinking was a salutary development, and one that still stands as the foundation of evolutionary thought today. In retrospect, however, Dobzhansky's and Mayr's proposals about the human fossil record are only two examples, among an infinite number in all walks of life, of a seemingly ubiquitous aspect of human behavior: the urge to caricature any good idea by taking it to its most ludicrous extreme. Nonetheless, to paleoanthropologists of the time, burdened by then with a different genus or species name for almost every fossil in the human evolutionary record, these notions came as a breath of fresh air—with the result that they were enthusiastically embraced.

We'll continue this discussion in Chapter 5. For now suffice it to note that paleoanthropology fell as completely under the sway of the Synthesis as did all other fields of evolutionary study. So mesmerizing was the elegance of the Synthesis to evolutionary biologists of all stripes that it took several decades for the realization to sink in that the simplicities of the Synthesis, seductive as they were, painted an incomplete picture of the complexities of the evolutionary process. In hindsight it's not surprising that the first murmurings of dissent emerged from paleontology, the very field which the Synthesis had made the intellectual Cinderella of evolutionary theory.

 Species and Punctuated Equilibria
Not all paleontologists had bought into the Synthesis, and many had been vaguely aware for years that species tend to come and go rather abruptly in the fossil record, rather than changing steadily over the eons. Nonetheless, ever since Darwin's time those who studied fossils had been in the habit of ascribing this pattern to the legendary incompleteness of that record: the expected intermediates between them simply hadn't been found. Well, of course, the fossil record *is* incomplete and always will be. Only the tiniest fraction of all the individuals that have ever lived have been preserved to be found and studied by paleontologists. To give us a reliable idea of the patterns of evolution, however, the record doesn't have to be anywhere near complete in a literal sense. The fact of the matter is that the record isn't all that bad.

Realizing this, in 1972 two young invertebrate paleontologists, Niles Eldredge and Stephen Jay Gould, suggested that we should look at morphological gaps in the fossil record as reflections of

17

Two views of how evolution occurs.

On the left is represented "phyletic gradualism", whereby species gradually transform over time into other species. In contrast, the notion of "punctuated equilibria" (right) sees change as episodic, species being essentially stable entities which give rise to new species in relatively short-term events.
Illustration by Diana Salles; after Ian Tattersall, The Human Odyssey *(Prentice Hall,* 1993*).*

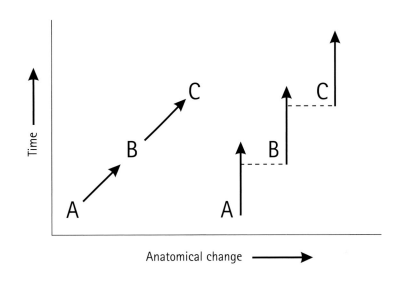

real phenomena, rather than simply as artifacts of incompleteness. To replace (or at least to supplement) the traditional view, to which they gave the name "phyletic gradualism," they proposed an alternative model of the evolutionary process, which they dubbed "punctuated equilibria." [Plate 17] To make a long story short, Eldredge and Gould pointed out that a striking pattern of species stability existed among the fossil animals they studied—trilobites (ancient sea-bottom-dwelling invertebrates) and Bermudan land snails, respectively. The fairly good fossil records available to them didn't show the expected pattern of gradual change over long periods of time. Instead, distinctive species appeared suddenly and then lingered more or less unchanged for a good period of time (several million years in the case of

the trilobites). Eventually, these species exited from the record as abruptly as they had arrived, to be replaced by closely related species. As I will discuss shortly, new species appear to originate most often in isolated populations of existing species, with geographically limited distributions. Rarely have they emerged in the places where their fossil records happen to be preserved. The pattern of abrupt appearance and replacement, moreover, appeared to apply widely in paleontology as a whole; expectations of gradual change simply were not borne out by general paleontological experience and could not continue to be justified by the "woeful" incompleteness of the fossil record. In this way Thomas Henry Huxley's doubts of more than a century earlier were finally and fully confirmed.

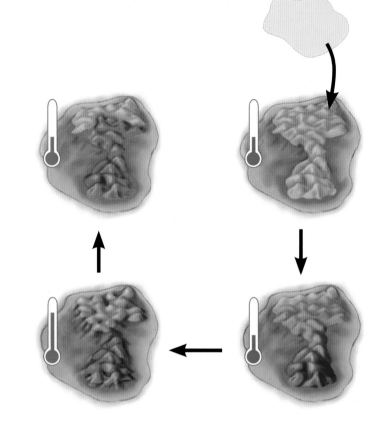

18

Stages in a hypothetical event of allopatric speciation.

Reading from top right: a species invades a new region (in this case, an island). It quickly colonizes all cool mountainous areas, avoiding the warmer lowlands. When the climate warms the population becomes divided geographically, as cool habitat is restricted to the highest mountain tops. Each reduced population follows its own adaptive path, and in one or both genetic change also occurs that disrupts reproductive continuity. When the climate cools again and the populations expand and are reunited, they do not interbreed. Instead, they find themselves in competition, and one begins to displace the other.
Illustration by Diana Salles.

Species thus turned out to be bounded entities in time as well as in space, with origins, life spans, and extinctions. And the greater part of most species' existence was characterized by nonchange, a phenomenon that Eldredge and Gould termed "stasis." This realization raised a problem as thorny as it was familiar: if species were not simply a passive consequence of gradually accumulating adaptive change, as the classic Darwinian view supposed, how *did* they originate? To explain the origin of species, Eldredge and Gould turned to a notion that had actually been most fully developed by the arch-Synthesist Ernst Mayr. As a systematist, Mayr was acutely aware of the discontinuities in nature—the discreteness of species—and he was deeply concerned by the question of their origin. In this quest he invoked what is known as the allopatric model of speciation, which depends on the fact that all widespread species exist as series of local populations. [Plate 18] Often these populations show some degree of physical differentiation from each other, the result of chance factors or

of local adaptation under natural selection. Such populations are often distinguished as "subspecies," with their own formal names. Subspecies names are formed by adding a third italicized name to the two names (genus and species) that identify an organism to the level of species. Thus, to those who believe that Neanderthals are simply a variant of our own species, the appropriate name is *Homo sapiens neanderthalensis*.

However much they might differ in external appearance, local populations of the same species are able to interbreed where their ranges come into contact. Where such populations are geographically separated, however—that is, where they are allopatric—genetic differences may occur that lead to reproductive isolation between them. If such reproductive isolation arises, two species will exist where only one existed before. It is important to understand that the sort of genetic reshuffling that produces reproductive isolation is not necessarily—or even at all—the same kind of genetic change that accompanies physical differentiation.

Nevertheless, the two may occur in tandem or in sequence and normally there is some type of physical differentiation between the two populations when speciation intervenes. The critical test comes, however, when the two species find themselves in contact once more. If they avoid mating with each other, the case is clearcut. But if they have not acquired behavioral or other mechanisms that discourage them from mating, their separate status will become evident only from failure to produce offspring, or from lowered fertility and/or viability in those that are produced. When physical contact has not been reestablished, there is obviously plenty of room for debate about whether the two populations really represent two separate species.

Under the Synthesis this process of speciation was seen as a more or less passive result of adaptive differentiation to different habitats, requiring an indeterminate amount of time. But Eldredge and Gould pointed out that in geological terms, speciation is a short-term event, taking at most tens of thousands of years, in contrast to the hundreds of thousands or millions of years that species tend to endure in the fossil record. What's more, as already noted, the types of genetic change involved in speciation—the establishment of reproductive isolation—are not necessarily those that apply in the accumulation of gradual adaptive change. It's easy to appreciate this when you consider that some closely related species are often

difficult to tell apart by eye (especially in the skeletal parts that are preserved in fossils), while other species accumulate a lot of morphological differentiation without speciating—precisely what Huxley was complaining about all those years ago. The paleontologist Otto Schindewolf later raised this difficulty, too, but was unable to integrate his observation into a convincing general view of the evolutionary process.

Even today, speciation is truly the "black box" of biology. Especially because gradual shifts in gene frequencies and the accumulation of mutations under natural selection are conducive to mathematical modeling and manipulation in genetic experiments, we now know quite a lot about how adaptive changes may occur within species. But we have not yet fully penetrated the spectrum of genetic events that give rise to speciation, although it is clear that many different processes may be involved in the establishment of reproductive isolation. These processes may range from tiny changes in the DNA molecule that controls heredity, through changes in the chromosomes (the structures in the cell's nucleus into which DNA is packaged), all the way up to major processes of individual development and behavior patterns, including interindividual signaling. Whatever speciation consists of in any specific case, however, we know that it is a short-term event in geological terms. We also know that speciation is very likely to be random with respect to adaptation.

All this, of course, is very different from what the classical Darwinian view suggests. In the early days of the theory of punctuated equilibria, when biologists were just coming to terms with this new perspective, Eldredge and Gould were often accused of being against the notions of adaptation and selection. Such accusations were profoundly unjustified; the question was and is a matter of the level at which natural selection and adaptation take place. Instead of acting across species as wholes, these processes function at the level of the local population. As we've seen, every widespread species straddles a range of more or less different environments, and the economic business of survival and reproduction is affected by local conditions. It is through each population's response to those locale-specific circumstances that many genetic novelties become fixed in local populations, and as geneticists have long known, this process is facilitated by small population size.

There is an important corollary of allopatric speciation viewed in this way. Since new species originate within old ones, and speciation itself may not result in much, if any, visible change, new species cannot look very different from their parent species. This similarity in appearance often makes species difficult to distinguish by eye, both in the living world and especially in the fossil record, where there is a much more limited range of evidence. Thus, differences between the closely related species that come and go

in the fossil record can be hard to detect, which in turn makes it easy to mistake the turnover of species for gradual change. Another complication is that competition between new species and their parents or other close relatives undoubtedly produces trends, such as increasing brain size among humans, for instance, or reduction in the number or size of toes in the feet of horses. Such trends can also be mistaken for gradual, stately change.

The notion of slow, directional change, taking place over the eons as lineages improve their adaptation to existing environments or adapt to gradually changing ones, flies in the face of what we know about the stability of environments over time. Through the geological ages, environments do not remain stable or change slowly. Climates and habitats tend to fluctuate in short-term episodes, and in a changing environment there are easier alternatives than changing adaptations. For example, you can move to a more congenial habitat, or, in the worst case, become extinct. At the same time, climatic change produces precisely those conditions that promote speciation (when habitats fragment) and extinction (when habitats recoalesce, and species that were formerly separate come into contact again and find themselves in competition with each other). In the second case, species are winnowed by competition in much the same way that individuals are sorted by natural selection, thereby producing the trends mentioned above, which are often regarded as one of the great proofs of the classical Darwinian view of evolution.

Of course, species are not static between episodes of speciation. Over their lifetimes, as we've seen, species differentiate geographically, which at least sets the stage for potential morphological differences between descendant species. But, I'll repeat, species are unlikely to respond directionally to a consistent set of selective pressures unless their environments remain static, and stasis of habitats certainly has not applied to human populations over the past couple of million years or more. In addition, each new species encounters new environments as it spreads. It is in this light that we can best understand the evolutionary setting in which the Neanderthals emerged.

The period during which these humans lived—the late Ice Age—was a time of extreme environmental and geographic fluctuation, not least in the Neanderthals' Eurasian homeland. During this span sea levels rose and fell as ice sheets grew and melted, cutting off islands from the continents and rejoining them. Vegetation zones moved south and north, down mountain massifs and up. The ice sheets themselves expanded and contracted over the landscapes, cutting humans off from previously inhabited areas and reducing corridors between diminished inhabitable ones—then reuniting them again. Because these are precisely the conditions most likely to produce speciation and competition between new species, it is highly

likely, even just in principle, that the human evolutionary record during this period was a lot more complicated than received paleontological wisdom, based on classical Darwinian precepts, would have it. This conclusion is reinforced by the fact that over time we see major morphological changes in the human fossil record, whereas morphological differences between very closely related species tend to be rather small. This fact suggests that more speciations took place in human evolutionary history than we have customarily supposed, and that we should expect to find evidence for a great variety of extinct human species in the fossil record. It may, indeed, turn out to be that *Homo neanderthalensis* was simply one—albeit the best-known—of a whole group of closely related species that arose in Europe and western Asia over the course of the late Ice Age. Traditionally, however, our expectation has been quite the reverse.

Thus we return to the point I made at the beginning of this chapter. This brief review of the history of evolutionary thought doesn't merely set the stage for the view of the Neanderthals that I personally espouse, for knowing how ideas of the evolutionary process have evolved is the key to understanding how the Neanderthals have been—and continue to be—interpreted by paleoanthropolgists generally. This holds equally true for interpretation of the rest of the human fossil record, which we'll look at in Chapter 4■

3

Fossils, Dates, and Tools

THE Neanderthals survive in the form of fossils, an intrinsic part of the geological record that preserves, if in an irregular fashion, the history of Earth and life. In a very real sense fossils are the facts of the history of life. And like any history, the fossil record needs to be calibrated so that at the very least we know in what order events occurred, even if we can't specify their exact dates. So before we set the background to understanding the Neanderthals by briefly recounting what preceded them, let's pause for a moment to look at what fossils are, and at how they are dated.

What Are Fossils?

Technically, a fossil may be any evidence of past life. Ancient footprints, for example, are fossils. But the vast majority of vertebrate fossils consist of the hard remains of dead animals—for all intents and purposes, bones and teeth. These are the body parts that best resist wear and tear on Earth's surface after their possessor dies. Such wear and tear results from a multitude of factors, for when an animal dies its carcass is prey to many kinds of destructive forces. Many animals, for instance, are killed by predators that consume the muscles, intestines, and other soft parts of their victims and that may crunch the bones, too; if they don't, a scavenger likely will. Scavengers, of course, also attend to animals that die spontaneously, unless the death occurs in a particularly sheltered spot. Thus, even before wind and water do their destructive work, the unconsumed bones of dead animals are usually damaged and scattered across the landscape. Hence, if they are to be preserved at all, they must quite rapidly be covered by protective sediments, for instance in marshes or at the edges of lakes or rivers. If the sediments are right (not too acidic, for example) and continue to build up, the bones will be incorporated into the accumulating rock record, and their constituents will eventually be replaced by infiltrating minerals—the process of fossilization.

Most fossils will stay buried, never again to see the light of day. And those that eventually come under scientific scrutiny are a fraction of the fossils that are exposed again at Earth's surface by the erosion of the enclosing rocks. Only a fraction are found, because fossils become subject to erosion themselves as they appear at the surface, and they must be discovered and collected by someone who recognizes their significance in the short time before they are entirely destroyed. Given the vagaries that bones experience during this long, complex process, it is not surprising that complete skeletons are very rare, that even individual bones are seldom preserved in their entirety, and that the most commonly found mammal fossils consist of isolated teeth (dental enamel is the toughest substance in the body) or of pieces of jaw with only a few teeth present. [Plate 19]

At least in its later stages, the human fossil record is unusual because human remains are not infrequently found in

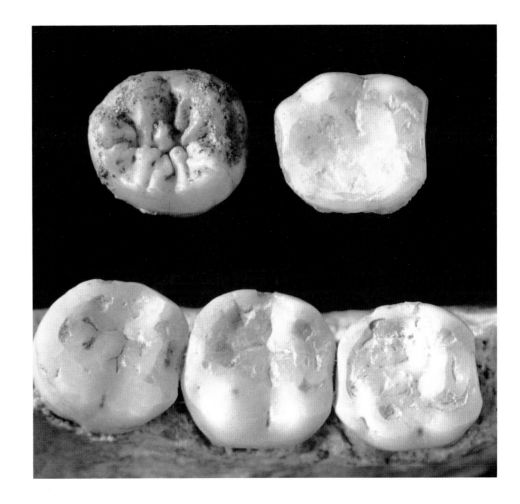

19
Neanderthal lower molar teeth, from the Grotta Breuil (top) and the Grotta Guattari (bottom), Monte Circeo, Italy.

Teeth are important to paleontologists because they are durable and fossilize well. Neanderthal molar teeth are not notably diagnostic, although their crowns are large compared to the modern average and they more commonly have unseparated roots and enlarged pulp cavities. Like other late Neanderthal teeth from southern Europe (the Breuil fossils may be less than 40 thousand years old), these are relatively small.

Courtesy of Giorgio Manzi, Museo di Antropologia "G. Sergi" (Dipartimento di Biologia Animale e dell'Uomo), University of Rome "LaSapienza".

cave settings that are somewhat sheltered from the elements. In some places bones, including those of humans, were accumulated by scavengers or carnivores; at other sites the shelter from the elements offered by cave mouths or rock overhangs made these places attractive for human habitation over the longer or shorter term. In these sheltered places the preservation of relatively complete skeletons, though far from ensured, is more probable than in open-air sites, and it becomes more probable yet when deliberate burial—occasionally practiced by the Neanderthals—is involved.

 Relative Dating
Fossils are found in sedimentary rocks, rocks composed of compacted particles weathered from other rocks. Because sediments build upward with time, fossils found low in any given sediment pile are older than those found higher up. In principle, this relative positioning provides a means of ordering fossils by age—a procedure known as "relative dating" because it doesn't allow you to assign an age in years, but merely to say which fossils are older or younger than which others. Determining even the relative age of a fossil is rarely that

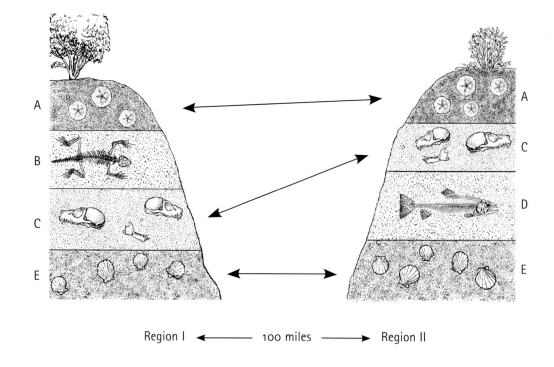

20
How biostratigraphic dating works.

Sedimentary rocks build upward with time, but the record is seldom complete in any one place. This diagram shows how the fossils contained in such rocks can allow incomplete sequences from different areas to be integrated into a more comprehensive scheme.
Illustration by Diana Salles.

A

B

C

E

A

C

D

E

Region I ⟵ 100 miles ⟶ Region II

simple, however, because sedimentary sequences are normally quite local, and the fossils of interest may occur in a variety of places. Thus, where it is impossible to trace physical connections between one rock sequence and another, some indirect means of correlating them is needed. Traditionally, this indirect correlation between sediments has come from comparing the fossil faunas they contain, because the distributions of individual species are generally much wider than those of rocks belonging to any given local sequence. [Plate 20] Even though individual species may have long life spans, if two geographically separated rock layers contain a reasonable proportion of species in common, they can be reckoned to be about the same age. At the same time, the succession of faunas in local geological sequences can tell you in which order they lived. Although

putting all this information together is a rather rough-and-ready process, it is the basis on which the general framework of world geological history was impressively built up, and such "biostratigraphic" dating has held an occasional surprise for practitioners of more "modern" dating techniques.

 Chronometric Dating
The ability to determine ages in years for fossils dates only from the middle of the twentieth century. The first such "chronometric" method was the radiocarbon technique, which became available in the early 1950s. This approach is based on the fact that every living organism contains a constant proportion of radioactive (unstable) carbon to stable carbon. The radioactive carbon "decays" at a constant rate to the stable state, but it is continually renewed as

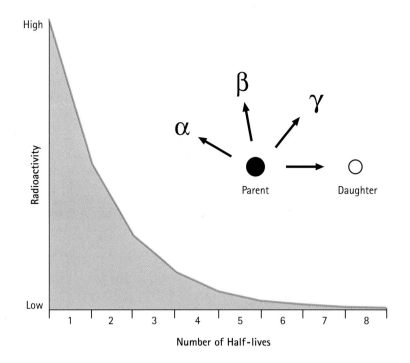

21
Radioactive decay.

Radioactive isotopes (unstable forms of elements) decay to stable "daughters" by emitting radiation or particles or both (upper right). The rate of such decay is expressed as the "half-life", the time it takes for half of the atoms in a system to decay in this way. The result is an exponential decay curve (lower left) which drops rapidly at first, then declines more slowly.
Illustration by Diana Salles, after Tjeerd Van Andel, New Views on an Old Planet: A History of Global Change, *2nd ed. (Cambridge University Press,* 1994*).*

long as the organism stays alive. [Plate 21] When the organism dies, though, the "radiocarbon clock" begins to tick as the quantity of radioactive carbon in its remains starts to decline. Because this decline is proportional to time, exact measurement of the ratio of radioactive to stable carbon provides a way of determining how long ago the organism died. Unfortunately, radioactive carbon decays rather rapidly, so after about 40,000 years have elapsed, too little is left to measure precisely. This method, then, is limited to the very latest stages of human evolution. What's more, bone itself is technically difficult to date, and until very recently large samples of it had to be destroyed in the dating process. Actual human fossils therefore weren't dated; instead, organic materials—charcoal being a particular favorite—associated with them were.

A decade after the introduction of radiocarbon dating, another chronometric technique appeared on the scene. This method, known as potassium-argon (which has since been supplanted by closely related techniques), involves the measurement in rock samples of argon gas that accumulates as radioactive potassium decays (again, at a constant rate). Although potassium is geologically abundant, for a variety of technical reasons this approach is rarely practical for anything but volcanic rocks. Fossils themselves cannot be dated directly in this way, but fortunately, undisturbed tuffs (consolidated volcanic ashfalls) and lava flows represent instants in time. When found in a continuous sedimentary sequence, tuffs and lava flows can be considered contemporaneous with any fossil-bearing rocks that may lie immediately above or beneath them. The snag is that radioactive potassium decays very slowly, so it takes a long time to accumulate enough argon to measure accurately. Thus, even if there are volcanic deposits in close association with the rocks containing the fossils of interest (which there often aren't), they cannot be dated accurately unless they are older than a few hundred thousand years.

For many years this limitation left a yawning gap in time between the time ranges of radiocarbon dating at the younger end and those of argon-based techniques at the older end. This gap, alas, includes most of the time range of the Neanderthals. Recently, though, a rash of new techniques has revolutionized our understanding of the sequence of events in this period. One of the most exciting of these developments is thermoluminescence (TL) dating. This method relies on the fact that bombardment of crystalline minerals by natural radiation leads to the trapping of free electrons in defects in their crystal structures. Assuming that all other factors are equal and can be controlled for, the accumulation of trapped

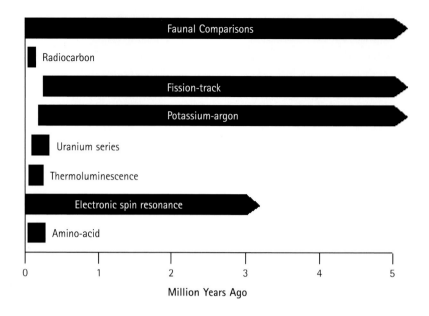

22

Ranges of faunal and chronometric dating methods.

Different dating methods have different time ranges within which they are applicable. This diagram summarizes the ranges of the major methods in use today.
Illustration by Diana Salles; after Ian Tattersall, The Human Odyssey *(Prentice Hall, 1993).*

electrons is proportional to passing time. Of course, paleoanthropologists are rarely interested in when such minerals themselves were formed; but heating and certain other processes empty electron traps and thus set the "clock" back to zero. The number of electrons accumulated since the clock was reset in this way can be determined by measuring the amount of light emitted by escaping electrons when an object of interest is heated again; from this information a date can be derived. Flints burned in fires made by early humans have proven a particular favorite for dating using this method.

Dates of up to about 150,000 years ago are possible using TL, but a related technique, known by the daunting name of electron spin resonance (ESR), can potentially take us much further back in time. [Plate 22] Like TL, ESR works by measuring the accumulation of trapped electrons, but the measurement is done in a different way. Unlike TL, ESR is applied to materials that were formed contemporaneously with early humans, rather than to objects whose clocks were reset when those early humans lived. Calcites (redeposited limestones) are one material of choice; dental enamel, the current front-runner, is another. Both TL and ESR depend among other things on the ability to measure radiation exposure precisely, which of course limits the situations in which they can be applied, but they have assumed a steadily growing importance in paleoanthropology.

Another, rather different approach is

known as uranium-series, or U-series, dating. Unstable uranium atoms decay at regular rates to "daughter" products, notably thorium-230. Uranium is soluble in water; thorium is not. Limestones formed in fresh water contain uranium but no thorium. Any thorium measured thus must be the result of uranium decay, and the ratio of uranium to thorium in the sample will, after much calculation, reveal the age of the specimen. Many archaeological sites are in limestone regions, and the ability to measure the ages of stalagmites, travertine layers, and similar structures that commonly form in caves holds much promise. In addition, other calcium-containing objects, such as mollusk shells, bones, and teeth, at least potentially can be dated using this approach.

The armory of techniques now available to paleoanthropologists for determining the ages of fossils is now greater than ever before—and improving rapidly. Such developments promise much excitement for the future, particularly in the case of the Neanderthals, most of whom are too old to be dated accurately by radiocarbon dating techniques.

 The Archaeological Record
At least as important as the fossil record in understanding our early history and that of our relatives is the archaeological record of human and prehuman behavior. A brief summary of the various cultures that have been identified in the Paleolithic period, or "Old Stone

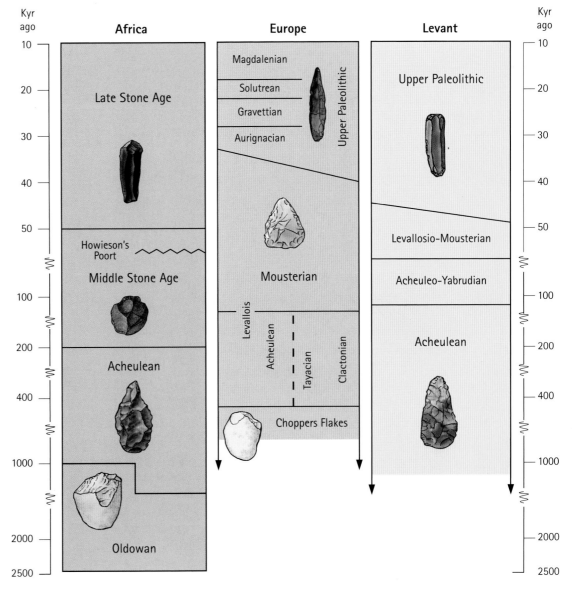

23

Succession of Paleolithic cultures in Africa, Europe and the Levant.

Archaeologists have developed different terminologies for the successive Paleolithic cultures in different areas of the world. This chart shows the approximate temporal equivalence of three major regional cultural sequences.
Illustration by Diana Salles

Age," may thus be useful. The Paleolithic (now dated between about 2.5 million and roughly 10,000 years ago) was the era of human history during which stone tools were shaped solely by flaking. It was succeeded at different times, in different places, by the Neolithic ("New Stone Age"), when stone tools were typically brought to their final shape by grinding and polishing. The term "Paleolithic" was introduced to help categorize ancient European lithic cultures, and although its use has been broadened to other areas of the world, some parallel terminologies have been adopted within it for the sequence of Old Stone Age cultures in different areas. I have tried to minimize the number of such terms used in this book, but it's impossible to avoid a fair number of names and cultures. [Plate 23]

The earliest stone tools are assigned to a culture named the Oldowan, for Tanzania's Olduvai Gorge, where such implements were first identified. At Olduvai these simple tools appear in the fossil record at about 1.8 million years ago, and they have now been found widely in other African sites ranging between about 2.5 and 1 million years in age. The tools consist of small cobbles, or "cores" (typically about 3 or 4 inches long), off of which small, sharp flakes have been knocked by blows from a hammer stone. Although several different kinds of "tools" have been identified among the cores, the principal products of toolmaking appear to have been the flakes. Rudimentary though these are, when made from the right type of rock such small implements are remarkably efficient cutting devices.

At about 1.6 million years ago, while Oldowan-type implements continued to be made, we see the introduction in

Africa of the Acheulean stoneworking culture, to which tools for the first time were made in a set and regular pattern, evidently conforming to a mental template that existed in the mind of the maker. Typical of the Acheulean were the teardrop-shaped handaxe, the straight-ended cleaver, and the sharp-pointed pick. These tools were flaked on both sides of a large core and were much larger than Oldowan core tools: most were more than six inches long, some more than a foot. With time, Acheulean tools became thinner, more symmetrical, and extremely finely made. By about 350,000 years ago, Acheulean tools were being produced in Europe, but this technology appears never to have penetrated as far as eastern Asia.

The Oldowan and Acheulean traditions are classified together as Lower Paleolithic industries. Following the Acheulean is a very fuzzy transition in both Europe and Africa to industries of the Middle Paleolithic, which probably emerged a little more than 200,000 years ago. The Middle Paleolithic was characterized by the manufacture of prepared-core tools, in which a core was preshaped so that a single final blow would detach a single large flake that was more or less in the form of the final tool. This approach had the advantage of yielding a long cutting edge that was continuous all around the tool. The exquisite control of stone flaking that the technique demanded was often achieved by using "soft" hammers, made of materials such as bone (which had occasionally been used for hammers

in the later stages of the Acheulean), and by the use of an intermediate punch between the core and the hammer. The best-known example of Middle Paleolithic technology is the Mousterian industry typical of the Neanderthals (and, in some places, of the earliest *Homo sapiens*). In France the Mousterian is known back to about 150,000 years ago, in some places possibly even further; its last known occurrence, in Spain, is about 27,000 years ago. Many different forms of Mousterian stone tools have been identified, most of them made on flakes of one kind or another. Mousterian craftsmanship is often of a very high order.

The final stage of the Old Stone Age is the Upper Paleolithic, introduced by *Homo sapiens* at different times in different places. Stoneworking of extraordinary accomplishment was joined by the use of antler, bone, and other materials in making utilitarian and decorative objects. Most stone tools were made on "blades"—flakes more than twice as long as wide, which were reworked into a large number of specialized implements. Art, symbolism, and notation appeared for the first time, and as we will see, there is evidence for the complex use of living spaces. The earliest evidence for the Upper Paleolithic in Europe comes from sites in Spain and Bulgaria, dated to about 40,000 years ago, when a culture known as the Aurignacian appears. In France, where the record is preserved best, the Upper Paleolithic is divided into four successive cultures; in other areas the sequence is rather different. The earliest French Upper Paleolithic culture, as elsewhere in Europe, is the Aurignacian, dating from about 32,000 to 28,000 years ago. This culture is followed by the Gravettian (about 28,000 to 22,000 years ago, or 18,000 years ago or even later in some places), the Solutrean (22,000 to 18,000 years ago), and the Magdalenian (18,000 to 10,000 years ago). Each of these cultures is technically defined by particular implement types, but they are equally distinctive in their artistic traditions.

In western France, in the period between about 36,000 and 32,000 years ago, we find a few occurrences of a lithic industry known as the Châtelperronian. This industry has both Middle and Upper Paleolithic aspects, but is now widely regarded as a terminal development from the late Mousterian industry. Apparently associated with Neanderthal physical types, the Châtelperronian may be the culture of Neanderthals who had observed the handiwork of Upper Paleolithic people.

The end of the Upper Paleolithic in Europe coincided with the final warming at the end of the last Ice Age, about 10,000 years ago. As the climate became milder, forests replaced the open tundra, with its vast herds of grazing mammals. Along with these mammals disappeared the economic base that had supported the enormously productive cultures of the Upper Paleolithic. A succession of materially poorer Epipaleolithic cultures followed in Europe, while the focus of technological innovation shifted to the east, where settled agriculture was on the brink of emerging.

I must clarify one more thing before we embark on the story of human evolution. This story involves changes that were both biological and cultural, against a time scale that is calibrated geologically. We are thus forced to think in terms of several different kinds of chronology. Geologically, things are not too complicated: All of the human history discussed in this book took place during the Pliocene epoch, which ended about 1.8 million years ago, and the Pleistocene epoch (roughly, the period of the Ice Ages), which extended from 1.8 million years to about 10,000 years ago. The Neanderthals arose toward the end of the Middle Pleistocene (a long period extending from 950,000 to 128,000 years ago) and endured through most of the Late Pleistocene (128,000 to 10,000 years ago). (We'll look at Pleistocene geological events later.) Cultural traditions changed periodically throughout the Pleistocene, yielding the sequence of cultures, mostly defined by the implements that typified them, that I just outlined. Biological innovation, by contrast, is measured by the appearance of new species, whose names we will learn as the story proceeds. Although biological, geological, and archaeological events all took place against the same background of passing time, they measure its passage in different ways. To that extent they are independent of each other■

4

Before the Neanderthals

THE Neanderthals represent a short and rather late phase in the entire long history of human evolution. Although this phase is important and relatively well documented, its full significance is hard to appreciate without at least a brief consideration of all the evolutionary events that preceded it. That's what this chapter is about.

In the Beginning

The human story starts not with fossils, but with a series of environmental changes that began to affect the world between about 7 and 6 million years ago. During this period large quantities of herbivores—committed grazers, adapted to open environments—begin to be found in the fossil record. This change amounted to a major episode of faunal replacement. Numbers of browsing species declined as the grazers expanded, and many of the genera that today are characteristic of open savanna habitats first appeared. To date, though, no human or convincingly prehuman fossils from this time are known. The geological deposits that might contain such specimens are not exposed at Earth's surface, or are at the least unknown or unexplored. We can, though, reliably surmise that the human family arose in Africa, because all the evidence we have of the first half of its history is confined to that continent. For want of fossil documentation, however, we can only guess the exact timing and nature of the changes that led to human emergence. What we can infer is

that about 7 million years ago the African climate began to become drier and more seasonal, causing an expansion of open savanna habitats and a dramatic reduction in the area covered by forest.

No doubt the human forerunners were four-legged forest dwellers, even though they probably didn't show many of the pronounced specializations (extremely long arms and curved hands and feet, for example) for living in trees that apes of today show. Just this lack of specialization is probably what permitted their successors to flourish at the edges of forests and on the fringes of the expanding savannas, even as their relatives who would give rise to today's apes remained confined to their ever-shrinking forest refuges. This points up the fact that, given the tendency of environments to fluctuate, anatomical and behavioral specialization is always a risky strategy in evolutionary terms. Both speciation and extinction rates seem to be higher among specialists than among generalists; but while *Homo sapiens* and its precursors clearly fall on the generalist side, this hardly justifies the minimalist stance taken by many paleoanthropologists on recognizing species in the human fossil record.

The virtual absence of fossils of the appropriate age means that exactly how our prehuman ancestors accomplished the transition in habitat and lifestyle from

forest to savanna remains unknown. The earliest possible hominid species that has been described, *Ardipithecus ramidus* from the 4.4-million-year-old site of Aramis in Ethiopia[3], was found in sediments indicative of a fairly heavily wooded environment. Whether this environment represents the preferred habitat of *A. ramidus* is not clear. Recall from our discussion of how evolution operates that, rather than having distinctive ecological niches, species tend to be spread over a number of local environments. Thus, Aramis may not have represented the environment in which *A. ramidus* arose. Unfortunately, the known fossils—a handful of isolated teeth and some skull and long bone fragments—tell us nothing about the adaptations of *A. ramidus*. Differences between its teeth and those of its later relative *Australopithecus afarensis* are certainly enough to suggest that this was indeed another species, but more than this is hard to say. We cannot, for instance, yet affirm with total confidence that *A. ramidus* walked upright.

The most dramatic evidence of early uprightness comes not in the traditional way, from fossil bones, but instead from a very unusual type of fossil: footprints preserved in volcanic ash. [Plate 24] In 1976 a paleontological team led by the archaeologist Mary Leakey discovered footprint trails left about 3.6 million years ago by a variety of animals at the northern Tanzanian locality of Laetoli. Soon afterward, a remarkable sixty-foot-long trail was found—undoubtedly made by upright-walking bipeds that strode across the landscape pretty much as we do today. This was an astonishing find, for while most people would probably agree that the most interesting thing about our ancient ancestors was how they behaved, behavior normally cannot be observed directly in the fossil record. Behavior must be inferred, indirectly, from bony structure. At Laetoli, however, behavior itself was preserved. There's been argument about the number of individuals who left their footprints behind at the famous Laetoli Site G (there were at least, and probably only, two) and about precisely how similar their feet were to our own. There's no doubt, however, that we are dealing here with the traces of upright striding animals, quite unlike any ape. [Plate 25] The 3.6-million-year-old bipeds

3   The same form may also be known from the similarly-aged site of Tabarin, in Kenya. If so, the appropriate name for this species is probably *Ardipithecus praegens*.

of Laetoli had crossed a major adaptive threshold, and by crossing it they had gained admission to the human family.

So much for how they walked. Exactly what were these creatures that trudged through the volcanic ash at Laetoli all those years ago? Although it's not possible to associate the footprints with any particular fossil species with a hundred percent certainty, it's a fair bet that the prints were made by members of the early human species whose bones were also found at Laetoli in deposits about the same age as the tracks. These remains are unimpressive in themselves, consisting mainly of a handful of partial jaws, but they provide a vital link to a much larger—indeed, uniquely large—series of hominid fossils found at about the same time some thousand miles to the north, at Hadar, in the Afar region of Ethiopia. Dating from between about 3.4 and 3 million years ago, these specimens were collected, starting in 1973, by a group led by the American paleoanthropologist Don Johanson, in collaboration with French colleagues. Among the first of the Hadar hominids to be found, and certainly the most famous, is "Lucy," a forty percent complete skeleton of a young female found in 1974. Complementing her are the "First Family," the jewel of the 1975 season: a collection of fossil fragments representing the remains of at least thirteen individuals—who may all have perished together in a flash flood—along with many more fossils. The latest find, culminating twenty (interrupted) years of

work at Hadar, is a partial skull that largely vindicates a reconstruction made in the 1970s from various unassociated bits and pieces.

In the late 1970s Johanson collaborated with Tim White, who had been given the job of studying the Laetoli early hominid remains, to try to figure out where the Laetoli and Hadar fossils—the only human or prehuman remains known from the 4- to 3-million-year period—stood in the evolutionary scheme of things. After much argument they decided that although these fossils varied greatly in size, only a single species was represented among them—a species they named *Australopithecus afarensis*. The great size disparities between the smallest and largest fossils were ascribed to sexual dimorphism—differences between the sexes. Modern humans are only slightly dimorphic in this way, but some hominoids, notably gorillas, are very strongly so. The argument for a single strongly dimorphic species didn't go over well with everyone, but in the longer term it has been sympathetically received. Today most paleoanthropologists are content to recognize just the one species *Australopithecus afarensis* among human fossils of this time span. Males of the species stood about four and a half feet tall and weighed more than a hundred pounds; females were up to a foot shorter, weighing in at perhaps sixty pounds. Most scientists are also prepared to go along, at least provisionally, with Johanson's and White's notion that *A. afarensis* is the "stem" species from which all later hominids diverged.

Australopithecus afarensis is, then, the closest thing we have to the progenitor of our human family. What kind of creature was it? As is probably inevitable, even though we know it walked upright, and thanks to Lucy we know a lot about its skeleton, there's still controversy about how it lived and moved. The anatomist Owen Lovejoy, who carried out the original analysis of Lucy's skeleton, thinks of her as a virtually perfectly adapted biped. Randy Susman and colleagues from the State University of New York at Stony Brook point to the rather long, slightly curved hands and feet as evidence for arboreal activity, suggesting that these hominoids habitually slept in trees for safety, and perhaps got a lot of their food there, too. Certainly, even as an upright biped *A. afarensis* did not have a body exactly like ours; for example, the legs were proportionately shorter than ours are, and the chest tapered sharply upward.

Above the neck *A. afarensis* differed from us even more strongly. Indeed, paleoanthropologists tend to describe these hominoids as "bipedal apes." Most important, in contrast to modern humans, these early hominids had large faces that projected in front of small braincases. The brains these skulls contained were in the modern great ape size range (about a third the size of ours today), although the small stature of these early hominids meant that, as a proportion of body size, the brains of *A. afarensis* may have been a bit larger than is typical of apes. The superficially apelike protruding face is at least in part a reflection (as it is in apes) of a large set of teeth that prolonged the dental rows on either side of the mouth. In contrast to those of apes, the canine ("eye") teeth of *A. afarensis* are reduced, although they still project slightly beyond the adjacent teeth. The incisor teeth in front of them are quite large (in apes, a characteristic that is associated with fruit eating), and the premolars and molars behind them are of very substantial size, with flattish chewing surfaces. The entire dental arcade, though long, bends in a little toward the front, forming a curve that was neither parabolic like ours, nor parallel-sided as in the apes. The total effect, however, is more humanlike than apelike.

These bipedal but small-brained creatures may have used pieces of wood for, say, digging, but there's no evidence that they made stone tools, as (much) later humans did. With no archaeological record to go on, then, we are limited (footprints aside) to what we know about their anatomy and their environment in making inferences about how they behaved. The arid, exposed grasslands in which those Laetoli bipeds left their prints appear not to have been typical of the habitats frequented by *A. afarensis* (though their presence in this unusual environment is consistent with the notion that a major motivation for moving out into the savanna was to get from one well-watered forest fringe to another). The preferred habitat of these hominids was probably much closer to that represented by the sediments at Hadar: a mosaic of river- and lakeside forest and woodland that combined the benefits of the ancestral forest environment with the new opportunities represented by the expanding savannas. These early bipeds probably fed and took shelter in the more forested areas, venturing out into the more open grasslands to scavenge and perhaps to grub for roots and tubers. They may well also have gone after large insects and small vertebrates such as lizards; and if their behavior at all resembled that of the chimpanzees studied at Tanzania's Gombe National Park, they may have quite regularly hunted smaller mammal prey such as colobus monkeys and baby antelopes. Such an economic existence would have allowed *A. afarensis* to capitalize on the combination of its ancestral climbing abilities, which had not been entirely lost, and its new capability for upright locomotion on the savanna.

But why upright locomotion at all? In some way this new adaptation must have allowed these early humans to exploit the new conditions ushered in by the drying trend in the climate. There were, however, plenty of quadrupeds that did very nicely in just those conditions without the need for dramatic change in posture. Why did the ancestral hominids opt for such a radical solution? Owen Lovejoy, who analyzed Lucy's skeleton, has offered an explanation that ties in with the human tendency to form pair bonds among adult

males and females. We have seen that evolutionary success equates largely with reproductive success. Lovejoy suggests that, in an environment where food resources are widely scattered, females would have enhanced their reproductive success by forming permanent bonds with a particular male. Although females who were nursing offspring would have suffered from decreased mobility, this handicap would have been handsomely compensated for by ties to a male who could roam widely and carry food back to her and her infants. Upright walking would have freed the hands of the males to carry food around in this way, and the motivation for doing so would have been the knowledge that the offspring they were thus supporting were their own.

Variants of the food-carrying hypothesis have been around for a long time, but they are far from the only theories offered to explain bipedalism. Other interpretations, for example, have centered on the relative mechanical efficiency of bipedal versus quadrupedal locomotion (much debated). My current favorite is a hypothesis advanced by the English physiologist Pete Wheeler, who suggests that moving out from the shelter of the forests exposed the early hominids to physiological demands that their ancestors never had to face. In the broiling heat of the tropical savanna, the vertical rays of the sun impose a heat load on the human body that has to be shed somehow, because regulation of body—and especially brain—temperature is critical to overall

Sun's rays
(vertical in tropics)

cool
breezes

high off
ground

heat radiating from ground

well-being. The easiest way of dealing with excess heat is to ensure that you receive as little of it as possible in the first place, and the best way of doing this is to stand upright. [Plate 26] By adopting this posture you minimize the heat-absorbing area of your body that is exposed to the sun's direct rays: effectively, this area is reduced to the tops of your head and shoulders, in contrast to the massive area of the head and the back that is exposed by a four-footed posture. What's more, the upright posture has two other advantages. First, the area of the body that is available to radiate away accumulated heat (metabolic heat as well as that absorbed from the sun) is maximized. Second, this heat-radiating area is raised high off the ground, away from heat radiating upward (anyone who has walked barefoot on hot ground knows how much heat that can be), to where cooling breezes can assist in heat dissipation.

This physiological explanation for the adoption of the upright posture has the added advantage of explaining another unique human feature: our hairlessness (actually, the reduction in size of our hairs, of which we have as many as any ape; it's just that most have become insignificantly tiny). Along with the sweat glands distributed extensively over our bodies, this lack of hair gives humans an unparalleled body cooling mechanism. We keep our body temperatures under control in hot conditions by the evaporative cooling of sweat and by the direct radiation of heat, processes that are obstructed by a hairy coat. Together, uprightness and hairlessness thus make up a single physiological package that was without question a huge advantage to any hominoid venturing out onto the savanna, even if the main reason for moving there was to get from one area of forest edge to another. Leaving the shelter of the forests (apart from the fact that they were shrinking) probably had other advantages, despite the evident dangers on the savanna for relatively slow-moving and small-bodied hominoids. For example, leopards routinely park partially consumed prey on the branches of savanna trees and leave them there (out of reach of terrestrial scavengers) for hours at a time while they roam around the landscape. What better protein source for a hominoid with intrinsic climbing abilities as well as the ability to move long distances out in the sun without overheating (and, presumably, with plenty of chutzpah)?

The Southern Ape of Africa

Before the discovery of *A. afarensis*, the earliest hominids known came from a number of unusual sites in and around South Africa's Transvaal region. We now know that these fossils date from about 3 to 1.5 million years ago. The sites consist largely of underground caves into which detritus from the surface fell through fissures in the ground. In this way the subterranean cavities became filled with a mixture of dust, rocks, and bones washed in from above, and the rubble became cemented by lime into a rock-hard "breccia." Because deposition of this kind is isolated from the more general sequence of geological events, such sites are particularly hard to date. The only practical way of doing so at present is to compare the fossil faunas they contain with firmly dated faunas from elsewhere. Unfortunately, the complex histories of infilling and erosion of the South African caves left them with stratigraphies that are hard to interpret, as well as an apparent jumbling of faunas of different ages.

The earliest of the hominid species from the South African breccia cave sites is *Australopithecus africanus* (literally, "southern ape of Africa"), which was first named in 1925 from a juvenile skull and brain cast found at the locality of Taung. Adult specimens were later found at the sites of Sterkfontein and Makapansgat. [Plates 27 and 28] These sites span the period from about 3 to 2 million years ago. As far as we can tell, *A. africanus* did not differ conspicuously from *A. afarensis*. Like *A. afarensis*, individuals of this species were less than four feet tall but were clearly upright bipeds, despite

27 and 28

Two *Australopithecus* crania from Sterkfontein, South Africa.

Below is Sts 5, the classic cranium of *A. africanus*. Above is Sts 71, probably representing another species. Both are about 2.5 million years old.

Photographs by Gerald Newlands.

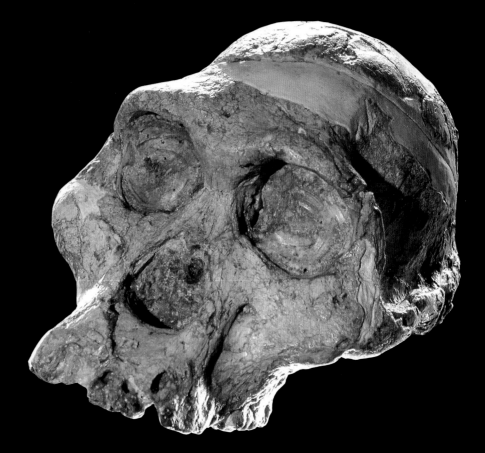

their rather primitive body proportions. At about 440 ml in volume, their brains were a little larger than those of *A. afarensis*, but their faces still protruded markedly, and their teeth were broadly similar to the latter's.

Early studies at Makapansgat by Raymond Dart, who had described the Taung child and named the species *A. africanus,* convinced him that these early humans were hunters. Dart arrived at this conclusion because the bones of other mammals found alongside those of the hominids were broken. Indeed, he identified some of the specimens as tools, components of what he called the "osteodontokeratic" (bone, tooth, and horn) culture of *A. africanus*. These hominids, Dart once wrote, were "murderer[s] and flesh-hunter[s]," whose predacious tendencies led to the "blood-spattered, slaughter-gutted archives of human history." Picked up by popular writers, these speculations led to the notion that humanity was born of a lineage of "killer apes," "red in tooth and claw," as the playwright and journalist Robert Ardrey once wrote. The reality, however, appears to have been less dramatic. The fragmentary nature of most of the bones (including those of *Australopithecus*) found in the breccia sites was the result of natural processes—including the activities of carnivores, notably leopards, among whose victims the hominids seem to have numbered. As for the hominids themselves, microscopic examination of chewing wear on the teeth of *A. afarensis* suggests that

these early humans were herbivores, consuming both fruits and foliage. Of meat in the diet there's little evidence, although they are as likely as *A. afarensis* to have consumed small mammals. But killer apes in any dramatic sense these certainly were not.

 ### The "Robusts"

With just *A. ramidus, A. afarensis,* and *A. africanus* to go on, we would be hard-pressed to make a case for splitting versus linearity in the early hominid fossil record. Sites yielding the latter two species, however, may just overlap at the 3-million-year point; but the record is too sparse to allow certainty. However, another, more distinctive, early hominid is also known from South Africa: one that testifies that a major split did occur in the human lineage before about 2 million years ago; exactly when, we'll get back to in a moment. [Plate 29] Sometimes regarded as just another species of *Australopithecus,* if a highly distinctive one, this new hominid is now more commonly known by its original name, *Paranthropus robustus,* to reflect its differences from the preceding early humans. Found at the breccia cave sites of Kromdraai and Swartkrans, dated to about 1.9 to 1.5 million years ago, *P. robustus* is distinguished by a massive chewing dentition, with greatly expanded molars and premolars. The front teeth (the incisors and canines) are, however, greatly reduced compared to those of *A. africanus*, so the faces of *P. robustus*

29
**Paranthropus robustus cranium
from Swartkrans, South Africa.**

The best preserved cranium (Sk 48)
from this classic site; probably about
1.7 million years old.
Photograph by Gerald Newlands.

30
Scene of *Paranthropus robustus* near Swartkrans, South Africa.

In this reconstruction of ancient life, set about 1.7 million years ago, a group of *Paranthropus* disports itself on the open high veld. It is likely, if not entirely certain, that these hominids used bones and horn cores for digging, as shown here.
Mural painting in American Museum of Natural History by and © Jay Matternes.

31

Fragment of polished horn core from Swartkrans, South Africa.

This and similar objects from Swartkrans, dating to about 1.7 million years ago, bear scratching and polishing attributed to their use as digging tools—plausibly by *Paranthropus*.
Photograph by Willard Whitson.

are distinctly shorter from back to front than those of *A. africanus.* The facial architecture is heavily built to withstand the stresses generated by the great grinding dentition. Brain size tends to be a little larger than that of *A. africanus,* but it's hard to estimate it as a proportion of body size, because not very much of the body skeleton is known. The brain was, however, small enough that the huge chewing muscles tended to meet at the midline of the braincase, forming a "sagittal crest" reminiscent of those in some gorillas. Because of the heavy structure of their skulls, these hominids are often referred to as "robust," although it's been pointed out that we don't know whether this description applies to their body build as a whole.

Unlike the more "gracile" (lightly built) omnivore *A. africanus, P. robustus* has a remarkable dentition that has led to a lot of speculation that its diet was restricted to extreme herbivory. Dental wear analysis suggests that the "robusts" habitually chewed on tougher, and perhaps grittier, objects than the "graciles"

did, but Fred Grine of the State University of New York at Stony Brook has argued strongly that this does not mean that *A. africanus* ate more meat. If both forms were largely herbivorous, then, why the great difference in chewing apparatuses? Perhaps the key lies in changing climate. In South Africa the graciles lived substantially earlier than the robusts did, and in the intervening period the local climate became drier and the vegetation sparser. Whereas *A. africanus* lived in wooded to bushy environments, *P. robustus* inhabited more-open grasslands, and its dentition was well suited to masticating the tough, gritty foods—plant rhizomes, tubers, and so forth—offered by a habitat of this kind. [Plate 30] The Transvaal Museum's Bob Brain has identified bone and horn-core fragments at Swartkrans that have been polished by wear in exactly the way that occurs when such objects are used for digging up roots. [Plate 31] I hasten to add, however, that there is no other firm evidence for tool use by either *Australopithecus* or *Paranthropus*—though it has

Cranium of *Paranthropus boisei.*

Dated to about 1.8 million years ago, this is the original "*Zinjanthropus*" cranium (OH 5) from the lowest levels of Olduvai Gorge, Tanzania. *Photograph by John Reader.*

been claimed that *Paranthropus* was responsible for some crude stone tools found at Swartkrans. Most authorities, however, think that these tools were more probably made by another hominid – whom we'll meet shortly – whose remains were also found at the site.

East African "Robusts"

Almost immediately after the initial description of *A. afarensis*, the debate began as to whether *P. robustus* and its relatives (which we'll discuss in this section) had descended from this early form or from the long-known *A. africanus*. As any ancestor must be, both *Australopithecus* species were less specialized than their putative descendants. The 1985 discovery in Kenya of a robust skull 2.6 million years old, however, tipped the balance in favor of the older *A. afarensis*. Unfortunately lacking teeth, this specimen is unlike later robusts in having a strongly projecting face. The details of its anatomy, however, along with its large masticatory musculature and supporting architecture (including a sagittal crest), make plain where its affinities lie. Other bits and pieces from Ethiopia dating in the 2.8- to 2.2-million-year range appear to belong to the same species. The name now generally applied to this species, *Paranthropus aethiopicus*, comes from one of the Ethiopian fossils.

Wherever and whatever its own origins, *P. aethiopicus* is putatively ancestral not only to *P. robustus*, but to a species of robusts that is widely known from sites in eastern Africa that date from about 2.2 milion years ago to a little less than 1 million years ago. This new form rocketed to fame in 1959, when paleoanthropologist Louis Leakey, Mary Leakey's husband, reported the discovery of the "*Zinjanthropus*" cranium at Olduvai Gorge in what was then Tanganyika (now called Tanzania). [Plate 32] The celebrity of this specimen grew shortly thereafter, when in the first application of potassium-argon dating to the human fossil record, it acquired the then mind-bogglingly ancient date of 1.8 million years. Subsequent finds of this robust hominid have ranged from other sites in northern Tanzania, to various parts of northern Kenya and southern Ethiopia. The new *Paranthropus* has been aptly described as "like *P. robustus*, only more so," with an even more massively constructed skull, more-expanded chewing teeth, and tiny canines and incisors.

The environments inhabited by *P. boisei,* as this species is called, vary considerably. At Olduvai the fossil deposits were laid down in a lakeside setting; around the lake reeds and trees flourished, but they yielded quite rapidly to an arid grassland. In Ethiopia's Omo River basin the climate dried out markedly during *P. boisei*'s long tenure, although forest presumably persisted throughout along the watercourses that laid down the fossiliferous deposits. Thus, in eastern Africa the appearance of *Paranthropus* did not coincide, as happened in South Africa, with a marked climatic deterioration. Most instructive, however, is that

as far as we can tell, *P. boisei* remained virtually unchanged for more than a million years during which there was noticeable climatic change. When finally the once abundant *P. boisei* died out, apparently leaving no descendants, it looked very much like it had in the beginning. *P. boisei* had not, it appears, done much if anything to adapt physically to the drying conditions in which it found itself. Presumably its disappearance was in response to a different factor entirely: its inability to compete successfully with yet another hominid, one that we will read about next.

The Earliest *Homo*?

In the year after the discovery of the "*Zinjanthropus*" skull at Olduvai, the remains of another kind of early human were found nearby, in deposits also about 1.8 million years old. [Plate 33] By the time of this discovery, recognizable stone tools had been known at Olduvai for almost half a century,

but few authorities had accepted Louis Leakey's initial claim that *Zinjanthropus* (a.k.a. *P. boisei*) had made them. The new hominid, however, was another matter, for here was not just another variation on the robust theme. The fossils consisted of a partial lower jaw and some cranial bones from a young individual, along with some bones belonging to the body skeleton. In 1964 Leakey and two colleagues used these fossils, together with other specimens found later, as the basis for describing the new species *Homo habilis* ("handy man"). This introduction of the new species caused quite a furor, especially because, while it was extremely distinct from *Zinjanthropus* and was certainly more plausible as a potential toolmaker, the new species did not differ much from South Africa's *Australopithecus africanus*. When all was said and done, the physical differences between these two boiled down to a somewhat larger brain in *Homo habilis* (the partial braincase had a volume of about 680 ml) and some

33

The type specimens of
Homo habilis.

The 1.8 million years-old type
specimens of *Homo habilis* from
Olduvai Gorge. After years of
controversy, this species is now
generally accepted (if unwisely) as
an early member of our own genus.
Photograph by John Reader.

distinctions in the shape of the premolars. This is not a great deal to base a new species of *Homo* on, to be sure; *Homo habilis* thus remains to this day a focus of debate.

What about the tools that the new hominid from Olduvai had made? In a word they were rather crude, consisting of small pebbles with flakes bashed off of them using another stone. [Plate 34] Mary Leakey developed the notion that several distinct forms of such Oldowan tools could be recognized, and that the Oldowan toolmakers had created an entire "kit" of tools devoted to various purposes. More-recent research has indicated, how-

ever, that it was the sharp flakes rather than the "cores" that were generally used as tools. The artifacts that Mary Leakey had thought were deliberately shaped seem to be no more than by-products of flake production. Those small and deceptively simple flakes are, however, formidable tools: experiments have shown that even a large, thick-skinned mammal such as an elephant can be skinned and butchered using them. [Plate 35]

Elementary as they were, these first stone tools must have made a substantial difference in the lives of those who made them. Of course, the first tools known to archaeologists are not necessarily the first tools that were ever used by human ancestors, for not all kinds of early implements would have been made of the sort of hard material that is likely to survive over millions of years. It's quite possible, for example, that the earliest tools of primitive hominids were simple digging sticks, used by our remote precursors to grub up roots and tubers out on the savanna. But the availability of cutting tools must have changed the rules of the game radically; certainly, it made an enormous difference in the foods potentially available. Earlier human ancestors may well have scavenged edible parts from animals they found dead, and have eaten small beasts that they caught, but the first toolmakers were able to butcher the carcasses of large animals and to extract a wide variety of high-protein foods from them. What's more, the ability to detach body parts would have enabled these comparatively small-bodied hominids to spend a minimum of time in the dangerous open savanna, for as bipeds they would have been able to carry the parts away and consume them in the relative safety of the trees. Early stone tools were not used solely for butchery, however. The edges of tools wear in different ways depending on how the tools are used. Microscopic analysis of such wear has shown that these simple tools were employed in shaping wood and cutting softer plants, as well as in slicing meat and tendons.

One other intriguing aspect of early toolmaking may give us some insight into the cognitive abilities of the toolmakers. Not all types of stone are equally well suited for making tools, and even though they made their implements in an ad hoc manner, the first toolmakers were clearly selective in terms of the stone they used. They didn't simply pick up any old kind of rock that came to hand; indeed, the nearest natural source for the stone tools found at any given site commonly was a mile or two, or even more, away. Early toolmakers thus obviously anticipated their needs, carrying stones of the appropriate sort around with them over quite large distances before making tools as required. It appears that they did not make the tools first and take them with them as they foraged, for archaeologists have been able to piece together complete cobbles from cores, flakes, and waste fragments found at sites where animals were butchered. The tools themselves were made on the spot, even though their use had been foreseen. Maybe this isn't surprising, for intact cobbles would have been a lot easier to carry around than piles of cores and flakes.

While the remains named *Homo habilis* were quite rapidly accepted as those of the first Olduvai toolmaker, the concept of *Homo habilis* as one of us had a bit of a rough ride at first. How could something as primitive as this be accepted as a member of our own genus? Not until 1972, when the Leakeys' son Richard found a remarkable 1.9-million-year-old cranium at East Turkana in northern Kenya, did *Homo habilis* begin to be generally

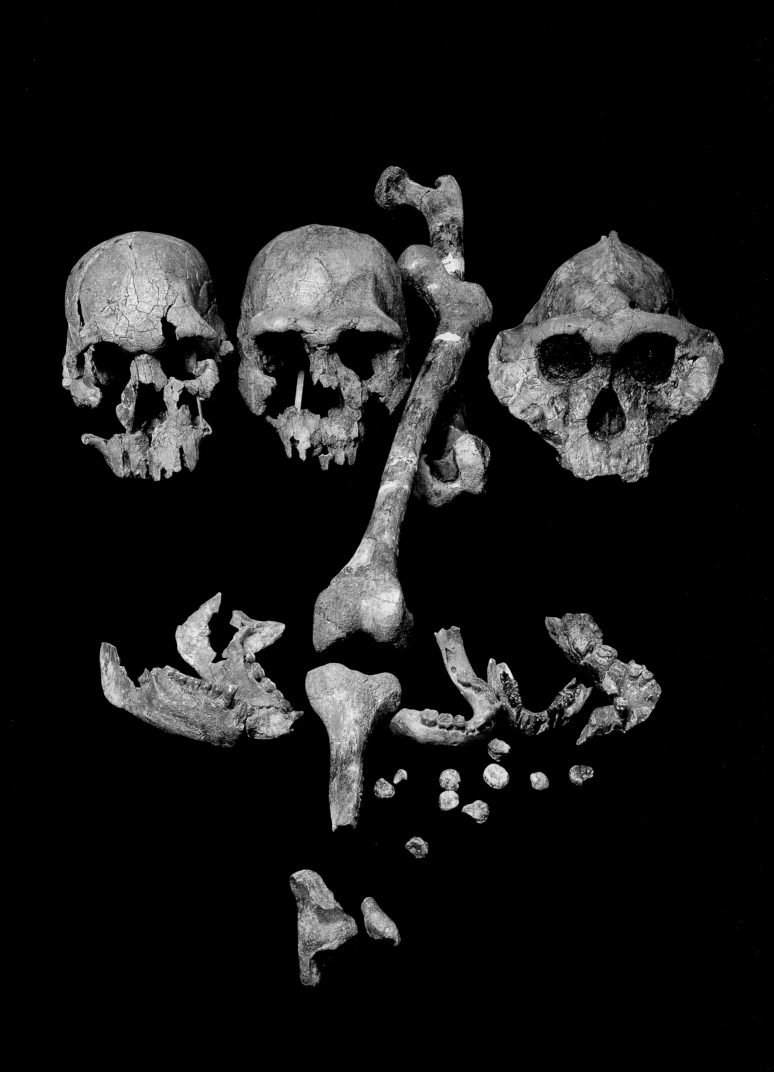

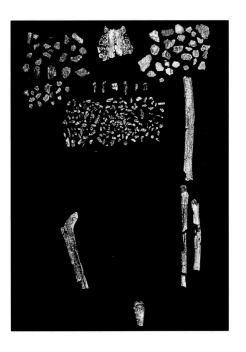

37
Fragmentary skeleton O H 62 from Olduvai Gorge, Tanzania.

This is the only associated skeleton yet known of *Homo habilis*. Incomplete and fragmentary though it is, it provides evidence of strikingly primitive limb proportions. About 1.8 million years old.
Courtesy of the Institute of Human Origins.

36
Composite of three hominid crania and postcranial bones from East Turkana, Kenya.

The remarkable 1.9 million years-old cranium KNM-ER 1470 (left) convinced the world in the 1970s that *Homo habilis* is indeed a distinct species. This is ironic, since this specimen is nowadays increasingly regarded as representing the distinct species *H. rudolfensis*. At center is KNM-ER 3733, now widely viewed as belonging to the species *Homo ergaster*, and on the right is KNM-ER 406, representing *Paranthropus boisei*.
Photograph by John Reader.

accepted as an early member of our genus *Homo*. [Plate 36] The new cranium, known by its museum catalogue number, KNM-ER 1470, was remarkable principally for its large brain size, estimated at a volume of about 750 ml. Because it was distinct in other ways from any *Australopithecus* or *Paranthropus* species, after a period of initial uncertainty (prolonged for several years by an inaccurate belief that it was 2.6 million years old) this specimen became widely thought of as the quintessential example of *Homo habilis*. Meanwhile, in 1973 an exceptionally complete cranium of about the same age, dubbed KNM-ER 1813, was found at East Turkana. Although this specimen initially impressed its discoverers by its resemblance to South African *Australopithecus africanus,* its teeth are reminiscent of those collected at Olduvai Gorge, and it is now often considered to be a female *Homo habilis*, with 1470 representing the male. Notably, however, the rather lightly built cranial vault of 1813 is quite small, with a volume not much more than 500 ml.

It's ironic that, in assuming the mantle of *Homo habilis*, 1470 became the specimen that convinced most scientists both of the validity of this species and of its proper placement in the genus *Homo*. For in retrospect, we can say with some confidence that 1470 does not belong to the species that left its bones at the bottom of Olduvai Gorge. On the other hand, 1813, along with other specimens from East Turkana, quite plausibly does; and it may well be that a cranium from 1.6-million-

year-old deposits containing stone tools at South Africa's Sterkfontein also represents *Homo habilis*. Nonetheless, *habilis* remains somewhat problematic as a member of *Homo,* not just because of the small brain size of 1813, but because of the extraordinary primitiveness of a skeleton discovered at Olduvai in 1985. [Plate 37] Found at about the same stratigraphic level as the original *Homo habilis* material, and thus about 1.8 million years old, this skeleton is highly fragmentary. It is complete enough, though, to show that the individual was very small, not much more than three feet tall, and possessed short legs and long arms, much like those of *A. afarensis*—if not more so. Primitive body, somewhat *Australopithecus*-like skull, small brain size: not exactly the portrait of an early species of our own genus, at least as envisaged by me and a growing number of my colleagues. Still, there's not much doubt that *Homo habilis* made tools during its decently documented span on Earth, from about 1.9 to 1.6 million years ago. The identity of the very first toolmaker, however, remains in doubt. The earliest stone tools that have been identified, which come from sites in eastern Africa about 2.5 million years old, are not associated with fossils that could give us clues to their maker. What's more, any hominids at all from this time period are in very short supply.

Specimen 1470 remains for the time being in the genus *Homo,* although it is increasingly recognized as representing a distinct species, *Homo rudolfensis.* Some limb bones from East Turkana that are presumably associated with *Homo rudolfensis* (if only because they don't look like others attributed to *Homo habilis*) show a more modern, less *Australopithecus*-like anatomy. Despite a more "advanced" body structure, however, few would be so bold as to hold *Homo rudolfensis* out as the ancestor of later humans. As already noted, any ancestor must necessarily be more primitive than its putative descendants, and the skull of *Homo rudolfensis* has a number of specialized features. The more (indeed, excessively) primitive *Homo habilis* makes a better early representative of our lineage, even if it doesn't make a lot of sense to place it in our own genus.

At present the grab bag of fossils that we have from the period around and following 2 million years ago thus seems above all to suggest that hominid species proliferated remarkably at about this time. Instead of a gradual transition from *Australopithecus* into *Homo,* we have evidence for at least one major lineage split (leading to *habilis* on the one hand, and to *rudolfensis* on the other), and possibly for more. The problem is that we are seeing only a fraction of the total picture, making it difficult for us to discern exactly how many species are represented among the fossils we have in hand, let alone how many hominid species existed at this time. Even more obscure is where our own ancestry lies. A clearer view will

have to await not only more fossils, but also a definitive sorting into species of the ones we have. At around 1.9 to 1.8 million years ago, then, the picture is confused, but we do not have to wait long for the appearance of a convincing contender for early membership in our genus.

The First Modern Biped

Work by Richard Leakey's team in the region around Kenya's Lake Turkana led to the recovery during the 1970s and 1980s of a series of hominid fossils unlike any we've discussed so far. Starting with some pieces of lower jaw, this material soon included a couple of crania known as KNM-ER 3733 and KNM-ER 3883. [see Plate 36] The more complete of these, 3733, has a braincase volume of about 850 ml, a relatively lightly built and upwardly arching cranial vault, distinct if small ridges above the eyes, a reduced face, and a humanlike if large (compared to us) set of teeth—unfortunately incomplete. Dated to about 1.7 million years ago, 3733 was not comparable to any species of *Australopithecus*; rather, it invited comparison with *Homo erectus,* a species described from Java late in the nineteenth century by the Dutch paleoanthropologist Eugene Dubois. [Plate 38] The material available to Dubois consisted of a skullcap, a complete femur with a bony outgrowth on it, and some fragments of femoral shaft. The femur (which was only dubiously associated with the braincase) was hardly distinguishable from that of a modern human (hence Dubois's choice of

38

"Java man."

The *Homo erectus* skullcap discovered by Eugene Dubois at Trinil, Java, in 1891. At least 700 thousand years old; perhaps substantially older.

Photograph courtesy of John de Vos.

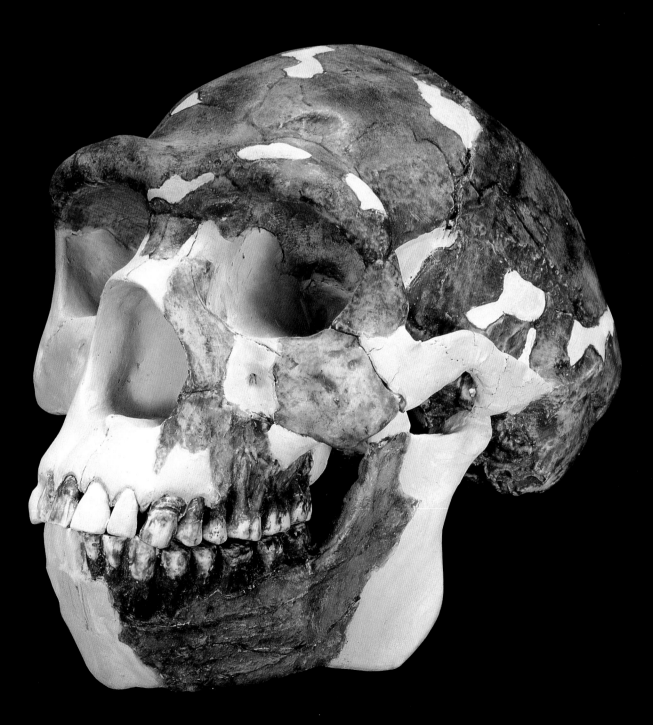

39

Reconstruction of the skull of "Peking Man".

This new reconstruction of the skull of *Homo erectus*, made at the American Museum of Natural History, is based on male skull fragments from Zhoukoudian, China, the originals of which were lost during World War II. Perhaps 300 thousand years old.
Reconstruction by G. J. Sawyer; photograph by Craig Chesek.

the species name *erectus,* "upright"), but the skullcap was another matter entirely. It was long, low, and made of thick bone; it was sharply angled at the back and decorated with pronounced ridges above where the eye sockets had been. Dubois estimated that its brain volume had been about 900 ml (940 ml by more recent estimates). In the 1890s this was unprecedented material, and to receive it Dubois created the new genus *Pithecanthropus* (ape-man), the name reflecting his view of this strange creature as an evolutionary intermediate between apes and humans. Since the 1950s, however, the species has customarily been included in our own genus, *Homo.*

Human fossils from Java have been notoriously resistant to accurate dating, largely because the sites where they were found were often not accurately pinpointed. It is now believed, however, that the age of the skullcap is 700,000 years or more, and since Dubois's time other early humans of this general kind have been discovered in Javan deposits that are both considerably older (a million years or in some cases apparently a lot more) and younger. "Peking Man" from Zhoukoudian in China is younger, specimens dating from perhaps 400,000 to 250,000 years ago, but it clearly belongs in the same species. [Plate 39] The Zhoukoudian sample of almost a dozen crania (lacking faces, unfortunately) is particularly interesting for the range of brain sizes it embraces, between about 850 and 1200 ml.

From the beginning, resemblances between the new specimens from East Turkana and those from Zhoukoudian were remarked upon, despite the great time gap between them. But although the resemblances are clear, *Homo erectus* has some specialized features—notably the long, flattened skull and the thick bone from which it is made—that the East African form does not. What's more, Asian *Homo erectus* is also specialized in ways that *Homo sapiens* is not. Thus, while majority opinion probably still inclines toward placing all of these fossils in *Homo erectus,* the whole group being broadly ancestral to modern humans, there is a growing tendency to separate the Kenyan form into its own species, *Homo ergaster.* This species makes a good putative ancestor for both *Homo erectus* and *Homo sapiens,* but the three don't appear to form a linear sequence. Rather, *Homo erectus* seems to be a specialized Asian offshoot— one that eventually became extinct—from the human lineage.

Thus, the limelight falls on *Homo ergaster.* What was this ancient relative of ours really like? That question was answered with a vengeance in 1984, when an astonishingly complete skeleton of an adolescent member of this species was discovered in 1.6-million-year-old sediments to the west of Lake Turkana. [Plate 40] This unfortunate individual is thought to have been 9 years old when he died in a swamp, where his remains sank rapidly into the mud, safe from dismemberment by scavengers. Because he was at about the stage of development that modern

Skeleton of the "Turkana Boy".

Dated to about 1.6 million years ago, this skeleton of an adolescent *Homo ergaster* from West Turkana, Kenya, is the earliest to show essentially modern body proportions.
Photograph of mounted cast by Dennis Finnin and Craig Chesek.

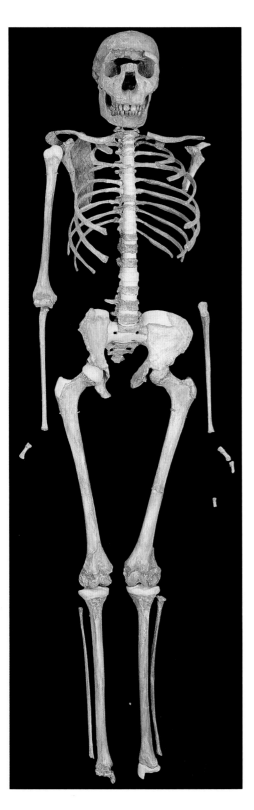

adolescents reach at 11 or 12 years of age, his height at death, about five feet four inches, was well below the six feet or so that he would have reached as an adult. What's more, he was extremely slim and long-limbed, quite the opposite of the conventional picture of the squat, heavily muscled *Homo erectus* that had been built up on the basis of the few limb fragments known. Indeed, the "Turkana Boy" was proportioned very much like the people who inhabit the Turkana region today, whose slender bodies are built to shed the heat load imposed by the merciless tropical sun under which they live.

The Turkana Boy's skeleton is thus the earliest we know of in the human fossil record that was proportioned much as ours are today—although there are certain differences in detail. For example, the Turkana Boy was not broad-chested as we are, but had an upwardly tapering thorax that gave him narrower shoulders than we have—apparently a minor holdover from a more arboreal past. The canal that carries the spinal cord down from the brain through the vertebral column was constricted, something that has been interpreted as evidence for limited control of voluntary respiration. In turn, this may suggest that the Turkana Boy was unable to manipulate as precisely as we do the air column that resonates to produce the sounds associated with modern speech. Another difference from us is that his thigh bones had rather long necks, possibly to compensate for what in a female would have been a small birth canal.

This last characteristic accords with the rather limited brain size which we know from specimens 3733 and 3883, as well as from the Turkana Boy, was typical of this species.

Lifeways

Homo ergaster was thus an early human species that was modern in most respects from the neck down, but that possessed a brain of only modest size and a skull with primitive characteristics. *Homo ergaster* occurs at East Turkana in the narrow time band of about 1.8 to 1.5 million years ago. Of course, this is just its *known* span; significantly younger sediments aren't preserved in the Turkana sequence. However, it is enough to show that during at least parts of this short period and in this limited area an amazing variety of hominid species existed. Early advanced humans with bodies very much like our own lived alongside *Paranthropus boisei*, *Homo habilis*, and *Homo rudolfensis* in the Turkana region. That's a lot of hominid species all making do in the same environment. What was *Homo ergaster* doing differently that allowed it ultimately to triumph at the expense of the other three species? At the beginning, at least, apparently not much. The early stone tool kit from Turkana doesn't look a lot different from the one that accompanies *Homo habilis* at Olduvai, nor do the archaeological sites themselves suggest that any major innovation in, say, hunting techniques, was going on. Here, then, we have the second intimation in the

41

Acheulean stone tools.

These tools, from Site WK in Bed IV, Olduvai Gorge, Tanzania, include some classic handaxes and cleavers. *Photograph by John Reader.*

fossil record—the first being the almost certain lack of marked physical difference between the first toolmakers and their predecessors—that physical and technological innovations have not gone hand in hand in human evolutionary history.

In the Turkana case, of course, we see a major physical innovation in the absence of technological change, rather than vice versa. But either way the theme of the decoupling of biological from behavioral change in hominid evolution was established early and was to become a pervasive motif in the human story. On the surface, the arrival of a new species might seem to be the simplest explanation for the introduction of a new technology, but if you take a moment to think about it, you'll realize that the pattern we see is not really surprising. Where else can innovation take place than within an existing species? Ultimately, any new technology has to originate with an individual—and how different could that individual be, physically or mentally, from his or her parents and children?

Not until about 1.5 million years ago, at which time *Homo ergaster* had been around for perhaps a quarter of a million years, do we pick up evidence for a major change in the archaeological record at Turkana and elsewhere in Africa. Around that time a new type of stone implement appears, exemplified by the handaxes and cleavers of the Acheulean tradition, named for Saint-Acheul, France, where such tools (albeit from much later in time) were first identified in the 1830s.

[Plate 41] Resulting from the conscious shaping of a stone core to a predetermined form, presumably by members of *Homo ergaster,* these implements were the first to be made to a standard pattern that must have existed in the toolmaker's mind before knapping began. The more modest Oldowan tradition was not abandoned as this improved technology was adopted, however. The teardrop-shaped handaxes and the broad-ended cleavers, from about six inches to a foot or more long and shaped on both sides to an uninterrupted edge, continued to be accompanied by simpler cores and flakes for several hundred thousand years or more—and the flakes struck off in the process of making handaxes were also used. This side-by-side existence of two different types of tools exemplifies yet another aspect of technological innovation, namely, the tendency of old technologies to persist alongside the new, often for extended periods.

The Acheulean handaxe has aptly been described as the "Swiss army knife" of the Paleolithic, efficiently serving such functions as cutting, scraping, hacking, and digging. Yet there's very little to indicate that its introduction ushered in substantial change in the lives of its inventors. The use of a "mental template" to produce Acheulean handaxes, picks, and cleavers does contrast strikingly with the ad hoc Oldowan process of producing sharp flakes as and where needed, and Acheulean tools are often found in huge quantities, as if they were made at specialized workshops. These two pieces of evidence hint at some kind of cognitive leap on the part of the Acheuleans. So, presumably, do the earliest potential intimations of the control of fire, which first turn up at about the same time. But although earlier interpretations suggested that *Homo erectus* or its contemporaries actively hunted large animals (by driving them into swamps where they became mired and vulnerable, for instance), few archaeologists are prepared to conclude today that these early humans ever systematically hunted the bigger mammals. Probably they were simply doing what their predecessors had done (scavenging, foraging for plant foods and invertebrates, and maybe hunting small mammals and other vertebrates)—only a little better.

This, of course, raises the question of why their brains were larger in proportion to body size, if only a little—for brain enlargement, it should be noted, is not an unalloyed blessing. The brain devours energy more hungrily than any other body system and has to be kept at a particularly constant temperature by elaborate mechanisms. The energetic downside of brain enlargement is thus evident; but the upside is at present an area for outright speculation. Maybe the ability to form mental templates changed the rules of the game by placing a premium on abstract intellectual skills, thereby profoundly influencing future biological and cultural developments. Perhaps even subtle technological advances—advances not necessarily discernible in the rather coarse

archaeological record—extended evolutionary advantages to individuals able to exploit them. These advantages could ultimately have affected the capacities of the small groups in which early humans lived, and among which evolutionary sorting might well have been intense in a climate—hence habitat—that was becoming increasingly unstable.

 ### Technological Advances
Not long ago it was reckoned that only about a million years ago did early humans leave Africa for the first time. New dates from Java of 1.8 and 1.6 million years for a couple of hominid specimens (which unfortunately are rather undiagnostic as to species) suggest, however, that this event must have taken place considerably before then, as does the discovery of a probably 1.6-million-year-old hominid jaw from a site in ex-Soviet Georgia. There's no doubt, however, that the next significant development in hominid technology awaited the 1-million-year mark. But even then, what we see is essentially a refinement of the basic technique for making handaxes; these became thinner (hence more efficient at cutting) as a result of the invention of "platform preparation," a method of manufacture whereby the edge of the axe was initially made blunter to provide a surface at which more force could be aimed to produce the final working edge.

Along with this somewhat counterintuitive technique, we occasionally find tools that must have been made, for the first time in stoneworking, by using "soft hammers" made of substances such as wood or bone. These materials, more yielding than the brittle stone that had uniquely been used for hammers up to that point, allowed a much subtler approach to toolmaking than had been possible previously. What kind of human introduced this significant advance? Again, it's not known, for the fossil record is a bit scanty at this point. Maybe these toolmakers, in Africa at least (in Asia the tool record at this point is exceedingly poor, though it's clear that handaxes never really caught on there), were *Homo ergaster*. Or perhaps they looked more like Olduvai Hominid (OH) 9, a skullcap that the Leakeys had found at Olduvai Gorge in 1960. Bigger and bulkier than the Turkana skulls, with a brain capacity of not much less than 1100 ml, and later in time, at about 800,000 years ago, OH 9 can be squeezed into a broad definition of *Homo erectus* that also embraces the Turkana and eastern Asian materials. This notion, however, is one of convenience rather than of biological reality, and the place of OH 9 within the larger scheme of things remains to be satisfactorily worked out.

Early Europeans—and Others

Since the *Homo ergaster/Homo erectus* group is represented in both Africa and eastern Asia, you might logically expect to find members of it in Europe as well, where a crude stone tool record extends back toward a million years ago, perhaps even further. Not so. Although for years it has been debated whether *Homo erectus* occurred in Europe, by now it is pretty clear that fossils from that region, known back to about half a million years ago, belong to another group entirely, though exactly which group remains a matter of contention. It's clear to me that these fossils are typical neither of *Homo erectus* nor of *Homo sapiens*. However, since received wisdom admits no intermediates between these species, two principal schools of thought have developed among paleoanthropologists. One (mainly in the English-speaking world) feels that because the fossils in question do not belong to *Homo erectus*, they must belong to *Homo sapiens*, albeit as an "archaic" form. The other (mainly French) school notes that because these specimens are not *Homo sapiens*, they must be regarded as an "advanced" form of *Homo erectus*. The adherents of both interpretations would deny, with cogent arguments, that their reasoning is as simplistic as this outline suggests, but there is nonetheless no rational explanation for this dichotomy other than the power of received wisdom, for these fossils belong to an entirely distinct species (perhaps, indeed, more than one).

The fossils in question are a motley assortment of specimens dating from about 500,000 to 250,000 years ago. The earliest one is a single lower jaw found in a gravel pit at Mauer, near the German city of Heidelberg, in 1907. [Plate 42] Lower jaws are notoriously difficult to

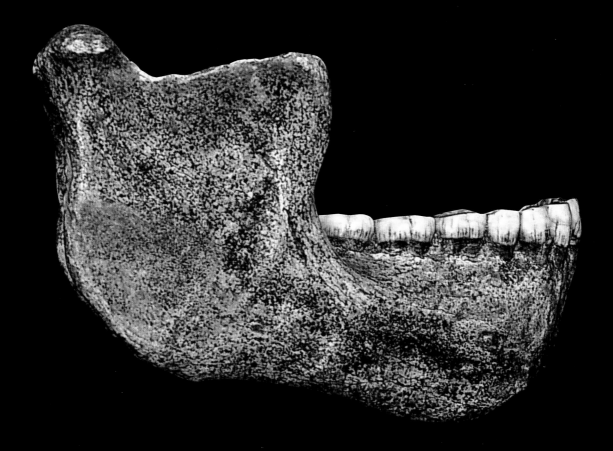

43 *left*
The Arago cranium.

Dated to about 400 thousand years
ago, this specimen and others from
the cave of Arago, near Tautavel,
France, are among the best-
preserved fossils of European *Homo
heidelbergensis.*
Photograph by John Reader.

44 *right*
**Cranium of *Homo heidelbergensis*
from Petralona, Greece.**

Uncertainly dated (perhaps to
around 450 thousand years ago),
this cranium is the best example we
have of *Homo heidelbergensis* from
Europe.
Photograph courtesy of George Koufos.

classify to the level of species, however, and we have to wait for the
400,000-year mark to find more-
complete European material that
gives us a better idea of what the
species involved was like. This evidence is furnished most dramatically by the cave of Arago, near Tautavel in the French Pyrenees, where
during the past quarter century several dozen mostly fragmentary hominid
specimens have been found. [see Plate 90]
The best of these is the face and part of
the skull vault of what has been claimed
to be a male individual, though this has
been disputed. [Plate 43] This fossil, with
a brain volume of almost 1200 ml, quite
closely resembles a more complete but
very poorly dated cranium found at the
Greek site of Petralona in 1960, which has
a brain of about the same size. [Plate 44
and see Plate 91] Together, these fossils
reveal a hominid with a more "inflated"
looking cranium than any possessed by
Homo erectus, although it still recedes
behind marked brow ridges that (in the
Petralona specimen) harbor large frontal
sinuses. These ridges are, however, more
individually arched above each eye than
in the Asian form. The back of the skull is
more rounded than in *Homo erectus*, and
the cheeks are inflated somewhat as in
Neanderthals, though the face itself is
flatter. Tools found in association with
these hominids are generally pretty crude;
the bulk of the implements consist of
simple cobble "chopping tools" and small
flake tools such as points and scrapers.

The species represented by
the Petralona and Arago fossils
should probably be called *Homo heidelbergensis*, for the name originally applied
to the Mauer jaw. But this species is not a
purely European phenomenon. The site of
Bodo, in northeast Ethiopia, for instance,
has produced a face and partial braincase
of an even more robust but essentially
similar hominid that may be as much as
600,000 years old. [Plate 45] And a
mining locality at Kabwe, in Zambia, has
yielded an extremely well preserved
cranium of comparable aspect. [Plate 46]
Like the Bodo specimen, this one is not
well dated, but it may be as much as
400,000 years old. Bones of the body
skeleton from Kabwe agree with fossils
from Arago and elsewhere in indicating a
body structure that was robust but, in
essentials, of modern build. Half a world
to the east, the Chinese site of Dali has
produced an as-yet inadequately
described cranium that appears to fall
into this group. Once more only very
approximately dated, this specimen may
be around 200,000 years old, perhaps
less. Other specimens from this time period, about 600,000 to 200,000 years ago,

45 *above*
Partial cranium from Bodo, Ethiopia.

Over 600 thousand years old, this cranium is probably a robust representative of African *Homo heidelbergensis.*
Photograph by Donald Johanson; courtesy of Institute of Human Origins.

46 *right*
"Rhodesian Man" cranium from Kabwe, Zambia.

This poorly dated cranium, probably at least 300 thousand years old, is the best-preserved representative of *Homo heidelbergensis* from the African continent.
Photograph by John Reader.

47

Cranium 4 from Atapuerca, Spain.

This is among the most complete of the human crania from the "Pit of the Bones" at Atapuerca, which have been described as having certain proto-Neanderthal characteristics. About 300 thousand years old.
Photo by Javier Trueba, © Madrid Scientific Films; courtesy of Juan-Luis Arsuaga.

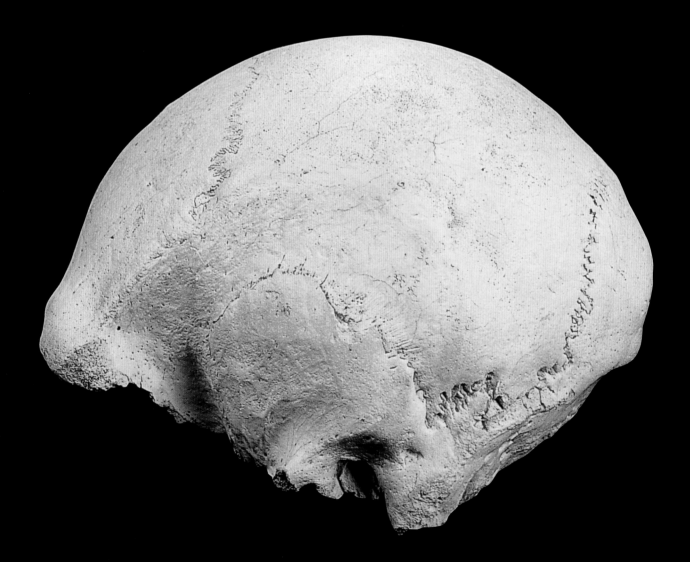

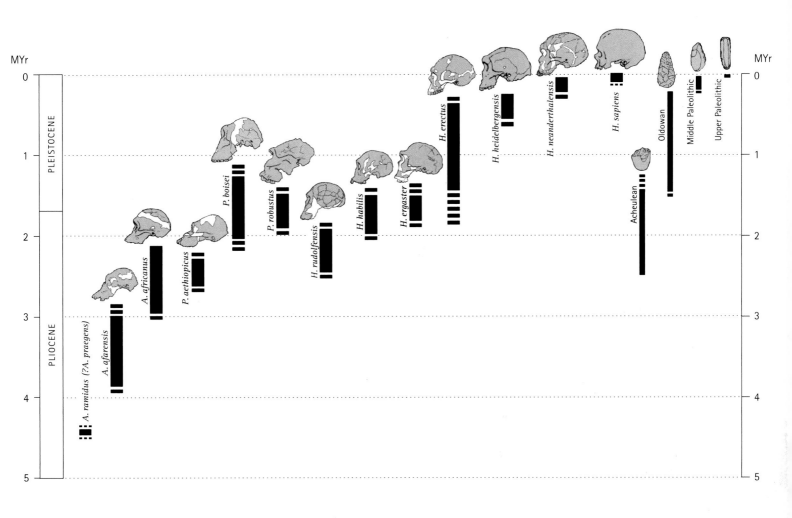

MYr
0

PLEISTOCENE

1

PLIOCENE

2

3

4

5

MYr
0

1

2

3

4

5

A. ramidus (?A. praegens)

A. afarensis

A. africanus

P. aethiopicus

P. boisei

P. robustus

H. rudolfensis

H. habilis

H. ergaster

H. erectus

H. heidelbergensis

H. neanderthalensis

H. sapiens

Acheulean

Oldowan

Middle Paleolithic

Upper Paleolithic

48
Chart showing the stratigraphic
ranges of the various hominid
species discussed in this book.
Bear in mind that known
stratigraphic ranges invariably
underestimate true ranges, and
that some are subject to
uncertainties in dating.
*Illustration by Diana Salles; after
Ian Tattersall,* The Fossil Trail
(Oxford University Press, 1995*).*

fall less certainly into the species *Homo
heidelbergensis.* These include a distorted
skull from Steinheim, in Germany, that
dates back to a quarter million years ago
or maybe substantially more [see Plates
66 and 67]; the rear end of a skull from
Swanscombe, in England, that is probably
of similar age [see Plate 92]; and a partial
skull from Lake Ndutu, in Tanzania, that
is about 350,000 years old. Recently, a
group of fossils from the Sima de los
Huesos site in the Atapuerca Mountains
of Spain, has been described as potential
early Neanderthals. [Plate 47 and see
Plates 94 and 95] An ESR date on a
calcite deposit overlying these specimens
has yielded an age in excess of 300,000
years, but it is uncertain how this deposit
relates to the bones themselves. Deciding
what species the Atapuerca fossils belong
to will have to await detailed study.

Homo heidelbergensis is a plausible
descendant of *Homo ergaster,* as well as a
potential ancestor of Neanderthals and

Homo sapiens, although some of the
other specimens just mentioned, notably
those from Steinheim and Swanscombe,
have also been debated as possible Neanderthal precursors. [Plate 48] We'll come
back to this tricky issue in Chapter 7.
Meanwhile, what do we know of life
during this period of human prehistory?

As we've seen, the stone tools from
the cave of Arago are generally simple,
with only the odd handaxe-like tool at
best. The site was, however, one at which
Homo heidelbergensis lived at least spo-
radically; some twenty habitation layers
have been identified at the site, associated
with a series of different climatic phases
varying from cold and dry (hence a rather
treeless environment) to more temperate
and humid, with more trees. Throughout,
there are abundant animal remains that
suggest that at least some hunting was
going on, though once again it's difficult
to be more specific than that. A better
idea of life in Europe around this time

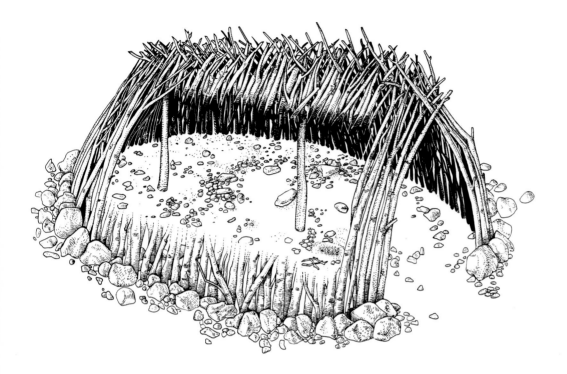

49

Reconstruction of one of the hut-like structures from Terra Amata, southern France.

Perhaps 400 thousand years old, these shelters, built on the ancient Mediterranean beach at Terra Amata, were as much as 25 feet long. The cutaway reveals an interior containing a circular hearth and debris from stoneworking.
Illustration by Diana Salles, after a concept by Henry de Lumley.

may come from the French site of Terra Amata, which lies within the city limits of Nice. Also about 400,000 years old, this site was interpreted by its excavators as a seasonally occupied beach camp at which early humans built shelters, although not all archaeologists agree with this interpretation. If the standard reading of the site is to be believed, however, the rudimentary huts of Terra Amata were surprisingly large, up to about twenty-five feet long and more than twelve feet wide. [Plate 49] They consisted of saplings embedded into the ground at the periphery of the hut and brought together at the top. Whether these structures were once waterproofed with animal hides is debated, although they probably were not. Interestingly, the interior of the best-preserved hut emplacement has disclosed the remains of an ancient fireplace—one of the earliest well-documented instances of a hearth, though there are hints of fire use as early as about 1.4 to 1.5 million year ago in Africa. Controlled use of fire in hearths most certainly represented a significant advance in

hominid life, so it's very surprising that once the practice was established, early instances of this kind are so rare in archaeological sites. Inside the shelter were numerous broken animal bones, from beasts of a variety of sizes, but remarkably, few if any seem to have been burned. Butchery certainly went on, however, and the numerous stone tools found, most made from the rather unsuitable local limestone beach cobbles, included bifacially flaked handaxes as well as implements of more primitive aspect.

The technique for thinning handaxes introduced about 1 million years ago appears to have been the last major technological advance for an extended period of time. Not until the period between about 400,000 and 200,000 years ago (dating is vague) do we find another major innovation in toolmaking technology. However, this development involved a major conceptual leap. Handaxes had been useful tools, and their widespread use in vast numbers in Europe and Africa over a long span of time testifies to the success of this technology. In the final analysis, however, handaxes are not a great deal more useful for most tasks than large, sharp-edged flakes are, so eventually traditional handaxes shaped on large cobbles were superseded by a superior type of flake tool. Tools of this new kind were produced by preforming a stone core in such a way that a single large flake of desired shape could be detached from it by a single blow, normally using a soft hammer. [Plate 50] Making such tools required a great degree of skill and knowledge on the part of the toolmaker; skill that paid off in the production of an implement that had a long, sharp, continuous cutting edge almost all the way around its periphery. Flakes made from "prepared cores" were not always the end product; such "blanks" were often "retouched" by gentle flaking to produce a range of final products. The manufacture of implements of this kind also required raw materials that could be relied on to fracture in a particularly predictable way. For this reason they are most common in regions abounding in such substances as flint and chert, which possess just this quality.

Exactly what the humans who first made prepared-core tools looked like is unknown, although it seems a reasonable guess that the technique originated in a local population of *Homo heidelbergensis*, and probably in Africa. The Neanderthals, of course, were not an African phenomenon, having initially evolved somewhere in Europe or western Asia. But in the end it was they, successors to *Homo heidelbergensis*, who became the ultimate masters of this toolmaking technique, producing a wide variety of beautifully crafted flake tools.

Having looked briefly at the long background from which they emerged, let's return now to the Neanderthals, first by examining how our knowledge of them has developed over the almost century and a half since they first came to scientific attention■

50

Prepared core with flake tool detached.

Flint replica of a Middle Paleolithic flake and core, showing the long continuous edge produced by this technique.

Replica by Dodi Ben-Ami; photograph by Willard Whitson.

Discovery and Interpretation of the Neanderthals

51 *below*
View from the south of the "Neandershöhle" as it appeared in the mid-1830s, by J. H. Bongard.

The Neandershöhle was the largest and most famous of the series of caves in the Neander Valley that yielded the Neander Thal fossils in 1856.
Courtesy of Gerhard Bosinski

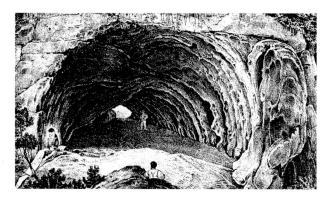

52 *right*
Portrait of Joachim Neander (1650–1680), by H. Ackermann.

This seventeenth-century composer and divine gave the Classicized version of his surname (originally Neumann) to the valley through which the Düssel river flows to the Rhine. In the valley walls was found the Feldhofer cave that yielded the original Neanderthal fossils.
Courtesy of Gerhard Bosinski.

 The Man of the Neander Thal
The Neanderthals' image problem is rooted in their history. Quite simply, a Neanderthal (*the* Neanderthal, in fact) was the first fossil form to be recognized as a somehow *different* kind of human, some three years before the publication of Darwin's great book *On the Origin of Species* ushered in the notion (and then only obliquely) that our species must have had an evolutionary past. In August of 1856, German laborers in search of lime blasted out the entrance to a small cave (the Feldhofer grotto) that lay high on the sheer wall of the Neander Valley (in German, *Neander Thal*), through which the Düssel river meanders to join the Rhine. [Plates 51 and 52] Within the cave the workers quickly exhumed the top part of a skull like none ever seen before: long and low, with a pair of large ridges arching over the now-vanished eye sockets. [Plate 53] Nearby they excavated some bones from the body of the same heavily fossilized and very robustly built individual. [see Plate 107] The workers didn't think anything much of these finds, assuming them to be the bones of a cave bear; but by great good fortune they set at least some of them aside for eventual examination by the local schoolteacher and amateur natural historian Johann Fuhlrott. Fuhlrott, to his eternal credit,

had the insight to recognize them for what they were: the remains of a previously unknown type of human. Guessing that what he had in his hands was part of what had at the time of its discovery been a complete skeleton, Fuhlrott returned to the cave with the workers, but it was too late. The grotto had been emptied of all evidence that might have revealed more about these remarkable specimens.

Fuhlrott might have had the insight, but he didn't have the connections to bring this remarkable new phenomenon

to scientific attention. So he took his finds to Hermann Schaaffhausen, professor of anatomy at the University of Bonn, and after a preliminary announcement by Schaaffhausen, the pair presented the Neanderthaler ("Neanderthal Man") to the world at a meeting of the local natural history society held in June 1857. [Plate 54] On this occasion Fuhlrott presented an account of the circumstances of discovery of the fossils, based on a careful questioning of the laborers who had found them. He emphasized the antiquity of the bones, as evidenced both by the thickness of the earth (some five feet) that had overlain them and by the fact that they were heavily mineralized and bore

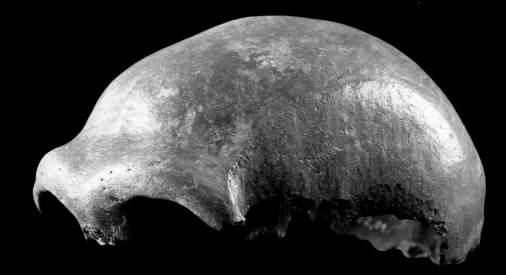

53
The Neanderthal skullcap.

The original skullcap from the Neander Thal, Germany, probably around 50 thousand years old. The discovery of this specimen in 1856 marked the effective beginning of the science of paleoanthropology, and the locality at which it was found gave its name to the entire group of extinct humans to which this volume is devoted.
Courtesy of the Rheinisches Landesmuseum, Bonn.

54

Hermann Schaaffhausen's 1857 illustration of the Neanderthal skullcap.

This lithograph accompanied Schaaffhausen's original description of the Neanderthal remains, on this page. The figures on the opposite page show a modern human skull of the most "barbarous" aspect that Schaaffhausen could find (note heavy brows).

branching mineral markings such as had been found, for instance, on the bones of giant extinct cave bears. The description and interpretation of the remains themselves fell to Schaaffhausen. Even though Darwin's great book had yet to appear, an active debate was then proceeding in Germany and elsewhere on whether or not life might in some way have developed through time as a result of some innate or external process. Indeed, five years earlier Schaaffhausen himself had written an article, entitled "On the Constancy and Transformation of Species," in which he had declared that "the immutability of species...is not proven."

At that time, Schaaffhausen had been concerned with theory, even philosophy; but in the Neanderthaler he was undeniably dealing with a fact that demanded explanation—that the Neanderthal skeleton, while human in many respects, including brain size, was nonetheless distinctly unlike anything he or anyone else had seen before. He provided an impressively detailed description of the bones, observing that their heavy build implied a strong muscular development, perhaps as a result of a physically demanding lifestyle. His attention was particularly drawn,

however, to the unusual shape of the skullcap, notably the low, narrow forehead and the large bony arches above each eye. He noted that these features, which he considered to be natural rather than the result of disease or abnormal development, were reminiscent of the great apes. Yet this clearly wasn't an ape, and if these strange features weren't pathological either, perhaps they were due to ancientness. So Schaaffhausen scoured the literature for accounts of comparable specimens among the reports of antiquaries who had dug up ancient skeletons. Even though he was unable to find anything that came close to matching the characteristics of his Neanderthaler, he eventually concluded that the bones belonged to a member of an ancient aboriginal tribe that had occupied Germany before the ancestors of its modern inhabitants had arrived there.

Since Schaaffhausen had to interpret his fossil in terms of the world as he understood it, this judgment was entirely rational, especially given that, according to Classical chroniclers (the authorities of record), Germany had in ancient times been peopled with wild and woolly tribes, each more savage than the last. Nonetheless, he was evidently not entirely happy with his conclusion that here were simply the remains of a barbarous ancient German. As he

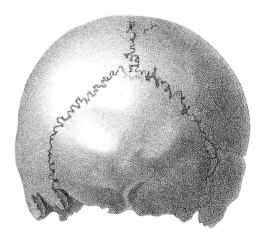

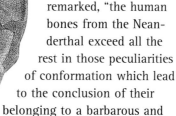

remarked, "the human bones from the Neanderthal exceed all the rest in those peculiarities of conformation which lead to the conclusion of their belonging to a barbarous and savage race." In hindsight, one can see how tantalizingly close Schaaffhausen came to an evolutionary perspective on his fossils, for he cleverly worked his notion of the mutability of species into his argument, stating that "sufficient grounds exist for the assumption that man coexisted with the animals found in the *diluvium* [Biblical Flood]; and many a barbarous race may, before all historical time, have disappeared, together with animals of the ancient world, whilst the races whose organization is improved have continued the genus." This was at least an incipiently evolutionary notion, but in 1857 the time was not yet ripe for the suggestion that the Neanderthaler, so close to us but yet so far, was anything other than an inferior version of our own species.

For controversy, however, the time is always ripe, and controversy aplenty was unleashed by Schaaffhausen's report. Unfortunately, the heavy guns were not on Schaaffhausen's side. In Germany the life

sciences were dominated at the time by Rudolf Virchow, the father of the modern study of cell biology and a doughty opponent of evolutionary thought in all its manifestations. Virchow's specialty was pathology, and pathology provided the explanation he preferred for the unusual appearance of the Neanderthaler. To Virchow, here were the remains of an ordinary human being cursed with a particularly unfortunate affliction, so he heartily endorsed the conclusions reached by Schaaffhausen's colleague on the Bonn faculty, Professor August Mayer—the very August Mayer who has gone down in history as the author of perhaps the most imaginative scenario ever dreamt up in the long history of human evolutionary studies.

Mayer's examination of the bones from the Feldhofer cave suggested several things to him. He noted, for example, that the thigh bones and the upper front part of the pelvis were somewhat curved, as in lifelong horsemen. These characteristics, he claimed, might also have been exaggerated by childhood rickets, a vitamin deficiency disease. The left arm had been fractured and had healed badly; and Mayer claimed that this injury was the key to the unusual shape of the skull: it was the constant frown brought on by the pain of the injury that had caused the formation of the bony ridges above the eyes! Putting all the evidence together, Mayer proposed that the remains were those of an unfortunate deserter from the Cossack cavalry that had paused near the

Rhine in January of 1814, before proceeding onward to attack France. This explanation conveniently incorporated many of the unusual attributes of the Neanderthaler, but it was totally deficient in accounting for any of them. Indeed, it flew in the face of what was already known about the bone pathology produced by rickets, in which Rudolf Virchow was an acknowledged expert. Yet even Virchow—who knew, for example, that rickets produces weakened bones, whereas those of the Neanderthaler were supremely robust—accepted the main elements of Mayer's analysis, and for years his support ensured that throughout the German-speaking world, pathology was the preferred rationalization for this strange phenomenon. The only convincing explanation of this strange behavior by a scientist of extraordinary gifts and achievement lies in Virchow's obsessive and politically motivated opposition to evolution—which by 1864, the year of publication of Mayer's diatribe, had become a subject of fervent debate in Germany.

 Neanderthals Abroad
The focus of rational discussion of the Neanderthaler thus shifted to elsewhere in the world, notably England, where the anatomist George Busk had published his translation of Schaaffhausen's article in 1861, together with an approving commentary. In England, as in France, the term "idiot" was sometimes heard in discussion of the

Neanderthaler, but the notion of pathology in Virchow's sense was generally ruled out. One of the first thoughtful English analyses came in 1863 from Darwin's defender Thomas Henry Huxley, in his famous book of essays entitled *Evidence as to Man's Place in Nature*. After careful consideration, and largely on the basis of its large brain size, Huxley found the Neanderthal skullcap to be "the most pithecoid [apelike] of known human skulls," forming "the extreme term of a series leading gradually from it to the highest and best developed of human crania." Thus, even though he wrote from a confirmed evolutionary perspective that allowed him to wonder, "In still older strata do the fossilized bones of an Ape more anthropoid, or a man more pithecoid, than any yet known await the researches of some unborn palaeontologist?," Huxley added little to what Schaaffhausen had already concluded. Perhaps this sketchy conclusion was inevitable, given that there was precious little genuinely ancient human fossil evidence to go on. Aside from the Neanderthaler itself, only one fossil specimen known to science was of comparable antiquity. This specimen was the skull of a two-and-a-half-year-old child found at Engis in Belgium in 1829, in association with the fossils of extinct animals. [Plate 55] The skulls of young—especially extremely young—Neanderthals and those of modern people differ from each other much less than do those of adults, and a demonstrably modern adult skull from the occipital regions, as far as the middle of the occipital foramen, with the squamous and mastoid portions of the right temporal bone entire, or nearly so, while the left temporal bone is wanting. From the middle of the occipital foramen to the middle of the roof of each orbit, the base of the skull is destroyed, and the facial bones are entirely absent.

Fig. 2.

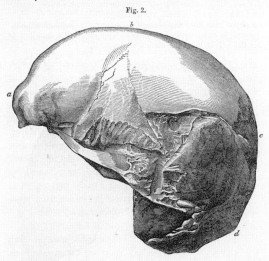

Side view of the cast of part of a human skull found by Dr. Schmerling imbedded amongst the remains of extinct mammalia in the cave of Engis, near Liége.

a Superciliary ridge and glabella.   *c* The apex of the lambdoidal suture.
b Coronal suture.   *d* The occipital protuberance.

" The extreme length of the skull is 7.7 inches, and as its extreme breadth is not more than 5.25, its form is decidedly dolichocephalic.

55

The Engis (Belgium) juvenile Neanderthal cranium.

This partial cranium of a two- or three-year old was discovered by Philippe-Charles Schmerling in 1829. It was the first Neanderthal fossil to be discovered, but it was not identified as such until a century later. Nonetheless, its ancientness was recognized from the start (it is now thought to be about 70 thousand years old), and this illustration was published by Charles Lyell in 1863, in his *Antiquity of Man.*
Courtesy of Peter N. Nevraumont.

Engis cave was wrongly thought to have been associated with the juvenile. Unfortunately, it was the former that monopolized scientific attention (including Huxley's). The juvenile was not correctly identified until 1936.

Not everyone was as cautious as Huxley. At the 1863 meeting of the British Association for the Advancement of Science, William King, professor of geology at Queen's College, Galway, championed the view that the Neanderthaler represented a separate species of *Homo, Homo neanderthalensis.* He was the first and, at the time, the only scientist to do so. This was a time in which (as Huxley's words imply), European savants considered some human populations to be less "advanced" than others (notably, than Europeans). The Neanderthaler, it seems, struck King as simply too benighted to belong even among the "lowest" races of *Homo sapiens.* Thus, in the published version of his speech that appeared the next year, King described the Feldhofer skull as resem-

bling that of a chimpanzee and hinted that a chimpanzeelike "darkness" had "characterized the being to which the fossil belonged." This description implied brutishness—even depravity—reflecting an undercurrent of belief about the moral status of the Neanderthals that lasted well beyond the nineteenth century. Apparently, the more King thought about it, the more he was impressed by the Neanderthaler's darker side, for he added in a footnote to his paper that since his initial statement, he had become "strongly inclined" to place the Neanderthaler in a separate genus. But while almost everyone would have concurred on the matter of the Neanderthaler's benightedness, nobody seemed any more impressed by this argument for generic distinction than by King's idea that here was a distinct human species.

Thus, during the first half of the 1860s just about every possibility was raised in explanation of the curious morphology of the Neanderthal fossil: pathology, idiocy,

56
The Gibraltar 1 cranium.

Recovered from Forbes' Quarry, Gibraltar, some time before 1848, and probably about 50 thousand years old, this was the first adult Neanderthal cranium to be discovered. Its affinities were not recognized, however, until after the Feldhofer Cave remains had been described.
Courtesy of The Natural History Museum, London.

trauma, the outer limit of normal variation within the human species, membership in a distinct species or even genus. The time had come for some winnowing of these possibilities. As it happened, the first incontrovertible piece of evidence that the Neanderthaler was not simply a freak occurrence came in 1863 when the anatomist George Busk, Schaaffhausen's translator, received a skull that had been found in Forbes' Quarry, Gibraltar, prior to 1848. [Plate 56] This specimen is of the same general type as the Neanderthaler, although it is built more lightly, possibly because it represents a female. Unlike the original Neanderthal specimen, however, this one possesses a face: large and modestly projecting, especially in the midline, with a wide nasal aperture and sharply receding cheekbones. Busk immediately appreciated the significance of the Gibraltar fossil, confirming as it did that the Neanderthaler did "not represent…a mere individual peculiarity." "Even Professor Mayer," Busk slyly continued, "will hardly suppose that a ricketty Cossack engaged in the campaign of 1814 had crept into a sealed fissure in the Rock of Gibraltar."

Even the splendid Gibraltar specimen, however, proved to be insufficient evidence to establish Neanderthals as a distinct type of human being—perhaps because Busk and his colleague Hugh Falconer, who commented on it in similar terms, never followed up with a complete description. Whatever the case, not until 1886, with the finding of two quite complete Neanderthal skeletons at the Belgian

site of Spy, did most authorities come around to Busk's point of view. Agreement was limited, however, to the fact that here was an ancient and distinctive type of human; the significance of this form continued to be debated. Even after pathology was removed from the picture by repetitive and consistent finds of humans of this type, it took several more years for the notion that they represented a "lower race" or "barbarous tribe" of *Homo sapiens* to be finally laid to rest. To this day, many paleoanthropologists are still unable to accept the idea that in the Neanderthals we have a distinct—and distinctive—species of human. This reluctance to consider Neanderthals a separate species is due in part to the historical accident that the first Neanderthal find was made and debated in a milieu in which its membership in a species other than our own was unthinkable to most, and in which there was no other human fossil evidence to assist in evaluating its peculiarities.

Also partly responsible for this hesitation, I think, is the entirely mistaken belief that, if we recognize Neanderthals as a separate species, we will have to endow the modern "races" of *Homo sapiens* with separate subspecies names. This misapprehension reflects yet another aspect of the insularity of human paleontology compared to other branches of vertebrate paleontology in general: from its very birth in the debate over the Neanderthal skeleton, paleoanthropology has been cursed with a *Homo sapiens*-centric point of view. Unlike other paleontologists, whose job is to unravel and explain the diversity of species in nature, paleoanthropologists have been obsessed by the single species *Homo sapiens*, by the variety within it, and by the attempt to trace its origins in a linear fashion into the past. That there is incontrovertibly only one human species in the world today has certainly fueled this fixation. There's no doubt in my mind, however, that the predominant outlook among paleoanthropologists today stems directly from a tradition that had its beginning in the Neander Valley on that August day in 1856 — at a time before there was an adequate evolutionary framework within which the extraordinary find could be interpreted.

 ### The Old Stone Age

While the anatomists were haranguing each other over the significance of a suite of peculiar bones, the antiquarians of Europe were hard at work creating the science of archaeology and establishing the chronology of the human cultural past at which we've already briefly looked. As early as 1819 the Danish archaeologists C. J. Thomsen and J. J. A. Worsaae proposed a division of European prehistoric time into successive Stone, Bronze, and Iron Ages. Then, in 1865, the English archaeologist Sir John Lubbock subdivided the Stone Age into the earlier Palaeolithic (Old Stone Age, characterized by chipped or flaked stone tools) and the later Neolithic (New Stone Age, with polished stone tools). Of these two periods the Palaeolithic was much the longer, so much so that it was eventually subdivided itself.

The initial subdivision was made by the French paleontologist Edouard Lartet, who noted that three of the sites that he had excavated in the Vézère River valley of western France did not "possess a uniformity in the production of human industry." As an expert in mammal fossils, Lartet opted to name the different periods of toolmaking that he discerned after the animals found with them: the Cave Bear period, Woolly Mammoth period, and so on. This system didn't go over well with the artifact-oriented archaeologists, however, and the French savant Gabriel de Mortillet soon established a chronology that recognized four distinctive periods of stone toolmaking in the French Paleolithic, each named for a site at which it was well represented. In later works de Mortillet expanded the number of periods to six.[4] First in time was the Chellean, which was characterized by massive handaxes and cleavers. This period was followed by the rather similar Acheulean, whose name today covers the Chellean as well. Next came the Mousterian, a sophisticated variant of the prepared-core technology. The Aurignacian followed, with bone points as well as stone tools made from long, thin "blades" struck from a cylindrical core. Then came the Solutrean, characterized by astonishingly finely worked "laurel-leaf" points; and finally, the Magdalenian,

4   Actually, de Mortillet recognized an additional, seventh, era of stone toolmaking at the beginning of the sequence. This he dubbed the period of eoliths ("dawn stones"), in which a remote hypothetical human ancestor, *Anthropopithecus*, had made an extremely rudimentary kind of stone tool, essentially just fractured pieces of rock. Even though there was in practice no way of distinguishing eoliths from any piece of naturally fractured stone, this concept was eventually adopted quite widely and caused great confusion before it became generally agreed that nothing that could be called an eolith could be regarded as evidence of human activity.

The Alpine glacial sequence.

Established by Penck and Brückner in 1909, this scheme of four glacial periods separated by warmer interglacials remained the basis of Pleistocene chronology in Europe until gradually superseded during the 1960s and 1970s by the oxygen isotope record.
Illustration by Diana Salles.

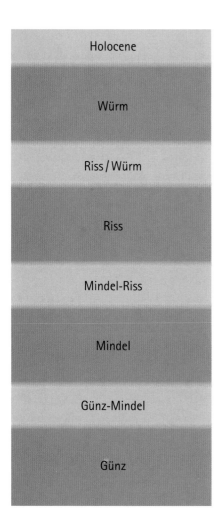

with many very fancy bone and antler tools, and much decoration of utilitarian items. Conventional practice today is to place the Acheulean in the period known as the Lower Paleolithic (which stretches back to the beginning of stone toolmaking, embracing, for example, the Oldowan of Africa as well). The Mousterian and some earlier traditions fall into the Middle Paleolithic, and the Aurignacian marks the beginning of the Upper Paleolithic. Here and there, a couple other names have over the years been added to the sequence, including the Châtelperronian, a stoneworking industry that fits uneasily between the Middle and Upper Paleolithic, and about which we'll learn more later.

The Ice Ages

During the nineteenth century a basic geological framework for Europe also developed. Geologists played an important role in establishing the great antiquity of humanity by demonstrating an association between the bones of extinct animals and the stone tools left behind by early people. Geologists of the period were also doing much to unravel the forces that had shaped the surface of Earth, and by the mid-nineteenth century it was becoming evident that a succession of glaciations (expansions of the polar ice caps) caused by cooling climate had done much to produce the landforms seen in the northern and high-altitude parts of Europe. De Mortillet quickly seized upon this view of fluctuating past environments. By the 1880s he was already

developing a scheme in which human physical and cultural evolution proceeded hand in hand with the seesawing climates of the Pleistocene epoch (the geological name for the period of glaciations, which we now know began about 1.8 million years ago, and which ended—if indeed it did, for there's no substantial reason to believe the glaciers will not return—with the retreat of the most recent glacial masses about 10,000 years ago). Near the beginning of the twentieth century, the classical account of Pleistocene glaciation in Europe was formulated by the Austrian geographers Albrecht Penck and Eduard Brückner. Working in the German Alps, which of course still retain a small icecap at higher altitudes, Penck and Brückner discerned evidence for four major glacial advances, during which the Alpine ice sheet swelled as the northern polar ice cap progressed southward. They gave a name to each of these advances: from oldest to youngest, they called them Günz, Mindel, Riss, and Würm. [Plate 57] The names themselves derived from four tributaries of the Danube beside which gravel terraces had been formed by meltwaters from the ice sheets. Between the four major glacial episodes, warmer "interglacials" had seen the retreat of the ice sheets. As the ice melted, the increased runoff of water had caused the rivers to cut down through the gravel terraces. Basing their estimate on the time thought to be necessary for the buildup and erosion of the various river gravels, Penck and Brückner hazarded that this

The rockshelter of Cro-Magnon.

Located in the southwestern French village of Les Eyzies, this site has given its name to the earliest modern humans who inhabited Europe.

Photograph by Ian Tattersall.

whole process of repeated cooling and warming had taken about 600,000 years.

Penck and Brückner's was a magisterial achievement, tying a vast quantity of disparate geological data into a coherent historical scheme. Although it eventually turned out that the Pleistocene was three times longer than they proposed and that the sequence of geological events within it was a good deal more complex, for more than half a century the scheme proposed by Penck and Brückner remained the framework within which hominid evolution in Europe was interpreted. What was most significant to paleoanthropology was the possibility this framework offered of developing a reliable relative chronology for fossil humans. The cave sites in which most of the early human (and particularly Neanderthal) remains were found could now at least in theory be placed in sequence by comparing the fossil animals they contained with those typical of glacial deposits of different times, in the manner described in Chapter 3. In addition, by 1909, the year in which Penck and Brückner's scheme was published, Neanderthal fossils had started to turn up in quite large numbers.

 ### The Record Expands

As the nineteenth century drew to a close, the human fossil record increased by leaps and bounds. As early as 1866 the first Neanderthal lower jaw—unfortunately incomplete and toothless—had been found at the Belgian cave of La Naulette, in circumstances that unques-

tionably indicated great antiquity. In 1868 came the famous find at the Cro-Magnon rock shelter in the Dordogne region of western France. [Plate 58] Here railroad laborers seeking fill uncovered at least five individuals (one an infant) who, because they were associated with Aurignacian tools and the bones of extinct animals, were undoubtedly of great antiquity but who had entirely modern anatomy. [Plate 59] These specimens were the first firm evidence of truly ancient modern-looking people, and their name, Cro-Magnon, ultimately was given to all the earliest *Homo sapiens* of Europe—of whom more evidence turned up much further east, at a couple of Moravian sites, in the 1880s. In 1874 some probably Neanderthal fragments were found at Pontnewydd, in Wales. This site still holds the record as the most northerly known occurrence of this species, as well as one of the oldest. A couple of years later more bits of evidence were found at Rivaux, in southern France. The most fuss, however, was provoked by a tiny fragment of juvenile Neanderthal lower jaw found at the Moravian site of Šipka in 1880. With impeccable credentials of antiquity that included ancient (Mousterian) stone tools as well as the requisite extinct animals, this specimen was fiercely attacked as pathological by the ubiquitous Rudolf Virchow. Hermann Schaaffhausen, on the other hand, defended the specimen as a genuine member of *Homo primigenius* (by then his preferred appellation for *Homo neanderthalensis*).

Skull of the "Old Man" of Cro-Magnon, France (right), compared with the skull of a La Ferrassie Neanderthal.

Discovered in 1868, the Cro-Magnon fossils provided the first convincing evidence of ancient modern humans in association with an extinct fauna. Bones from La Ferrassie were used by Marcellin Boule to cover parts missing from the La Chapelle Neanderthal skeleton, but he never properly described the ensemble from the site. Cro-Magnon about 30 thousand years old, or a little less; La Ferrassie probably about 20 thousand years older.
Photograph by John Reader.

As the old Virchow/Schaaffhausen wrangle over the Neanderthaler was being replayed with undiminished vigor, two somewhat complete Neanderthal skeletons from the Belgian site of Spy turned up to settle the argument. Again associated with Mousterian artifacts, and of undoubtedly great antiquity, the Spy specimens were studied by Max Lohest (one of their discoverers) and Julien Fraipont, both of the University of Liège. These scholars demonstrated beyond question that the skeletons were both "Neanderthaloid" and human, although with many "apelike" features, such as the brow ridges and receding foreheads already so evident in the Neanderthal and Gibraltar individuals. While the anatomy of the emerging Neanderthal type was undoubtedly unusual, however, there was now no way that such repetition in form could be ascribed to pathology. The specimens from the Neander Valley, Gibraltar, and Spy all belonged to a distinctive type of human, now extinct, that had once roamed from northern Europe to Gibraltar.

Like those of the Neanderthaler, the bones of the body skeletons from Spy were massively constructed and had large joint surfaces. From the anatomy of the leg bones, Fraipont and Lohest came to the conclusion that these individuals had walked upright, but with bent knees—just as, in fact, apes do when they stand up. Thus started the myth of the bent-kneed Neanderthals, a myth that was to endure more than half a century. But at least this myth was about a distinctive type of human that had lived widely throughout Europe and beyond in the remote past, and not one about a doubly mythical pathological idiot. *Homo neanderthalensis*—its original name resurrected by the American paleontologist and "Dinosaur Wars" protagonist Edward Drinker Cope—began to edge its way into the pantheon of vanished human species.

 The Big Picture
Neanderthal Man did not occupy this pantheon alone for long. In 1891 and 1892, far away in the Dutch East Indies, Eugene Dubois made his extraordinary find of the *Pithecanthropus* skullcap and femur (as we saw in Chapter 4), representing a yet more ancient and apelike precursor of humans. [see Plate 38] While Dubois himself didn't bother to compare his new fossils with any Neanderthal—for reasons best known to himself he clung to the pathological explanation for Neanderthal morphology—others did. Perhaps the bravest of the early commentators was the Dublin anatomist Daniel Cunningham, who took Dubois to task for not making this comparison, and who concluded as early as 1896 that the Neanderthals represented an intermediate stage in a lineage leading from *Pithecanthropus* to modern humans. This was very much a minority opinion at first, however, and the *Pithecanthropus* debate initially developed along lines very similar to those the Neanderthal debate had taken forty years earlier.

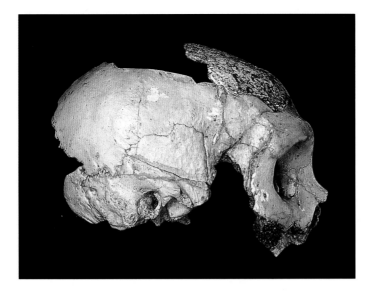

60
Partial cranium from Krapina, Croatia.

The best-preserved of the Neanderthal cranial fragments from this historically as well as paleoanthropologically important cave site. Probably about 120 thousand years old.

"Ancestors" photograph by Chester Tarka; courtesy of Jakov Radovčić.

With two distinctive fossil hominids in the ring alongside *Homo sapiens*, though, it's possible to see in hindsight that the time was ripe by the turn of the twentieth century for a general reappraisal of the evidence for human evolution. The most influential such reassessment was provided by the German paleontologist Gustav Schwalbe, who in the years straddling the turn of the century produced long monographs on *Pithecanthropus* and the Neanderthals (to him, *Homo primigenius*). Schwalbe firmly believed that both *Pithecanthropus* and the Neanderthals were distinctive extinct human species. At the time, both of these early humans were generally thought to have come from somewhere in the middle of the sequence of glacials (the Middle Pleistocene, now reckoned to have lasted from 950,000 to 128,000 years ago). On the grounds of morphology, however, Schwalbe thought that *Pithecanthropus* had to be older. Two major possibilities thus presented themselves: either *Pithecanthropus* was directly ancestral to both Neanderthals and modern humans, or *Pithecanthropus* gave rise to the Neanderthals, which in turn were ancestral to modern humans. A third possibility was that both fossil forms were side branches in human evolution, but Schwalbe didn't favor this interpretation, vacillating instead between the first two. What was most important to Schwalbe was that *Pithecanthropus*, *Homo primigenius*, and *Homo sapiens* formed a coherent series. Even if the fossil species were not the actual ancestors of *Homo sapiens*, how different from them could the ancestors themselves have been?

One person who was impressed by Schwalbe's morphological appraisal was the Croatian paleontologist Dragutin Gorjanović-Kramberger, who in the years following 1899 had been excavating a rock shelter in the town of Krapina, some 50 miles north of Zagreb. From the very beginning Krapina promised to be an archaeological site of exceptional importance. By 1906, the year in which Gorjanović monographed his finds, the locality had yielded several hundred hominid bits and pieces, among them a number of partial crania and fragments of the skeletons of infants and children, as well as of adults. [Plate 60] Gorjanović identified the remains as Neanderthal in type and concluded that *Homo primigenius* (he later converted to *Homo neanderthalensis*) stood in the direct line of ancestry of *Homo sapiens*. He also thought that, though quite variable among themselves, the Krapina fossils formed a roughly contemporaneous assemblage that dated from an early interglacial, either the Günz-Mindel or the Mindel-Riss (though he finally came around to the more accurate view that they were from the last, Riss-Würm) interglacial. [see Plate 57] In retrospect, it has turned out that the Krapina stratigraphy is quite complex. Although Gorjanović went into little detail in his monograph (quaintly, even for that day, titled *Diluvial Man from Krapina*), he kept elaborate stratigraphic notes on his excavations, which have allowed later researchers to gain a clearer picture of the history of the site—if not yet of its precise dating. Human remains apparently came from most stratigraphic levels and may span a long period from about 130,000 to 80,000 years ago. The bulk of the material is accompanied by a fauna typical of a warmer climate and probably comes from the main part of the last interglacial, between about 127,000 and 115,000 years ago; some later specimens probably come from milder periods within the last glacial itself, maybe around 100,000 years ago. All of the hominid fossils, however, are plausibly Neanderthal, and all were found in an at least broadly Mousterian archaeological context.

Cannibal Feasts?

Perhaps the most provocative of the conclusions that Gorjanović drew from his excavations at Krapina was that the fragmentary state of the human fossils was due to the practice of cannibalism. This was not the first time that the notion of cannibalism had been raised in connection with Neanderthals. Oddly enough, this suggestion appears to have first cropped up in the literature in the form of a denial by Edouard Dupont, describer of the robust Neanderthal jaw from La Naulette, that his specimen had been broken as the result of cannibalistic activities. Well-intentioned though they doubtless were, Dupont's protestations make it clear that the notion of Neanderthal cannibalism was already in the air by 1866, when he wrote. But perhaps this

is not surprising, for what other appalling practice could better confirm the bestiality of these creatures? Nonetheless, although Gorjanović pointed to hints of burning on some of the Krapina bones as additional evidence of cannibalism, the immediate response to his idea by western European and American colleagues was somewhat muted. Perhaps the mildness of this reaction was a result of other finds that were beginning to attract the limelight.

In retrospect, some of the most important of these finds were the fragmentary remains of several individuals discovered at the German site of Ehringsdorf, beginning in 1908. The find that really garnered widespread attention, though, was the single well-preserved lower jaw that was uncovered in a gravel pit at Mauer, near Heidelberg, in 1907. [see Plate 42] The mandible was massive, with, as the illustration shows, rather squat rami and a noticeably receding chin region. What's more, the jaw had been found eighty feet down in the glacial sediments of the pit, and was clearly of great age, much greater than that of any Neanderthal. The German paleontologist Otto Schoetensack promptly described it as a new kind of human, *Homo heidelbergensis*, older (from the Günz-Mindel interglacial) and more primitive than any yet known. There was thus plenty of food for thought for the paleoanthropological community, but even this remarkable discovery was overshadowed almost immediately.

61

Mural reconstruction of a Neanderthal group, painted by Charles R. Knight in 1920.

Set at a site (perhaps Le Moustier) overlooking the Vézère River in southwestern France, this mural, painted for the American Museum of Natural History, reflects the view of the Neanderthals prevalent at the time.

Courtesy of the American Museum of Natural History

 The Old Man of La Chapelle
Between 1908 and 1911, excavations at several cave sites in southwestern France produced semi-complete or multiple skeletons of Neanderthals, opening up new possibilities to paleoanthropologists. One of these sites was Le Moustier, the rock shelter in the Vézère River valley for which the Mousterian industry had been named. [Plates 61 and 62 and see Plates 109 and 110] Another was the shelter of La Ferrassie, not very far away, which over a period of years yielded quite complete skeletons of two adults and the more fragmentary remains of half a dozen infants and

juveniles. [see Plate 59] Historically most important, though, was the skeleton of an aged Neanderthal discovered buried in a small cave at La Chapelle-aux-Saints, some way to the east in the Corrèze. [Plate 63] The reason for the preeminence of this specimen was that it was chosen for detailed study by Marcellin Boule, Professor of Paleontology at the National Museum of Natural History in Paris, who published voluminously on it between 1911 and 1913. At the time, Boule's was by far the most comprehensive study ever attempted of Neanderthal anatomy and relationships, and, aided by the success of his book *Les Hommes Fossiles,* published

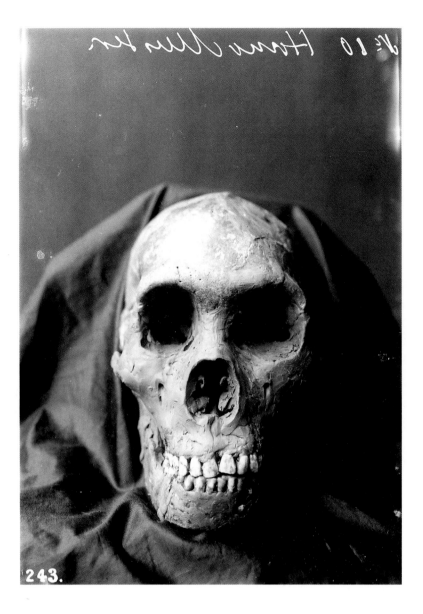

62
Adolescent Neanderthal skull from Le Moustier, France.

In 1907, the German antiquarian Otto Hauser discovered a more or less complete adolescent Neanderthal skeleton in the "lower shelter" of Le Moustier, the site from which the Mousterian stoneworking culture of the Neanderthals acquired its name. This 1909 photograph shows the skull as reconstructed by Hermann Klaatsch. About 50 thousand years old.

63
Skull and postcranial bones from La Chapelle-aux-Saints, Corrèze, France.

The skeleton of the "Old Man" from La Chapelle, now thought to be about 50 thousand years old, was misinterpreted by Marcellin Boule in 1908-11 to yield the classic caricature of the Neanderthals as shuffling, bent-kneed brutes.
Photograph by John Reader

in 1912 (and still in print in English as *Fosssil Men*), it set the stereotype of the Neanderthals for decades to come.

This was unfortunate, to say the least, for Boule had very definite ideas about the Neanderthals. One was that *Homo neanderthalensis* was a side branch in human evolution that had become extinct without issue. So far so good. But Boule also took pains to demonstrate that Neanderthals were anatomically inferior to modern humans in almost every way imaginable. He used the La Chapelle skeleton, its big brain notwithstanding (by his own reckoning its cranial capacity was more than 1600 ml), as the basis for an excruciatingly detailed portrait of the Neanderthals as beetle-browed, bent-kneed, sloping-necked, shuffling slouches with grasping feet and inferior brains. "What a contrast," he wrote in 1913, "with the…Cro-Magnons, [who] with their more elegant bodies, finer heads, expansive and upright foreheads…manual dexterity… inventive spirit…artistic and religious sensibilities…[and] capacities for abstract thought were the first to deserve the glorious title of *Homo sapiens*!" What's more, Boule believed that these demigods had already been in existence in Neanderthal times. Noting that there seemed to be a rather abrupt transition in France between the Mousterian stoneworking industries of the Neanderthals and the Upper Paleolithic cultures of the Cro-Magnons who succeeded them, he argued forcefully that the former had been wiped out by the more talented moderns.

If Boule was uncharitable toward the Neanderthals, toward *Pithecanthropus* he was downright hostile. In a long consideration of virtually every fossil that might conceivably have relevance to human evolution, he barely mentioned Java Man at all, dismissing it as a giant gibbon, just as Virchow had done years earlier. But if neither *Pithecanthropus* nor *Homo neanderthalensis* lay in the human lineage, then where had modern humans come from? Boule entertained two possibilities. One was Schoetensack's *Homo heidelbergensis*, but after due consideration Boule concluded that this jaw was too apelike to be his own ancestor and was instead the progenitor of the hapless Neanderthals. For the antecedent to *Homo sapiens* he was obliged, doubtless reluctantly, to look across the English Channel, to the village of Piltdown in the southern English county of Sussex.

The Piltdown Fraud

At the end of the first decade of the twentieth century, perhaps the most influential member of the British paleoanthropological establishment was the anatomist Arthur Keith. For reasons unclear to me, Keith's penchant was to believe, like Boule, in a very ancient existence of the modern human type—so ancient as to exclude the Neanderthals and even *Homo heidelbergensis* from modern human ancestry. In 1912, however, Arthur Smith Woodward, a fossil fish expert at the British Museum (Natural History), announced the discovery in a

gravel pit at Piltdown of pieces of an ancient human skull in association with some crude stone tools and various mammal fossils that suggested a possible pre-Pleistocene age. The ability to identify age in years was still far in the future, of course, but this relative age made the Piltdown specimen even older than *Pithecanthropus* was believed to be. Woodward's reconstruction showed the combination of a rather apelike jaw with a high but small braincase of less than 1100 ml capacity. [Plate 64] He named it *Eoanthropus dawsoni* ("Dawson's Dawn Man," for the Sussex lawyer who had first brought the pieces to his attention) and declared it to be the ancestor of modern humans. At the same time, the neuroanatomist Grafton Elliot Smith examined a cast of the inside of the braincase and announced that although the brain had been "simian" in certain respects, this was only to be expected in a human ancestor that was ultimately descended from an ape.

At first Keith was unreceptive to these interpretations, and his initial response was to produce a new reconstruction of *Eoanthropus* that was more humanlike, notably by shortening the face and adding a chin (which region was missing among the fragments), and by increasing the volume of the braincase. This was not a difficult task, for the available fragments lacked just those parts that would have allowed a definitive conclusion about the association of the cranium and the lower jaw. Woodward, however, parried the very next year with the discovery at Piltdown of a canine tooth that was not only large and apelike but that closely resembled the imaginary tooth that he had included in his reconstruction. This serendipitous tooth more or less settled the question in Woodward's favor, and by 1915 the notion that the pre-Pleistocene human ancestor had combined a humanlike braincase with an apelike jaw and face carried the day, in England at least.

Scientists elsewhere, however, were less sure. As early as 1915 the American mammalogist Gerrit Miller declared that the specimen simply combined an ape jaw with a human braincase. Eventually an uneasy compromise was reached, especially after Elliot Smith produced a third reconstruction boasting a brain size that lay between the Woodward and Keith estimates. This new Piltdown, which saved face among all concerned, swung general support behind the emerging "pre-*sapiens*" theory of human origins. According to this theory, at some remote time, probably in the Pliocene (the epoch that preceded the Pleistocene), the human lineage had split. One branch had led, via Piltdown, to *Homo sapiens*; the other had proceeded toward the ill-fated Neanderthals. As everyone now knows, of course, the Piltdown "fossil" was a deliberate hoax—by whom is uncertain—that combined a suitably modified ape

lower jaw with a judiciously fragmented human cranium. The fraud succeeded partly because it played into the preconception that because a large brain is the most striking characteristic of *Homo sapiens*, it is the characteristic most likely to have been possessed by our species' remote ancestor. And of course the idea that the "Earliest Englishman" was also the progenitor of mankind as a whole naturally appealed to the patriotic sentiments of English paleoanthropologists. The fact of the hoax, however, did not emerge definitively until after World War II. In the meantime, variants of the pre-*sapiens* notion proliferated, banishing the Neanderthals to a bit part in the human evolutionary story.

Bear Cults and Dark Rituals

As we'll see in a moment, there was one big exception to this banishment. And in any event, it's hardly possible to complain that the Neanderthals were ignored in the immediate post-Piltdown period. Indeed, they were rapidly acquiring a very interesting set of behaviors. For example, between 1917 and 1921, the amateur archaeologist Dr. Emil Bächler excavated the Drachenloch ("Dragon's Cave") site in the Churfirsten Mountains of Switzerland. No Neanderthal fossils were found there, but the Mousterian tools associated with them were, along with what Bächler considered to be evidence of Neanderthal ritual activity. Inside the cave were found the remains of many cave bears, *Ursus*

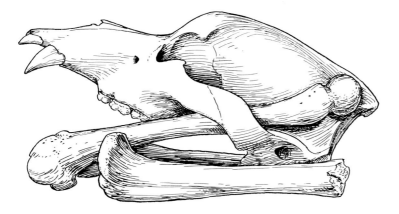

65
Cave bear skull with a femur thrust through its cheekbone.

Artist's reconstruction of the alleged artifact from the Drachenloch cave, Switzerland, as described by Emil Bächler. It now appears that this arrangement of bones resulted from natural processes.
Illustration by Diana Salles.

spelaeus : huge beasts that became extinct some 40,000 to 50,000 years ago. This discovery in itself is not unusual; the giant bears regularly hibernated—and sometimes died— in shallow pits that they excavated deep inside caves. But to Bächler there was something special about the way in which the bones were disposed.

In the interior of the cave he reported finding walls composed of piled-up stone blocks, with bear fossils enclosed behind them. What's more, he described several "cists": dry stone boxes sunk into the ancient cave floor, all filled with bear bones and capped with stone slabs. And one cave bear skull was found with a thigh bone thrust through the gap between cheekbone and braincase. [Plate 65] What conclusions did these findings imply? Bächler thought he had the answer in the behavior of the Neanderthals who had left their tools behind at the site. Scavengers' toothmarks on the bones showed that they had been meatless when buried, eliminating any likelihood that the cists were food caches; the only other apparent possibility was ritualized behavior. Thus began the notion of Neanderthal "bear cults," with bears the subject of worship or other ritual activities that maybe included deliberate sacrifice, and that must surely have involved some type of feeling for the spiritual. Perhaps not surprisingly, reports of similar presumed behaviors began to trickle in from other sites—and exotic customs of this kind meshed well, of course, with the darker side of Neanderthal nature as

exemplified by Gorjanović's alleged cannibalism.

Cave bears are pretty impressive things just as bones, and they must have been absolutely fearsome in life. The supposition that Neanderthals worshipped them or treated their remains as cult objects must certainly have endowed these extinct people with a profound fascination. To a scientific milieu that was still trying to come to grips with the Neanderthal phenomenon, there must also have been a certain comfort in the contemplation of a deeply human spiritual awareness in combination with "primitive" rituals such as those envisaged by Bächler. Familiar yet unfamiliar: these behaviors perfectly matched the equivocally human morphology of the Neanderthals. More-recent work, however, has shown that the reality of the bone accumulations of the Drachenloch was almost certainly much more prosaic than the picture Bächler painted.

Unlike Gorjanović at Krapina, whose excavations two decades earlier had been well ahead of their time in terms of detailed stratigraphic recording, Bächler employed an older approach to archaeology, whereby digging was delegated to gangs of laborers. The archaeologist did not supervise the excavation personally, but instead showed up from time to time to receive the foreman's report and admire the laborers' finds. Modern archaeologists shudder in retrospect, recalling, for example, how in 1909 much of the magnificent bas-relief animal frieze in the Upper Paleolithic shelter of Cap Blanc, maybe 13,000 years old, was hacked away before the laborers who were clearing the site realized that they had hit the shelter's rear wall. To add insult to injury, almost all the stratigraphy at Cap Blanc was lost as the workers violently attacked the tough calcified fill with their pickaxes. Nowadays archaeologists proceed with extreme caution, working with brushes and dental picks. They never remove an object they are excavating before its position has been recorded in all three dimensions, for the act of excavating a site inevitably destroys it, making it vital to preserve everything possible of the information it contains before the work is finished.

But this is now, and that was then. Bächler did not keep detailed records of the excavations at the Drachenloch, and was not even there when many of the most important cave bear discoveries were made. What he did was to report his *interpretations* of what his laborers found and of what he saw as the Drachenloch was dug, rather than the detailed facts on which those interpretations were based. Indeed, he presented different renditions on different occasions. What's more, Bächler's reports differ in significant details from the notes kept by his foreman, even though both apparently agreed on the essence of what was discovered. Thus, even though there was clearly no deliberate intention to deceive, it was not evidence for a bear cult that was reported from the Drachenloch, but rather a particular reading of the evidence, which was not itself clearly recorded.

Today, archaeologists are unanimous that the Drachenloch cave filling can be accounted for by natural processes. The "dry stone walls" of apparently piled-up rock slabs, for example, probably originated as single large blocks that fell from the cave ceiling and were later split apart along bedding planes by frost action. The concentrations of bones most likely resulted from the activities of the cave bears themselves as, generation after generation, they excavated clean nests to hibernate (and sometimes die) in. Even the cranium with the femur thrust inside its cheekbone is not something unexpected in a place where a lot of bones accumulated naturally. If, of course, the facts had been exactly as reported by Bächler, then it would be hard to deny entirely that some intentional activity on the part of humans had been involved. But if the aspects of his account that clearly involved imaginative reconstruction are eliminated, his interpretation fades. I have not belabored this particular case because Bächler was alone in his approach, but rather because he epitomized a practice that was once widespread in archaeology and that deeply affected (or perhaps reflected) early perceptions of the Neanderthals. In the wake of the Drachenloch finds, numerous other cases of Neanderthal "bear cults" and ritual behavior were reported; except maybe for the evidence in some cases of deliberate burial of the dead, however, none of these instances stands up to close scrutiny. The notions they enshrine still linger, though, as we'll see shortly.

Attention Distracted

The Piltdown "discovery" certainly hastened the demotion of the Neanderthals' significance that Boule had initiated with such vigor. In the United States, however, the Piltdown find had been viewed with particular suspicion, and one major figure in American physical anthropology wasn't buying Boule's interpretation at all. This was Aleš Hrdlickǎ, who was convinced that the Neanderthals lay in the direct line of human descent. In 1927, in a lecture to London's Royal Anthropological Institute, Hrdlickǎ defined the Neanderthal as "The Man of the Mousterian Culture," demonstrated to his satisfaction that the Mousterian had evolved gradually into the Aurignacian (hence Neanderthals had evolved into Cro-Magnons), and concluded that there was "less justification in the conception of a Neanderthal *species* than...in a Neanderthal *phase* of man." This declaration was to become an icon to certain later paleoanthropologists, but it didn't cause much of a stir at the time, perhaps because paleoanthropologists were becoming preoccupied by finds in Africa. The first of these was the Kabwe cranium (which even Woodward suggested, in 1921, "may revive the idea that Neanderthal man is truly the ancestor of *Homo sapiens*"). But the find that really claimed attention—most of it unfavorable—was Raymond Dart's 1925 discovery of the Taung child, the first specimen of *Australopithecus africanus* and something that was clearly more ancient than Java Man or the Piltdown specimen.

In the realm of human evolution the years between the Taung find and the outbreak of World War II were dominated by further *Australopithecus* and *Paranthropus* discoveries in South Africa, and by a stream of finds of "Peking Man" at Zhoukoudian in China. [see Plates 27, 28 and 39] Europe continued to produce fossils, however, among them the back part of a skull from Swanscombe, in southern England, which was faunally dated to the Mindel-Riss interglacial, earlier than any unequivocal Neanderthals (it has since been dated to about 225,000 years ago or more). [see Plate 92] With a large estimated brain capacity (1325 ml), this specimen was widely seen as reinforcing the "*presapiens*" hypothesis, whereby a Pliocene split in the human lineage had led to the Neanderthals on one hand and to the Piltdown specimen and modern humans on the other. Some authorities, though, noted Neanderthal-like characteristics in Swanscombe's occiput. In Germany a more complete if distorted and somewhat smaller-brained cranium was found in deposits of similar age at Steinheim, near Stuttgart. [Plates 66 and 67] Few at the time were sure how to classify this specimen, although lately it has become popular to view it as a proto-Neanderthal. In 1931 to 1933, the Dutch mining engineer W. F. F. Oppenoorth recovered a

66 and 67
Front and side views of the cranium from Steinheim-an-den-Murr, Germany.

Discovered in 1933 and well over 200 thousand years old, this somewhat distorted cranium is widely viewed as that of a Neanderthal precursor.
Photographs courtesy of the Staatliches Museum für Naturkunde, Stuttgart.

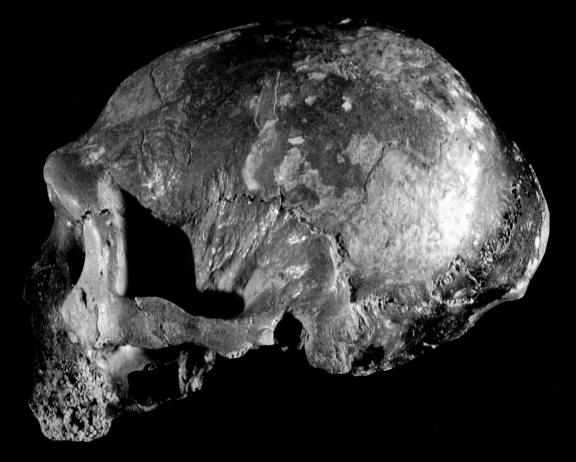

68
Side view of the Neanderthal cranium from Monte Circeo, Italy.

One of the best-preserved Neanderthal crania from southern Europe, this fossil is about 50 thousand years old. The Guattari cave from which it came is now regarded as an ancient hyena den, rather than as the site of cannibalistic rituals (see Plate 69)
Photograph courtesy of Ministry of Culture, Italy.

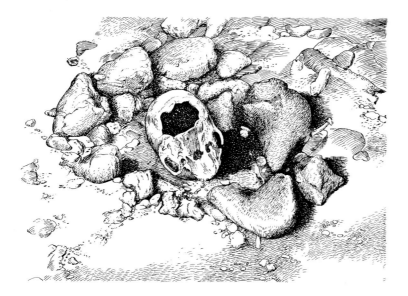

69

The "crown of stones" at the Guattari cave, Monte Circeo, Italy.

This redrawing of an illustration published by A.C. Blanc in 1939, shows the Neanderthal skull, seen at the left, inverted in a circle of stones. Billed originally as evidence for cannibal ritual, this post-hoc reconstruction is now thought to be fictional.
Illustration by Diana Salles, after A. C. Blanc.

series of braincases from a terrace of the Solo River in Java, at a place called Ngandong. These were initially referred to as "tropical Neanderthals," apparently implying no more than that the Ngandong population had played a role in the East equivalent to that played by the Neanderthals in the West. Nowadays the Ngandong skulls are seen as closer to *Homo erectus*, especially since they may be as much as 400,000 years old – much older than once thought.

More Cannibal Feasts

Some important Neanderthal discoveries were made in the period between the two World Wars. In 1926 a juvenile Neanderthal skull was found in Gibraltar, and in 1929 workers in a gravel quarry at Saccopastore, near Rome, found a rather lightly built Neanderthal skull that seemed to date from the Riss-Würm interglacial and was accompanied by typical Mousterian stone tools. [see Plates 97 and 98] Similar tools were found ten years later, and sixty miles to the south, in Guattari Cave on Monte Circeo. This cave also yielded the skull of a more heavily built Neanderthal from the last glacial. [Plate 68] What made this particular specimen a cause célèbre, though, was less the fossil itself than the supposed context. The original discovery had been made accidentally, by a workman, in almost complete darkness, and the skull – one of many bones lying on the cave floor – had been picked up and replaced on the ground by the time the paleontol-

ogist Alberto Blanc was called in. A reconstruction by Blanc showed the cranium lying inverted, a gaping hole in its base pointing straight up, within a "crown of stones." [Plate 69] Ignoring the fact that the cave floor was covered with stones and bones, and that there was no certainty about exactly where the skull had come from, Blanc built on the tradition of Krapina and the Drachenloch to spring to the conclusion that the Guattari skull represented the remains of a cannibal feast. The individual had been killed by a blow to the right side of the head; the head had been severed from the body and placed upside down in a ring of stones; the skull base had been broken open to extract the brain (exactly as the anatomist Franz Weidenreich had suggested had happened to the Peking Man skulls from Zhoukoudian); the empty braincase had been used as a drinking cup before being replaced on the floor; and the broken animal bones scattered around the cave had accumulated as the result of further sacrifices associated with this bizarre cannibalistic ritual.

We know now that Guattari Cave was in fact an ancient hyena den, and that the Neanderthal skull was simply one more of the numerous mammal bones with which it was littered. But Blanc's Guattari scenario struck a chord with many, for complex behavior of this kind, while mystifying and somewhat reprehensible, hinted at a sort of humanity. Thus, with the new perspective opened up by the large range of smaller-brained and undeniably more

70
Tabūn I skull from the cave of Tabūn, Israel.

Now thought to be over 100 thousand years old, this relatively lightly-built (probably female) Neanderthal skull comes from Layer C of the Tabūn cave. This site has served as a reference point for studies of the late Pleistocene archaeological sequence in the Levant.
Courtesy of The Natural History Museum, London.

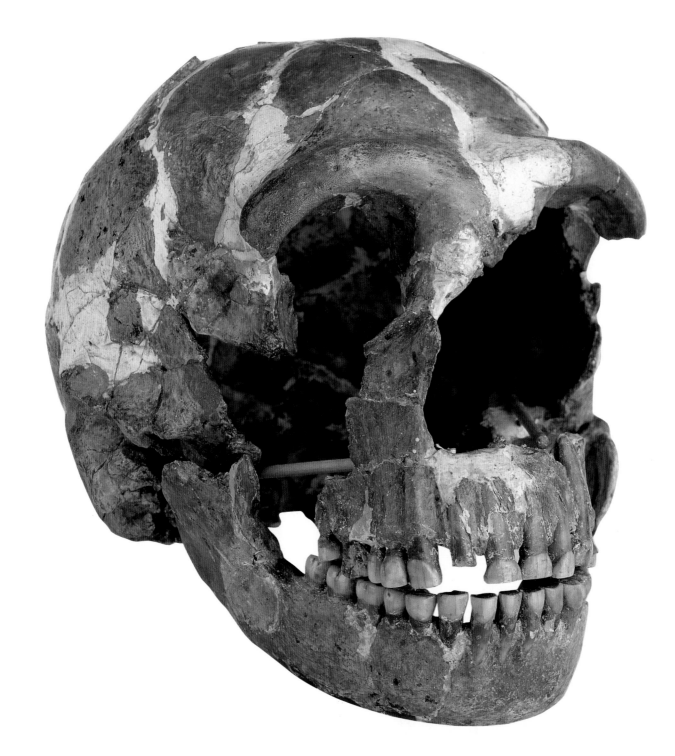

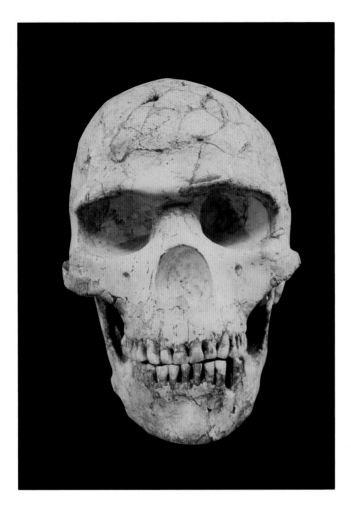

71

The Skhūl V skull.

The best preserved of several crania from the rock shelter of Skhūl, Israel. This specimen, almost 100 thousand years old, is of essentially modern form despite retaining some development of the brow ridges.

Courtesy of the Peabody Museum, Harvard University.

primitive human fossils that were known by 1939, it was becoming increasingly easy to see the Neanderthals as in some way human and capable of spiritual feeling. Indeed, in the very year of the Guattari discovery, the American physical anthropologist Carleton Coon produced an elegant profile reconstruction of the "Old Man" of La Chapelle, shaved and dressed in a hat, jacket, and tie, and looking for all the world like a coarse-featured *Homo sapiens*.

 Levantine Confusion

If the human evolutionary picture was made uncertain by the need to factor Piltdown into it, the waters were muddied even further by the interpretation of fossils discovered in Palestine (now Israel) between 1929 and 1934, when two sites on the western slope of Mount Carmel were excavated by the English archaeologist Dorothy Garrod. One of these, Layer C of the cave of Tabūn (now known to be more than

100,000 years old), produced an almost complete skeleton of a female human dating from the last interglacial. The skull of this individual was rounded at the back and was more lightly built than most western European Neanderthals, but otherwise it fit comfortably among them. [Plate 70] A presumed male lower jaw from the same site was quite heavily built, although unlike the female it did have a distinct chin–a modern feature. [see Plate 106] The associated stone tool industry was one of the local versions of the Mousterian. Some more-fragmentary human fossils came from the overlying Layer B, which contained a subtly different Mousterian tool assemblage. A few minutes' stroll away, the rock shelter of Skhūl yielded tools similar to those of Tabūn Layer C and several skeletons of quite modern anatomy, although with brow ridges a little heavier than is typical of today's human populations. [Plate 71] Despite minor faunal differences, the two sites were believed to be more or less

72

The cave of Zuttiyeh, Israel.

Spectacularly sited in a valley adjacent to Lake Tiberias (the Sea of Galilee), this cave has yielded a frontal bone, probably 125–150 thousand years old, that represesents a population antecedent to the Levantine Neanderthals.
Photograph by Willard Whitson.

73 a and b

The cave of Jebel Qafzeh, Israel.

First excavated in the 1930s, this site has yielded a rich trove of anatomically modern human fossils, dating from as much as 92 thousand years ago, that are associated with a Mousterian lithic assemblage.
Photographs by Willard Whitson.

contemporaneous. Apparently because of this, together with the similarity of the stone tools from the two sites, Arthur Keith and the American physical anthropologist Theodore McCown, who jointly described the Mount Carmel hominids, concluded that all the specimens from the two sites belonged to a single highly variable population. (On the grounds of morphology, Keith and McCown would certainly have had difficulty justifying this inference.)

But the time was clearly becoming ripe for blurring the distinction between Neanderthals and modern humans, anatomically as well as behaviorally, and the outlines of one currently popular schema of human evolution were beginning to come into focus. This framework is known as "Multiregional Continuity," and preaches the ancientness of the evolutionary roots of today's major human groups. Most significantly, Franz Weidenreich, the monographer of the Zhoukoudian *Homo erectus* fossils, was busy during the late 1930s developing the notion that the main groups of humankind had evolved independently from separate populations of *Homo erectus*. In Weidenreich's estimation, Java Man had ultimately given rise to modern Australians, Peking Man had evolved into modern Chinese, and forms such as Rhodesian Man (Kabwe) had gradually become modern Africans. He had a bit of difficulty explaining the apparent replacement of Neanderthals by moderns in Europe, but decided that the latter must have evolved from Neanderthals

elsewhere, then spread into Europe to supplant their own ancestor. This theory suited McCown and Keith, who saw a spectrum in Europe that ran from the "classic" European Neanderthals at one extreme, through the more lightly built Krapina types, via Tabūn and then Skhūl, to the Cro-Magnons. Noting the tendency for the "extreme" Neanderthal type to become modified from west to east until at Mount Carmel there was found a form apparently transitional to the modern, the pair proposed that the ancestors of modern Europeans had evolved in western Asia, even further east than Palestine. Thus were the Neanderthals somewhat awkwardly reworked into the tapestry of modern human evolution, as one end of a spurious morphological series that had *Homo sapiens* on the other.

McCown and Keith might have been more reluctant to lump together hominids of disparate appearance strictly on archaeological criteria if they had stopped to consider other finds that were being made in Palestine at about the same time. A very archaic-looking frontal bone was found at the cave of Zuttiyeh, near Lake Tiberias (the Sea of Galilee), in 1925, also in association with Mousterian tools. [Plate 72 and see Plate 99] Not long after, though, the finding of similar tools at the cave of Qafzeh, near Nazareth, led to excavations in which several skeletons of altogether modern morphology were ultimately recovered, although none was properly described until many years later. [Plates 73 a and b and 74 and see Plate 115] Not

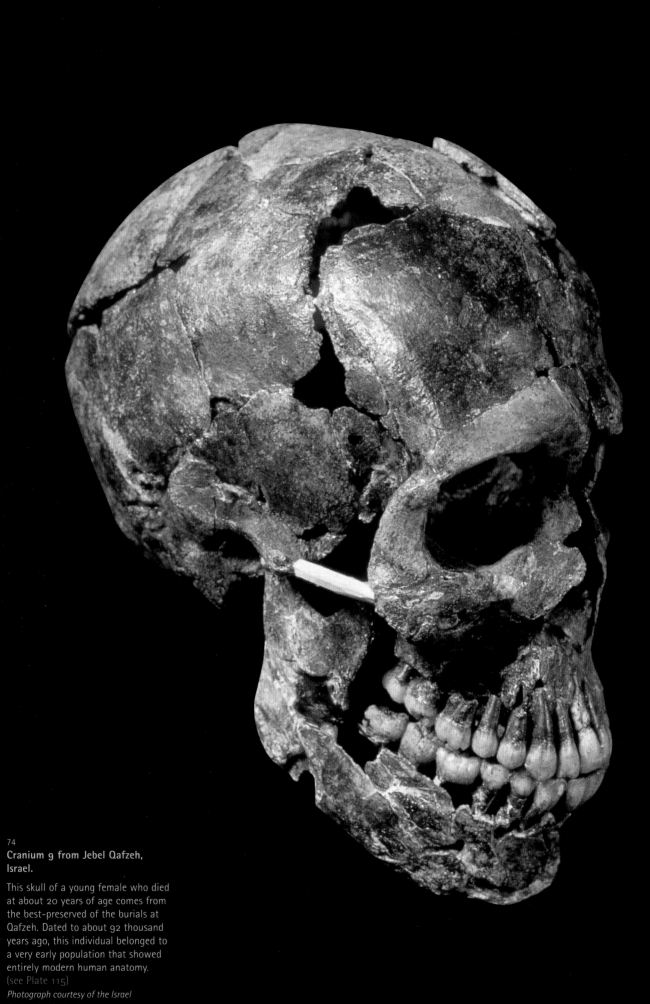

74
Cranium 9 from Jebel Qafzeh, Israel.

This skull of a young female who died at about 20 years of age comes from the best-preserved of the burials at Qafzeh. Dated to about 92 thousand years ago, this individual belonged to a very early population that showed entirely modern human anatomy.
(see Plate 115)
Photograph courtesy of the Israel Antiquities Authority.

until the late 1980s did the dating of this site to more than 90,000 years ago prompt some hard rethinking about modern human origins, but the evidence was already available by the late 1930s to show that tools and morphology do not go hand in hand. Clearly Hrdlička's definition of the Neanderthal as the "Man of the Mousterian Culture" was inappropriate, and the association of Upper Paleolithic industries with modern physical types, clear-cut as it was in Europe, did not necessarily hold elsewhere.

 ### Enter the Synthesis

The 1940s was the decade in which the ideas of the new Evolutionary Synthesis finally began to take hold, and as we saw in Chapter 2, the first of the triumvirate of the Synthesis to wade into the paleoanthropological fray was Theodosius Dobzhansky. His take on the Mount Carmel fossils was that they represented hybridization between Neanderthals and moderns (a possibility considered but rejected by McCown and Keith). In this case the two forms would have to be subspecies of the same species, for otherwise they could not have been interfertile. This meant in turn that the single species *Homo sapiens*, embracing as it did the wildly divergent Neanderthals and moderns, was extraordinarily variable. What's more, if *Homo sapiens* was so variable, earlier human species probably were too. It was thus hardly surprising that Dobzhansky was able to find no evidence in the human fossil record for more

than one species at any one time. His colleague Ernst Mayr heartily concurred with this assertion. Thus was born in paleoanthropology an era of "lumping" – the minimizing of the number of species recognized in the human fossil record – in which the Neanderthals were demoted to a mere subspecies of modern humanity, *Homo sapiens neanderthalensis.*

In this way the Neanderthals became an epiphenomenon that no longer demanded explanation in the way that *Homo neanderthalensis* had. Nonetheless, one very salutary result of the lumping approach was the disappearance of the plethora of names that had obscured the outlines of human evolution; and at the same time, spurious ancient hominids such as the Piltdown specimen, and some modern skeletons formerly thought to be of high antiquity, were being expelled from the human fossil record by the application of new analytical techniques. Together with a more refined appreciation of Pleistocene chronology, this systematic winnowing opened the way for a new appraisal of the fossil evidence for human evolution in Europe and western Asia. The first paleoanthropologist to apply this new perspective to the Neanderthals was Clark Howell, then of the University of Chicago, who published a series of papers in the early 1950s in which he examined the morphological differences between different Neanderthal populations and correlated these with their distributions in time and space. He proposed that a single lineage led from Mauer through

Swanscombe to Steinheim and then to an "early Neanderthal" group to which belonged such fossils as those of Ehringsdorf and Saccopastore. These latter specimens, from the Riss-Würm interglacial, had shorter, higher, and less strongly built skulls and hence were more like modern humans than were the later "classic" Neanderthals (Neander Valley, La Chapelle, La Ferrassie, Monte Circeo, and others) of the last glacial period. In addition, like McCown and Keith, Howell observed a trend toward lightness of skull build from west to east.

From all this emerged the notion that early and relatively lightly built Neanderthals had been widespread across Europe and western Asia during the last interglacial. The expansion of the ice sheets at the beginning of the Würm glacial had cut off the western population from that to the east, setting each on its own independent evolutionary path. In isolation, and under the influence of the harsh glacial climate, the western early Neanderthals had evolved into the "classic" forms, while the eastern population gave rise, via the Mount Carmel population, to modern humans. Ultimately, with the return of milder conditions, the moderns moved west to replace their Neanderthal cousins. This view ties in well with Ernst Mayr's model of allopatric speciation, in which the formation of geographic barriers is the key to the fixation of evolutionary innovations via the formation of new reproductively isolated populations—species. Conversely, the dissolution of such barriers formed the basis for the spread of new species and for the winnowing through competition that I spoke of in Chapter 2.

 Flower People and Subway Riders
During the 1950s new Neanderthal discoveries continued to come in, helping to fill out the picture painted by Howell. Between 1953 and 1957 the Columbia University archaeologist Ralph Solecki excavated the cave of Shanidar, in northern Iraq, recovering the remains of nine adult and juvenile Neanderthals—some of which appeared to be very much of "classic" aspect. [Plates 75, 76, and 77] One of the skeletons was that of an adult male who had suffered, perhaps since birth, from a disease that withered his right arm. Solecki pointed out that this individual could not have survived to a relatively advanced age without the active support of his social group. [Plate 78] Suddenly the Neanderthals became caring and humane, as well as spiritually aware. This new Neanderthal persona was made yet more compelling by the discovery of fossil pollen that suggested the individual had been buried with spring flowers. The subtitle that Solecki later chose for his popular book on Shanidar, *The First Flower People,* eloquently reflects how dramatically the Neanderthal image was changing.

With the Neanderthals becoming behaviorally more human almost by the minute, the time had obviously come for a reappraisal of their anatomy—

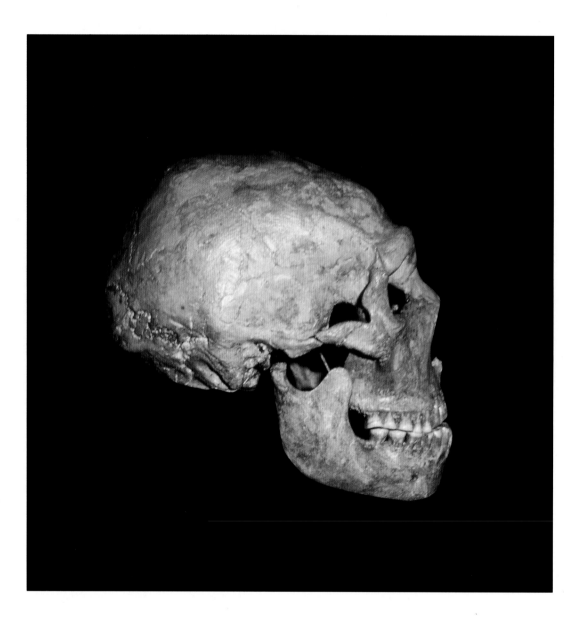

75 and 76

Front and side views of the Shanidar 1 skull, Iraq.

The best-preserved of several skulls from this important Neanderthal site. Erik Trinkaus has suggested that Shanidar 1, one of the more recent group of burials at this locality (about 50 thousand years), may have experienced some form of cranial deformation as an infant. The individual had also experienced damage to his left eye socket that presumably blinded him in that eye.
Photograph by Erik Trinkaus.

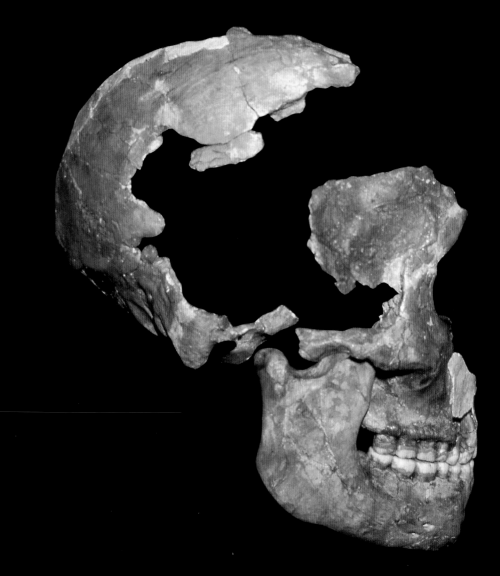

77

Side view of the Shanidar 2 skull, Iraq.

This specimen is among the earlier group of burials from Shanidar, estimated at about 70-80 thousand years old. These individuals have more prominent cheekbones than the later Shanidar fossils, which are some 20-30 thousand years younger.
Photograph by Erik Trinkaus.

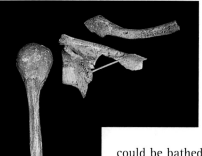

78
Bones of the right arm and shoulder of individual 1 from Shanidar, Iraq.

The abnormal shape of these bones has led Erik Trinkaus to suggest that the right arm of this Neanderthal was useless to its owner for most— at least—of his life (35 to 40 years). To have survived to this advanced age (for a Neanderthal) this individual must have received some form of support from his group.
Photograph by Erik Trinkaus.

perceptions of which, despite the odd murmur of dissent, remained until the mid-1950s largely in thrall to the unflattering image created by Boule. In 1955, however, the French paleontologist Camille Arambourg looked at the La Chapelle skeleton and could find no evidence to back up Boule's assertion of a slouching, bent-kneed posture, while the Swiss primatologist Adolph Schulz pointed independently to the inherent instability and hence improbability of that attitude. Two years later the anatomists W. L. Straus of the United States and A. J. E. Cave of England definitively demonstrated not only that the La Chapelle individual showed extensive effects of arthritis and age, but that many of the supposed differences from modern humans to which Boule had pointed did not exist. They concluded that, despite certain differences of detail from modern people, this Neanderthal had been an efficient upright biped. It was Straus and Cave who made the famous statement that if the Old Man of La Chapelle

could be bathed, shaved, and dressed in a suit, he would pass unnoticed in the New York City subway.

The 1950s also saw the introduction into paleoanthropology of radiocarbon dating. It turned out that its effective maximum of about 40,000 years places most Neanderthal sites out of the range of this technique, but largely as a result of the efforts of Harvard's Hallam Movius, a radiometric chronology of the latest Middle Paleolithic and the Upper Paleolithic was rapidly developed. It was found, for instance, that Mousterian artifact assemblages persisted in France up to about 32,000 years ago. The Châtelperronian industry, variously interpreted at the time as the work of late Neanderthals or early moderns, started somewhat before this and lasted to about 30,000 years ago. The Châtelperronian posed problems because, while flake tools were still important, about half the tools were made on long "blades," a hallmark of the Upper Paleolithic, whose first undoubted European industry, the

79

Châtelperronian tools from Laussel, France.

The Châtelperronian industry is probably associated with Neanderthals. Nonetheless it has some similarities with the Upper Paleolithic, as evidenced by the blade tools shown in the right column.

Photograph by Alain Roussot.

Aurignacian, began about 32,000 years ago. [Plate 79] At least to the satisfaction of many, the identity of the Châtelperronians was eventually revealed in 1979, by the discovery of a Neanderthal burial in Châtelperronian context at Saint-Césaire, in western France. [see Plate 102] The focus of debate has now shifted to whether Neanderthals independently invented blade-tool technology or copied it from invading *Homo sapiens.*

Regional Continuity

In 1947, in one of his last papers, Franz Weidenreich published a diagram that formalized his theory of the independent descent of the major modern racial groups from forms that we would now classify as *Homo erectus.* He was apparently still having difficulty with the European Neanderthals, for he left them out of his scheme. But he had no problem with identifying the Tabūn fossils as "typical Neanderthals," and deriving "Eurasians" (Europeans and western Asians) from such extinct people via the intermediate forms found at Skhūl. Weidenreich's scheme was picked up on a decade and a half later by the physical anthropologist Carleton Coon, in his 1962 book *The Origin of Races.* This work was widely and probably unfairly attacked for propagating a racist doctrine, but in many ways it was an impressive achievement, and it contained some new speculations on the adaptations of the Neanderthals as well as on their position in the human family tree as ancestors to modern

Europeans. Coon noted that, like other mammals, modern humans tend to be more stocky in build the further away from the equator they live. This build minimizes the surface area of the body compared to its volume, thus conserving precious body heat in cold climes. The short, bulky Neanderthals, Coon proposed, showed the ultimate adaptation to a frosty glacial climate. What's more, the large Neanderthal nose had served to warm the inhaled frigid air of the periglacial environment and thus to protect the fragile lungs below it. Ameliorate the climate, Coon implied, and a change in morphology toward the modern state would almost inevitably follow.

Two years after Coon's book was published, and while the brouhaha it unleashed was still going on, the American physical anthropologist Loring Brace launched a magnificently sweeping attack on everyone who would exclude the Neanderthals from modern human ancestry. He traced lingering tendencies of this kind to Boule's work at the beginning of the century, and castigated all concerned for being "anti-evolutionary." The core of Brace's argument was a view of human culture as the prime mover in human evolution. Broadly, he asserted that culture was the human ecological niche, and since according to ecological theory no two species could share the same niche, not more than one culture-bearing hominid could have existed at any one time. Brace's initial application of this contention was to the Neanderthals. Later,

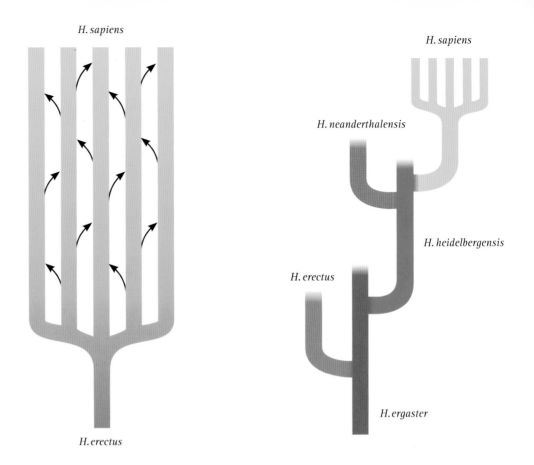

H. sapiens

H. sapiens

H. neanderthalensis

H. heidelbergensis

H. erectus

H. erectus

H. ergaster

80

Diagrammatic representation of the two leading notions of modern human origins.

This diagram contrasts the essential characteristics of the "Multiregional Continuity" and "Single Origin" notions of modern human emergence. The arrows at left represent interlineage gene flow. *Illustration by Diana Salles.*

however, he argued that there could only ever have been one human lineage, and that this lineage could only arbitrarily be broken up into segments such as *Homo erectus* and *Homo sapiens*. Picked up by others, this notion became known as the "single species hypothesis," and it was widely touted in the late 1960s and early 1970s until it was definitively disproved by the discovery, described in Chapter 4, of several different fossil hominids coexisting at East Turkana.

This disappointing discovery left several vocal paleoanthropologists looking for another cause in which to employ their talents. Given that their mind-sets were firmly fixed on gradual within-lineage change as the ruling theme in evolution, it's hardly astounding that they chose to take up the cudgels on behalf of Weidenreich's scheme of parallel evolution, tainted though it was by its association with Coon.

The essence of the resulting "Multiregional Continuity" theory was that, although the starting points to which the various modern human populations were traced belonged to *Homo erectus*, each regional population had evolved along its own distinctive lines but had exchanged enough genes with its neighbors to

remain part of the same species, all eventually becoming *Homo sapiens*. [Plate 80] A recent refinement, introduced to circumvent the problem of how different lineages could evolve separately into the same species, has been to combine *Homo erectus* into *Homo sapiens*. The Neanderthals have proven to be the least tractable group of extinct humans to work into the multiregional scheme because of their distinctiveness from, and their contemporaneity with, modern humans. The exercise of considerable ingenuity, however, combined with a firm if unfounded belief that their capacities, if not morphology, were just like ours, has allowed the Neanderthals to be shoehorned in, at least to the satisfaction of believers. For example, if the Neanderthals were a mere subspecies of *Homo sapiens*, they would have been interfertile with moderns. Thus, the story is that although the Neanderthals had done their own thing in Europe during the last glacial, their distinctive genes were simply "swamped" toward the end of the last glacial by those of the invading modern people who interbred with them. In support of this scenario, various "primitive" traits have been touted in a few very early fossil modern humans from eastern Europe.

Out of Africa

One problem with the multiregional hypothesis is that it flies directly in the face of what we know about how the evolutionary process works. As I pointed out in Chapter 2, the origin of new mammal species seems invariably to be associated with particular geographic areas. Back in the 1970s Harvard's Bill Howells had proposed a "Noah's Ark" model of human evolution whereby our species had a single and relatively recent origin; and during the mid-1980s it began to be inquired once more exactly where that origin might be sought. Africa rapidly became the prime candidate. An early proponent of the view that modern humans had evolved on that continent was the University of Hamburg's Günter Bräuer, who pointed out that the earliest fossil evidence for modern human anatomy was African. Neanderthals, in his view, were an indigenous European/western Asian development that was eventually displaced after the first moderns had left Africa.

The "Out of Africa" bandwagon really started rolling, however, after molecular analyses of living human populations were begun by The University of California at Berkeley's Allan Wilson and colleagues. These researchers looked at the DNA (the genetic material) carried in tiny intracellular structures called mitochondria. Most DNA is found in the nucleus of the cell, where half is inherited from each parent. Mitochondria, however, are located outside the nucleus and are inherited from the mother alone (since the mother's ovum is a complete cell, whereas the father's sperm – usually – contains only nuclear material). Because of this, mitochondrial DNA (mtDNA) is not jumbled up in each generation. Instead, mtDNA is passed from mother to offspring unscathed – except for mutations that may accumulate along the way – in an unbroken sequence that goes all the way back to an ancestral "Eve." Because the accumulation of mutations is in some way a function of time, the fact that modern human mtDNA is remarkably uniform, as was rapidly established, suggests a relatively recent origin for our species. What's more, diversity is highest among individuals of African ancestry, suggesting that Africans have been diversifying the longest, with other major geographic groups deriving from small populations that became established later in time – presumably after the diaspora from Africa.

By assuming an average rate of change of about three percent per million years, Wilson and colleagues initially came up with a molecular age for *Homo sapiens* of about 400,000 years – more than somewhat at odds with the fossil record. This age has been steadily modified, however, until the latest estimate of about 140,000 to 130,000 years sits fairly well with the admittedly rather sparse African fossil evidence. A pall has been cast over the mtDNA studies by the revelation of flaws in some of the early comparative analyses of the structure of mtDNA on which the "African Eve" hypothesis was also based; nonetheless, the diversity data do appear to be significant and do fit well with the fossil record.

How does all this affect the Neanderthals? If the distinctive anatomy of modern humans first evolved in Africa, then we must conclude with Bräuer that Neanderthals were a distinct and endemic European/western Asian group. And if *Homo sapiens* is a unitary species with its origins outside Europe and western Asia, then the Neanderthals were indeed a side branch in human evolution—our cousins, certainly, but neither our ancestors nor contributors of genes to the modern human population.

Very recently, new dates have emerged from the Levant that demonstrate that Neanderthals shared that region with anatomically modern people for a very long period of time. ESR dates on mammal teeth associated with the hominid remains from Skhūl (virtually modern human) and Tabūn (lightly built Neanderthal) have come out at around 100,000 years and 120,000 years, respectively. These dates match well with the new TL date on burned flints from Qafzeh (modern human) of more than 90,000 years. At the other end of the scale, Neanderthal sites in Israel such as Amud, excavated in the 1960s by a Japanese team, and Kebara, excavated in the 1980s by an international group, have come in with dates of about 40,000 and 60,000 years, respectively. [Plate 81 and 82 and see Plates 93, 100, 101, and 105] This range of dates indicates that Neanderthals and moderns overlapped in their occupation of the Levant for a period of

up to 60,000 years or perhaps more, though whether the two ever existed in exactly the same place at exactly the same time is harder to determine. Interestingly, the stone tool kits used by the Neanderthals and anatomical moderns were similar—they've all been classified as Mousterian—during almost that entire span of time. Recent work indicates that the first known Upper Paleolithic tools from the region appeared only about 47,000 years ago, at the site of Boker Tachtit in the Negev desert. These tools were non-Aurignacian (the Aurignacian showed up late in the Levant), and their method of manufacture hints at Middle Paleolithic technology, but there are no associated human fossils to say who made them. What seems significant, though, is that the last appearance of the typical Mousterian in the Levant occurred only a little later, at 40,000 years ago.

 ### Defining the Neanderthals

In this long historical chapter, I have not yet mentioned a single attempt to define the Neanderthals as a group distinguished from all other kinds of fossil humans. The reason for this is simple: the whole notion of Neanderthals as a distinctive entity developed at the level of intuition, rather than of rigorous analysis. Ever since the discovery of the original Neander Valley fossils, everyone knew that the Neanderthals were different—so different, indeed, that for more than a century it hardly seemed necessary to inquire exactly how they differed, or to

81 and 82

Side and three-quarter views of the adult Neanderthal cranium from Amud, Israel.

During the 1960s a Japanese team excavated a fairly complete Neanderthal skeleton at Amud. Dating from about 40 thousand years ago, this adult male is the latest Neanderthal known from the Levant. He was also the tallest Neanderthal known, at close to 6 feet in height.

Photograph courtesy of Israel Antiquities Authority.

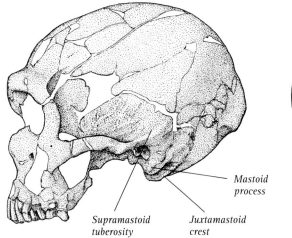
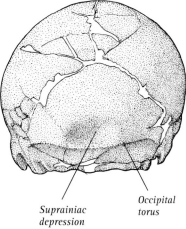

83

Some unique characters of the Neanderthal skull.

In 1978 Albert Santa Luca produced the first morphological definition of the Neanderthals, based on the characters shown here.
Illustration by Diana Salles.

Mastoid process

Supramastoid tuberosity

Juxtamastoid crest

Suprainiac depression

Occipital torus

provide anything other than an impressionistic definition of the group. Thus, not until 1978 did someone—Albert Santa Luca, then of Harvard—take the bull by the horns and point out that no adequate definition of Neanderthals existed. To redress this problem, he identified a "core group" of fossils (La Chapelle, La Ferrassie, Spy, and a number of others) that everyone agreed were Neanderthals and scrutinized them for features that they alone among hominids possessed. [see Plates 59 and 63] In the end he isolated four characteristics, shown in the illustration, that seemed to be unique to Neanderthals. [Plate 83] One of these is the occipital torus, a bony ridge that runs horizontally across the occipital bone at the rear of the skull. Above this ridge lies the oval suprainiac depression, another unique Neanderthal feature. Moving forward on the skull base, we find the third distinguishing feature, a very large and well-defined "occipitomastoid crest" (often known nowadays as the juxtamastoid crest) lying inside the mastoid process. The mastoid process is a bony structure (small in Neanderthals compared to modern humans) that projects downward behind and below the ear canal. Finally, high up on the mastoid process itself, Neanderthals show a distinct, rounded eminence, the mastoid tuberosity. Running upward and backward, this tuberosity is absent or differently developed in other humans.

These four traits may not look like much by which to characterize Nean-

derthals, especially since they are concentrated in one area of the skull. But they allowed Santa Luca to compare the Neanderthals with a variety of human fossils, from places as far apart as Ngandong in Java and Kabwe in Zambia, that had at one time or another been described as "Neanderthal-like." The ability to make such comparisons in turn permitted him to refute conclusively, for the first time, the notion of a worldwide "Neanderthaloid stage" of human evolution. It turned out that of all the potential Neanderthal relatives that Santa Luca looked at, only the Steinheim and Swanscombe fossils shared any of the defining Neanderthal features. [see Plates 66, 67, and 92] These observations supported earlier suggestions that these "archaic *Homo sapiens*," older than any full-blown Neanderthals, nonetheless stood in their ancestry. What's more, Santa Luca pointed out that since modern humans share none of the distinctive and specialized Neanderthal traits, it's highly unlikely that the Neanderthals were our ancestors. [Plate 84]

Other features have since been invoked in the investigation of Neanderthal uniquenesses, and it's clear that Santa Luca's investigation was just a start to what will need to be a thorough examination, in great detail, of what morphological features define our nearest relatives—and us. Nonetheless, Santa Luca's approach represented a real breakthrough. Although his contribution never quite attracted the attention it

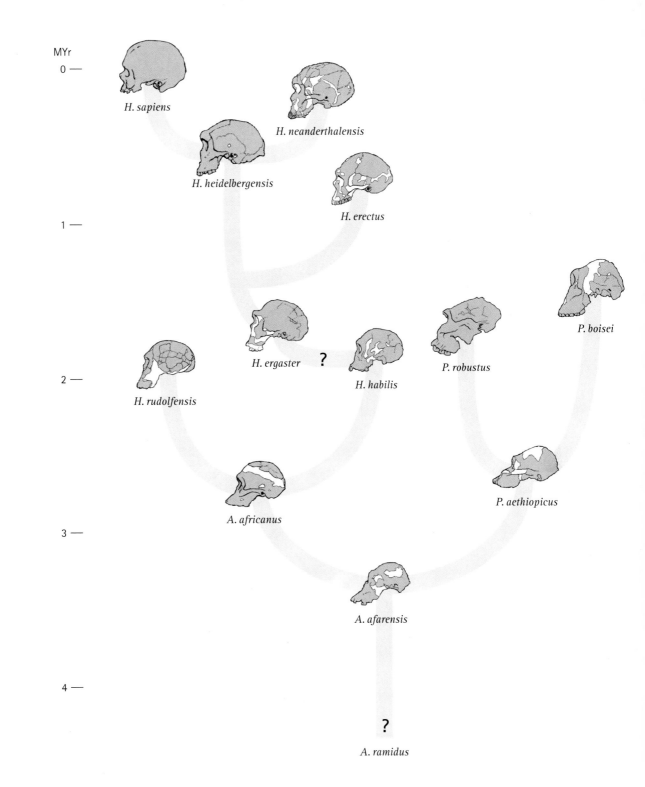

MYr

0 —

H. sapiens

H. neanderthalensis

H. heidelbergensis

H. erectus

1 —

P. boisei

H. ergaster **?**

H. habilis

P. robustus

H. rudolfensis

2 —

P. aethiopicus

A. africanus

3 —

A. afarensis

4 —

?

A. ramidus

84

The human family tree.

A summary of the approximate distribution in time and the probable relationships of all the hominid species recognized in this book. *Illustration by Diana Salles.*

deserved, it has been followed up by a few later workers, notable among them Jean-Jacques Hublin, of the Musée de l'Homme, in Paris, and Bernard Vandermeersch, of the University of Bordeaux.

The account in this chapter of the history of our emerging knowledge of the Neanderthals is far from exhaustive. Neanderthal remains, albeit mostly fragmentary, have been reported from many dozens of sites not yet mentioned, and Mousterian tools from hundreds more. Many investigators yet to be mentioned

have participated in their study. My intention has been to describe how our ideas about the Neanderthals have developed, and to show how we are still burdened in our perceptions of the Neanderthals by notions inherited from the past. There's no doubt that what we think today is inevitably shaped by what we believed yesterday, and this is something we should keep firmly in mind as we go on to look at the Neanderthals from our current perspective. But first, let's take a look at the world in which they lived ■

The Neanderthals' World

 The Ice Ages

The Neanderthals lived between around 200,000 and 30,000 years ago, during the period of extreme climatic fluctuation that characterized the later part of the Pleistocene epoch, colloquially known as the "Ice Ages." As we've seen, in 1909 the geographers Albrecht Penck and Eduard Brückner identified evidence for four major glacial advances and retreats of the Alpine ice cap, thereby setting the basic chronology of geological events through the 1.8 million years of the Pleistocene. [see Plate 57] This chronology they achieved by analyzing surface geology, and given that each glacial advance or retreat tends to scour or wash away the evidence of its predecessors, their achievement was monumental indeed. But for years the inevitable spottiness of the terrestrial evidence for glaciation posed a major obstacle to detailed understanding of the sequence of Pleistocene events, particularly on a global scale. Since the mid-1950s, however, an alternative approach to this problem has been developed, exploiting the fact that cores taken through the muds that accumulate on the seabed reveal a more or less unbroken record of deposition. Such marine deposition takes place at much more regular rates than does the deposition of sediments on land. What's more, the cores also contain microorganisms (notably those known as foraminifera, or forams for short) that record the relative temperature of the ocean at the time they were deposited.

How does this work? When alive, these tiny single-celled creatures float in the ocean and absorb two different forms (isotopes) of oxygen from the waters around them: ^{16}O and ^{18}O. [Plate 85] These two isotopes become incorporated into the tests (shells) of the forams in a ratio that varies according to the prevailing temperature. As the ice sheets swell during periods of cold, they "lock up" the lighter ^{16}O isotopes that evaporate preferentially from the surface of the seas. At the same time, the oceans, and thus the foraminiferal shells, become richer in the heavier ^{18}O. The shells of forams thus preserve a climatic record in the form of the ratio of oxygen isotopes they contain. When the forams die, their shells sink to the seafloor and become incorporated into the accumulating pile of mud, which later turns into rock. Rock cores raised from the ocean floor by drilling thus furnish a continuous record of climatic change that can be read by isotopic analyses of the foram shells.

A continuous record of fluctuating climate is one thing; tying these fluctuations to the passage of time is another. Most cases involve an elaborate process combining chronometric and relative dating with other geological techniques. The very top of the sedimentary column can be directly dated by radiocarbon; as I've noted, however, this method takes us back no more than about 40,000 years. Beyond this time, we find ourselves in a complex process of correlations, based on the fact that the direction of Earth's magnetic

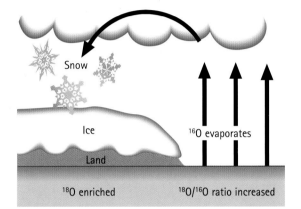

Snow

Ice

Land

^{16}O evaporates

^{18}O enriched

$^{18}O/^{16}O$ ratio increased

Glacial

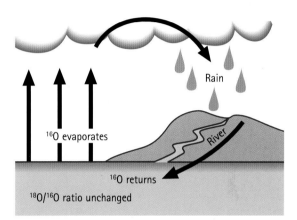

Rain

River

^{16}O evaporates

^{16}O returns

$^{18}O/^{16}O$ ratio unchanged

Interglacial

85

Oxygen–isotope analysis.

Past climates are reflected in the ratio of the oxygen isotopes ^{16}O and ^{18}O in the tests of tiny organisms found in cores taken from the ocean floor. These isotopes are derived by the organisms from the seawater in which they live. Since the lighter ^{16}O evaporates preferentially from seawater and is returned to the sea in smaller quantities when precipitation becomes "locked up" in icecaps, in colder times this isotope becomes rarer in the seas compared to ^{18}O.
Illustration by Diana Salles, after Tjeerd Van Andel, New Views on an Old Planet: A History of Global Change, *2nd ed. (Cambridge University Press, 1994).*

field reverses itself from time to time (a million years ago the needle of your compass would have pointed south). The direction of magnetism at the time rocks were deposited can be determined in the cores raised from the seabed. These directions can then be matched with those found in datable volcanic deposits on land, and a time scale can be constructed. From the point of view of those interested in Neanderthals, however, there's a catch. Since the beginning of the Pleistocene, there have been only four magnetic reversals (the last of which took place long before the Neanderthals came on the

scene). The oxygen isotopes, on the other hand, indicate that climates have warmed and cooled far more frequently. Thus, calibration of the isotope record has been refined using extrapolations from sediment thicknesses and from calculations based on various aspects of Earth's orbit and axial tilt, which affect climate by varying the amount and distribution of energy received from the sun.

During the last 1.8 million years Earth's climate has cycled on average from one warm peak to the next, via a trough of cold, about every 100,000 years—although early cycles tended to be

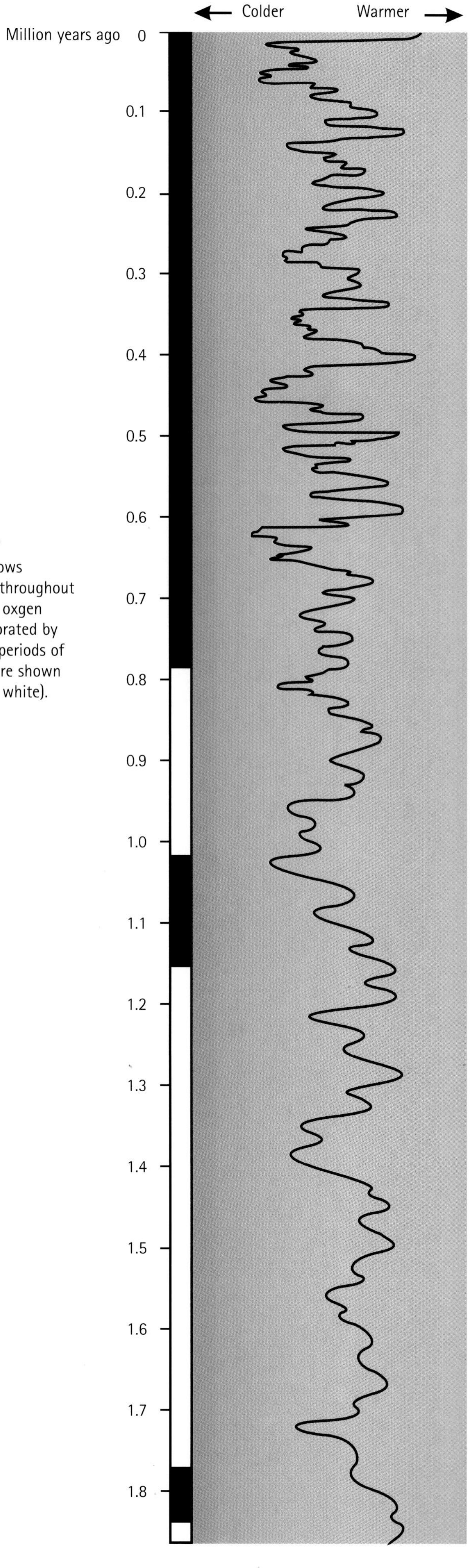

Million years ago

Colder ← → Warmer

0

0.1

0.2

0.3

0.4

0.5

0.6

0.7

0.8

0.9

1.0

1.1

1.2

1.3

1.4

1.5

1.6

1.7

1.8

86

Ice Age climatic change.

The curve on the right shows fluctuating temperatures throughout the Pleistocene, based on oxgen isotope analyses and calibrated by paleomagnetic reversals (periods of "normal" magnetization are shown in black; reversed ones in white).
Illustration by Diana Salles.

less extreme than later ones. There have thus been about fifteen glacial episodes since the beginning of the Pleistocene. [Plate 86] The general pattern is a slow buildup of ice to a glacial maximum, followed by a rather rapid warming phase—and breakdown of the ice sheets—at the end of each glacial cycle. But the record also shows fluctuations on an even smaller scale. Generally speaking, during the glacial periods the summers were not much cooler than they are today, but the winters were longer and much more severe—hence the buildup of ice. Toward the end of each glacial episode, the climate also generally became more arid. Interestingly, studies of the geographic distributions of forams adapted to cold water have also shown a fundamental 400,000-year cycle of general cooling (when forams adapted to colder water moved a long way toward the equator) and warming (signaled by reverse migration) superimposed on the 100,000-year pattern. Thus, we return in a roundabout way to the original four-glacial notion.

The oxygen isotope signal becomes less distinct as we move backward in time. The best record comes from the last 780,000 years, the time since the last geomagnetic reversal. In this period eight full climatic cycles have been measured. The last of these, which began about 127,000 years ago, is the time normally known as the Late Pleistocene. It includes the last interglacial, the last glacial, and the warmer period that we are in now. The present warm phase began about

10,000 years ago and is often known as the Holocene epoch. Some geologists, however, prefer to say that we are now simply in the Flandrian interglacial, and evidence from ice cores taken in Greenland and the Antarctic shows a reduced variability in climate over the last 10,000 years that does correspond to a true interglacial. Let's not forget, however, that in this relatively short period there have nonetheless been many climatic fluctuations, such as the "Little Ice Age" that peaked in 1650, or warmer periods like the one during which Hannibal and his elephants crossed the Alps through mountain passes that are now blocked by glaciers. The important thing to bear in mind, then, is that the Ice Ages were not a monolithic time of cold, inhospitable climates, but rather a temporal patchwork of environments. We should also remember that cold times were not necessarily hard times for humans living in northern latitudes. Great herds of large-bodied mammals out on the cold open tundra afforded a much easier target for early human hunters than did, say, small groups of red deer flitting between the forest trees in warmer periods.

Ice Age Environments

The period of the Ice Age that we know best—thanks to its comparative recency and to the fact that no later glaciations have yet come along to destroy the geological evidence for it—is the Late Pleistocene. This phase started about 127,000 years ago, as the last interglacial began with the rapid thawing of the extended polar ice cap and of more-localized ice sheets such as those that covered the Alps and Pyrenees. One of the consequences of this melting was an increase in the amount of water flowing into the oceans, which expanded as a result. Sea levels rose, forming islands where continuous land had been before. Great Britain is a case in point; its land connection to continental Europe was last disrupted about 14,000 years ago. At the warmest points in the cycle, sea levels may have been even higher than they are in the present interglacial, perhaps by as much as twelve or fifteen feet. As the climate ameliorated, forest expanded over areas that had previously been open tundra, and the nature of the fauna changed. The bones of hippos, for example, have been found in Britain at a site 200 miles north of the former ice sheet boundary. It's notable, however, that the fauna was quite different from what we are used to in the present interglacial, largely because there was a major extinction of large-bodied mammal species in northern Eurasia after (and perhaps because—though this is still debated) modern humans came on the scene. When the early Neanderthals roamed Europe during the last interglacial, hippos, rhinoceroses, and straight-tusked woodland elephants abounded on the landscape right up to northern England. Further north yet, where the landscape remained more open, reindeer were joined by huge mammals such as the two-horned woolly

87

Neanderthals at Le Moustier, France, about 50 thousand years ago.

This diorama at the American Museum of Natural History depicts three Neanderthals at this classic site during a relatively warm interlude in the last glacial. Dress is of course conjectural, although almost certainly Neanderthals wore clothing of some kind.
Photograph by Dennis Finnin and Craig Chesek.

rhinoceroses and the woolly mammoths. Among widespread smaller species were red deer, horses, wild cattle, and mountain goats (ibex), which would have been particularly attractive to human hunters in the fall, when they descended from the high mountains into the more hospitable valleys below. [Plate 87]

After about 115,000 years ago, a cooling trend set in, heralding a thinning of the forests and an expansion of grasslands that supported large herds of horses, wild cattle, and deer. In the European heartland of the Neanderthals, a mixed woodland habitat prevailed, with open spaces interspersed by forests, particularly in lowlands and along river margins. This cool temperate period was followed, in the period after about 70,000 years ago, by a fairly steep if irregular descent in global temperatures. In Europe and western Asia, this drop in temperature led to the disappearance of forest from all but sheltered areas, and to the advance from the north of an ice sheet centered on the Scandinavian peninsula. Humidity declined as the ice accumulated, and after about 40,000 years ago, fully glacial conditions reigned, as the European climate became dry and intensely cold. Mile by mile the polar ice cap progressed southward, until it had engulfed most of Ireland, half of England, and the entire coastal region of Europe east of Denmark. Forest gradually disappeared, to be replaced by open tundra with tussocky grasses, sedges, and low bush cover in sheltered areas.

With this change in vegetation came a southward movement of the Arctic fauna, which included reindeer, saiga antelope, woolly rhinos, chamois, steppe bison, musk ox, and woolly mammoths. Some of the more exotic mammals that characterized the glacial period included the giant cave bear, the cave hyena, and the cave lion, all larger than their surviving counterparts. Cave bears became extinct just as the temperatures were beginning the dive toward their minimum, some 40,000

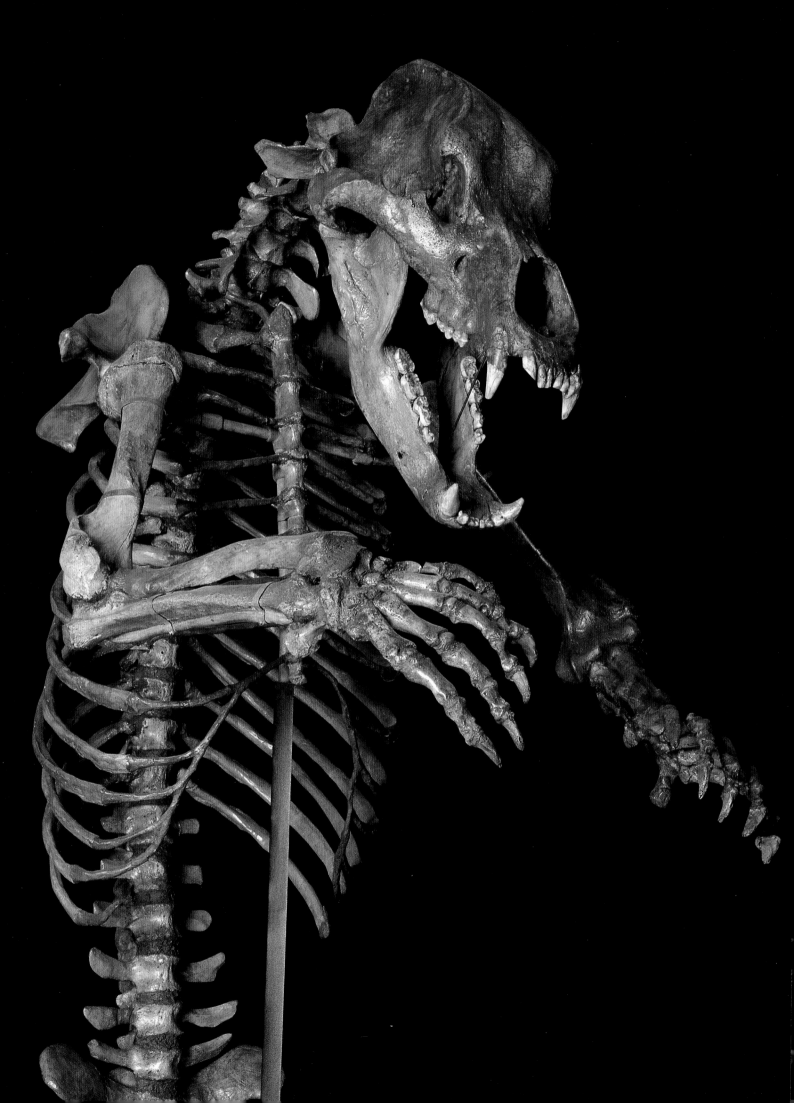

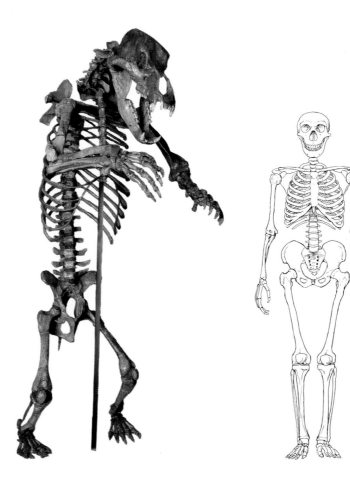

88
Cave bear skeleton.

Giant cave bears (*Ursus spelaeus*) became extinct slightly before *Homo neanderthalensis* did, but the two coexisted over most of the latter's timespan. Older scenarios frequently pitted Neanderthals against the fearsome bears, but it seems more likely based on their relative sizes (right) that the Neanderthals generally avoided them.
Photograph courtesy of the American Museum of Natural History.

years ago; the other two species survived almost to the end of the last glacial. [Plate 88] Between about 30,000 and 20,000 years ago, by which time Neanderthals had disappeared from Europe, conditions began to tumble to their coldest and driest, hitting bottom about 18,000 years ago. The resulting drop in sea levels exposed wide expanses of the continental shelves—including the maximum extent of the land bridge between Europe and unglaciated southern England—and in doing so exacerbated the cold continental climate, as the ameliorating influence of the seas receded. During the most intense phases of glaciation, it seems, large swaths of Europe were excluded from human habitation. Moravia, for example, where highly sophisticated Upper Paleolithic cultures had developed between about 28,000 and 24,000 years ago, has no archaeological sites from the millennia around the glacial maximum. Neither does England. This was probably true at other glacial maxima as well.

At about 14,000 years ago, Europe witnessed a marked amelioration in climate. Forests spread once more, and

by not much less than 10,000 years ago they had become the dominant vegetation type of northern Europe. The very rapidity of environmental change at this point may have helped unsettle the populations of the large mammals—woolly rhinos, mammoths, and so forth—that disappeared as the glaciers retreated, to such an extent that the species became vulnerable to modern human hunters. But the reasons for the megafaunal extinction of this time (which extended to the Americas and across Asia, as well as in Europe) will certainly continue to be debated.

At the risk of sounding repetitious, I'll reiterate that these environmental changes did not occur in smooth cycles. The period leading up to the last glacial maximum was one of extraordinary climatic swings, many of them quite short-term. Moreover, microclimates varied enormously from place to place. Neanderthals accommodated to a huge range of environments during their long sojourn on Earth, which is one reason for wondering to what extent they were as specifically "cold-adapted" as they have been portrayed.

89
Reconstruction of the giant "Irish elk".

Painting by Charles R. Knight, probably late 1920s. This huge creature, *Megaloceros*, was a common feature on the landscape during Neanderthal times. Not an elk, but essentially a giant fallow deer, *Megaloceros* occurred not only in Ireland but widely throughout Eurasia. The antlers of males could span as much as twelve feet, and weigh over a hundred pounds.
Courtesy of the American Museum of Natural History.

Resources

Archaeology has been described — not without some justification — as the study of ancient garbage. One of the earliest and most significant forms of garbage that ancient people left behind is the remains of the animals they ate. Along with stone tools, broken and butchered animal remains are the main features of most Old Stone Age sites. Thus, it is important to be able to distinguish whether agglomerations of animal bones are the work of humans or of carnivores or scavengers. In making such a determination, it's also important to know the composition of the living fauna at the time the ancient humans of interest were alive. Perhaps surprisingly, in view of the great environmental changes experienced by the regions occupied by the Neanderthals, in general the two main areas from which Neanderthals are known — western Europe and the Levant — each preserved its own typical fauna through most of the Late Pleistocene. In the west the dominant herbivores were mammoths, woolly rhinos, bison, boar, wild sheep and cattle, horses, reindeer, ibex, red and roe deer, saiga antelope, Irish elk, and musk ox, while carnivores included cave bears, cave lions, cave hyenas, arctic fox, and wolves. [Plate 89] Mammals typical of eastern faunas embraced hippopotamus; wild sheep and goats; red, roe and fallow deer; wild boar; steppe asses; wolves; hyenas; and jackals. Many of these animals were found throughout the domain of the Neanderthals, differing among regions principally in their frequency (which fluctuated, of course, along with the climate). But as the paleoanthropologist Chris Stringer and his colleague archaeologist Clive Gamble have recently pointed out, there is a distinct if gradual increase in certain species from west to east. Stringer and Gamble also point out that it is in the intervening area—central and eastern Europe—that the remains of carnivores are found in the greatest concentration. From this observation they deduce two things: first, that in this central area Neanderthals experienced more-intense competition from fellow predators than they did elsewhere; second, that the greater frequency of complete Neanderthal skeletons in western Europe and the Levant is due to reduced destructive activity occasioned by the lower numbers of carnivores.

This may be true, but later we'll look at the possible role of deliberate burial in the preservation of Neanderthal skeletons. It's certainly true that the distribution of herbivore bones—the remains of potential prey—at Neanderthal sites reveals that these humans were much more choosy about what they ate than were other meat eaters. In hyena dens, for example, there is a general pattern of nonselectiveness among the herbivore species represented by broken bones, whereas at Neanderthal sites it's usual for one or two prey species to preponderate. Exactly what those species were varied a lot from site to site, of course. Neanderthals occupied a vast swath of Earth's surface for a very long time, during which the climate at any one spot oscillated wildly. Some sites lie in mountainous regions, others on low plains. Some are hundreds or even thousands of miles from the sea; some are right on the shoreline. Some lie in deeply dissected topography where varied resources would have been available from the sheltered valley bottoms all the way up to the windswept plateaus and crags above; others are found in monotonous open expanses. Some are on the hospitable shores of the Mediterranean; others on the fringes of the frozen tundra.

Put all these variables together, and you'll realize that it's hard to make any broad generalizations about Neanderthal environments. It's even harder to generalize about their prey preferences or culinary tastes. It is possible, for instance, to say that in the west, favorite prey species included large-bodied herbivores such as bison and their close relatives wild cattle, while at mountain sites in the western Asian interior wild sheep and goats tended to be more numerous. By themselves, however, such differences do not suggest that Neanderthals of different regions exploited their environments in different ways. More likely, they reflect the availability of animal resources in local environments, and as we've seen, Neanderthal environments were remarkably varied. If we can say one thing from looking at the places in which they lived, it is simply that Neanderthals were highly adaptable. Clearly, these humans had the behavioral and technological wherewithal to cope with a wide variety of ecological circumstances that ranged from warm temperate to arctic. They were, like us, ecological generalists■

7

Evolution of the Neanderthals

Precursors of the Neanderthals
It's hard to say exactly when the story of *Homo neanderthalensis* begins. Most paleoanthropologists believe that Neanderthals evolved from a Middle Pleistocene population of *Homo heidelbergensis*, but the details—or even the broad outlines—of that event are unclear. The attractiveness of *Homo heidelbergensis* as an ancestor for later humans of all kinds stems essentially from its primitiveness—in other words, its lack of the anatomical specializations possessed by later hominids to which it might be linked.

Some of the difficulties in making the connection between *Homo heidelbergensis* and modern humans stems from the kind of organism that humans are. As I said at the end of Chapter 6, ecologically speaking humans are generalists, and generalists tend to speciate less than specialists do. Thus, our own family has probably spun off fewer new species than many other groups of mammals have—although on the other hand, the fluctuating climatic and geographic conditions of the Pleistocene certainly would have encouraged speciation, particularly in northern regions. [see Plate 18] What's more, because they cannot afford to kill off the animal populations on which they prey, carnivores exist in much lower individual numbers than do herbivores. As predators—or even as scavengers—humans were almost certainly rare on the landscape; thus, they are commensurately rare in the fossil record. The only elements that might potentially mitigate this basic fact

are cultural practices—such as deliberate burial of the dead—which may enhance the chance of preservation. As we'll see, however, burial appears to have been a rather uncommon practice among Neanderthals.

The upshot is that while we should expect a reasonable amount of speciation among humans during the Pleistocene, the total number of species involved may not have been enormous. Put this together with other considerations—such as that humans have generally been thin on the ground and thus necessarily have a rather sparse fossil record, that "sister" species do not tend to be separated by major anatomical distinctions, and that we are unlikely to find the large numbers of individuals of any species needed to identify patterns of morphological difference with total confidence—and it is far from surprising that the precise origins of the Neanderthals are not easy to discern. One thing, though, appears to me as close to certain as it can be: the Neanderthal lineage originated as a single population isolated somewhere in Europe or western Asia. We should not be surprised to find the source of that population hard to interpret in the period before the lineage's distinguishing characters were amplified by successive speciations.

From time to time it has been argued that some classic examples of *Homo heidelbergensis*, such as the 400,000-year-old Arago form (which was associated with a rather crude Early Paleolithic tool kit known as the "Tayacian", flake-based

90

Excavations in progress at the cave of Arago, near Tautavel, southern France.

This cave has produced a large number of fossils, mostly fragmentary but including much of a cranium, which document early hominid occupation in Europe around 400 thousand years ago.
Photograph by Ian Tattersall.

91

Front view of the cranium from Petralona, Greece.

Poorly dated (to about 450 thousand years ago), but excellently preserved, this is the most complete example of *Homo heidelbergensis* from Europe.
Photograph courtesy of George Koufos.

but lacking handaxes), resemble Neanderthals in certain respects. [Plate 90 and see Plate 43] Such features, however, may have been inherited from an older common ancestor and thus may not indicate a special relationship between the two species. Shared resemblance of this kind is also true of the massive and poorly dated Petralona skull from Greece, which has sometimes been cited as Neanderthal-like in the structure of its brow ridges. [Plate 91 and see Plate 44] Although like those of Neanderthals (and unlike those of *Homo erectus*), these ridges do follow the upper contours of the orbits and are continuous from one side of the brow to the other, they are significantly different in shape. They bulge at the middle of each orbit and thin markedly toward the sides instead of maintaining a

relatively consistent thickness as those of Neanderthals do. The brow ridges are also "crested" at the top, which is not the case among Neanderthals, and the cheeks are inflated instead of being hollowed out. All in all, the Petralona and Arago specimens show a coherent morphology that is shared with other *Homo heidelbergensis* specimens from Africa and perhaps from China, and that is distinct from that of the Neanderthals.

A few other European finds deserve mention, although it's not at all clear exactly where they enter the picture. A travertine quarry near Bilzingsleben, in eastern Germany, has yielded fragments of what was probably a single adult skull, as well as an extra tooth from an immature individual. Middle Pleistocene in age, possibly more than 280,000 years old, the skull is too incomplete to be pieced together, but the occipital bone, in particular, is extremely heavily built and sharply angled at the back. It has elicited (dubious) comparisons with *Homo erectus*, but its affinities are still very vague, and the key point is that this specimen does not resemble Neanderthals in any convincing way. The associated industry is flake-based, lacking handaxes, as is that found with another massive and inscrutable occipital, which may be around the same age, at the Hungarian site of Verteszöllös. Recently, a more lightly built partial skull, also of Middle Pleistocene age (say, 225,000 years, although the actual age might be as much as 100,000 years younger—such are the vagaries of dating in the Middle Pleistocene) has come to light at the German site of Reilingen. Remarkably, this specimen—with quite a high braincase—has an estimated cranial volume close to the mean for modern humans. Like Neanderthals, the Reilingen skull has a strong occipital torus, a distinct suprainiac depression, and a hint (unfortunately, it is broken in the critical spot) of a juxtamastoid crest. It's likely that this specimen has Neanderthal affinities of some sort; detailed studies will help with this determination, but additional finds would help more.

Until recently, then, the Swanscombe and Steinheim specimens have been the ones most frequently cited as the earliest potential Neanderthal precursors. Both of these fossils are well over 200,000 years old, but both present problems of interpretation. The Swanscombe specimen consists solely of the rear end of a skull whose original cranial volume is estimated to have been about 1325 ml. [Plate 92] Following its discovery in the 1930s, the specimen was initially interpreted as supporting evidence for a "pre-*sapiens*" lineage in Europe, marginalizing the Neanderthals. Intact, the skull would have been more highly vaulted than is characteristic of Neanderthals, with its maximum breadth higher on the sides (though not as high as in *Homo sapiens*). Nonetheless, there are some suggestions of Neanderthal morphology in the skull rear, notably in a hint of a suprainiac depression. The cultural associations of the Swanscombe specimen are, however, not Mousterian (though at 225,000 years old, there's no reason why anyone should expect them to be); stone tools found in the same deposits belong to a tradition called Clactonian. Like the Mousterian, the Clactonian was based on prepared-core technology, but nowadays it is regarded as an independent development out of the Acheulean.

Before we identify the archaeological associations of the early Neanderthal fossils, it's probably useful to digress a little to point out that there is some confusion in the terminology applied to the stoneworking technologies of the later Middle and earlier Late Pleistocene. Sometimes industries are referred to as "Levalloisian," meaning that they contain implements that were produced by the prepared-core technique, with extensive

92
Rear of cranium from Swanscombe, England.

Dated to over 200 thousand years ago, perhaps as much as 300 thousand years, two pieces of this partial cranium were discovered in 1935-6, and a third in 1955! The Swanscombe specimen is often viewed as a proto-Neanderthal. *Photograph courtesy of The Natural History Museum, London.*

preshaping of a core, including the production of a "striking platform" at which blows were directed (often by bashing the platform down onto a stationary "anvil") to detach one or more "Levalloisian flakes" with a flat upper and convex lower surface. The Mousterian tradition widely associated with the Neanderthals included Levalloisian technology, but Levalloisian implements are also found in some later Acheulean assemblages, perhaps as far back as 300,000 or 400,000 years ago (dating is vague). The term "Mousterian" has also been applied to several industries from northern Africa, outside the realm of the Neanderthals, because in both areas some Middle Paleolithic toolmakers produced similar tools. In both regions it is hard to say with any precision when such traditions started, because they are often recognized simply by a lack of the large handaxes and cleavers of the Acheulean—and these faded out with a marked lack of regularity.

In the Levant, the term "Levalloiso-Mousterian" has been applied to assemblages that are rich in Levalloisian flakes, but that are otherwise typically Mousterian, with small handaxes made on flakes, backed knives, side scrapers, and so forth. [Plate 93] The overall situation is complicated by the fact that prepared-core technology was introduced to different

places at wildly different times. Further, the proportion of different tool types in the "kit" varies greatly from site to site, depending presumably on the availability of materials, the nature of the activities carried out at the site, and a host of other influences that were independent of the specific cultural tradition of the toolmakers. In the face of this highly complex situation, it would be unfair to blame archaeologists for the lack of high definition in their characterizations of tool assemblages, and unrealistic to expect complete uniformity in the terminology they use.

Returning to the fossils, the Steinheim skull is remarkably intact, but regrettably crushed, to the extent that there's plenty of room for disagreement over its exact facial morphology. [see Plates 66 and 67] The skull itself is small and narrow, with a brain volume of only about 1100 ml. Its brow ridges, large nasal opening, and sloping forehead, however, might be viewed as incipiently Neanderthal features, as might the suggestion of a suprainiac fossa at the rear of the skull. Interestingly, though, this skull has recently been compared to a much older (about 350,000 years) and less complete specimen from Lake Ndutu, in faraway Tanzania. Archaeologically, the association of the Steinheim cranium with rather crude "pebble tools" has been disputed. About all that can be said of

94

Excavations in progress at the Sima de los Huesos ("Pit of the Bones") in the Atapuerca Hills, Spain.

A deep pit in this Atapuerca cave has recently yielded a large number of hominid fossils, mostly fragmentary. No artifacts are present, and how the fossils accumulated remains a mystery. The fossils are overlain by a flowstone dated to about 300 thousand years ago.
Photograph by Javier Trueba, © Madrid Scientific Films; courtesy of Jean-Luis Arsuaga.

the Steinheim and Swanscombe specimens at this point is that they do not sit comfortably together with typical *Homo heidelbergensis* fossils such as the Arago and Kabwe specimens, and that they are also not Neanderthal under any strict definition. Whether either or both specimens is incipiently ancestral to *Homo neanderthalensis* remains a toss-up.

An additional reason for thinking that they might not be Neanderthals is that by about 230,000 years ago, there were already more-plausible Neanderthals or Neanderthal relatives around. For years, the human fossils found early in the twentieth century at the German site of Ehringsdorf were believed to date from the last interglacial, by which time the Neanderthals had become well established. At Ehringsdorf a fragmentary skull and lower jaw, along with bits and pieces of several other individuals, were found in association with animal bones, invertebrates, and plant fossils that indicated a temperate environment of deposition.

New ESR and uranium-series dates have shown that these remains in fact come from an earlier interglacial, about 230,000 years ago, and new morphological studies have suggested strong Neanderthal affinities for the fossils. The associated tool kit, which lacks handaxes, consists largely of finely crafted bifacial points and scrapers long thought to be potential precursors to later Mousterian industries. In light of the new dates and interpretations of the fossils, this suggestion takes on added force, although as already noted, such a cacophony of stoneworking industries existed in Middle Pleistocene Europe that it's difficult to be categorical about anything.

All previous bets about Neanderthal origins are off, however, in the wake of a very recent series of finds at a site in the Atapuerca Mountains of northern Spain. [Plate 94] Known as the Sima de los Huesos ("Pit of the Bones"), this cave locality represents not a living site, but rather several cavities in which a mass of bones and rubble collected (but no stone tools). Most of the bones in the cave belong to a species of cave bear and some other carnivores, but some 700 human fossils, mostly fragments, are said to represent the remains of at least twenty-four individuals. Outstanding among these are an almost complete adult cranium, an adult braincase, and a fragmentary cranium of a subadult, all recovered in 1992. [Plate 95 and see Plate 47] Exactly how the human bones came to rest deep in this interior cavity (though perhaps closer to a now-collapsed ancient entrance) remains a mystery. One suggestion—on the face of it a bit implausible—is that all the individuals belonged to a single social group that was caught up in a catastrophe of some kind. They were all found beneath a flowstone that has been U-series dated to more than 300,000 years ago.

The Atapuerca human sample is reportedly quite variable in morphology, although at this writing only the three crania have been at all adequately described.

Each of the three is said to "anticipate" the Neanderthals in the morphology of the back of the skull (with a "rough" suprainiac surface, albeit no distinct depression). In the most complete specimen at least, the back of the skull seems quite rounded. The brow ridges are also said to be Neanderthal-like, although from available photographs they appear to have the peaked shape typical of *Homo heidelbergensis*, and a steep forehead is present. Estimated brain sizes range from 1390 ml in the adult braincase, through 1125 ml in the most complete skull, to about 1100 ml in the immature individual. Altogether, these specimens appear to be closer to *Homo heidelbergensis* than to the Neanderthals in morphology, though more-detailed descriptions and analyses will doubtless clarify the matter. Meanwhile, although the reported variability in the sample adds to the uncertainty, it would be unwise to dismiss the describers' notion that these specimens anticipate the Neanderthals in certain ways. The Neanderthals must have

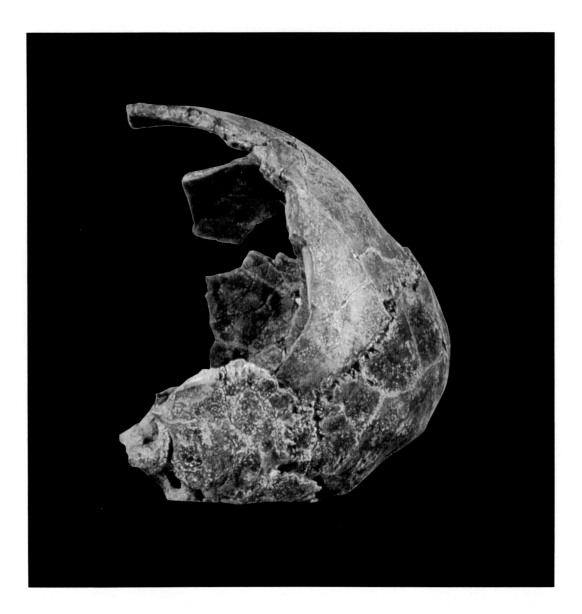

96

Rear of cranium from Biache, France.

About 150-175 thousand years old,
this cranium, though far from
complete, is typically Neanderthal in
preserved features.
Courtesy of Bernard Vandermeersch.

had antecedents that lived 300,000 years ago, and in the longer term this extraordinary sample of European early human fossils will doubtless play a major role in clarifying our knowledge of human evolution during this period.

The Early Neanderthals

The long period of intense cold around the peak of the next-to-last glacial (about 180,000 to 130,000 years ago) is when we first encounter human fossils that appear without a doubt to be Neanderthal in preserved features. The earliest evidence is sketchy, though, consisting of bits of two individuals from the northern French site at Biache-Saint-Vaast. Unfortunately, the principal specimen consists once again of only the back of a skull, together with a bit of upper jaw, from a small (presumably female) individual with an estimated cranial capacity of about 1200 ml. [Plate 96] Some bits of the front of a more heavily built skull were also recovered. Regrettably, the Biache human assemblage has never been studied as a unit, but the rear of the complete skull bears most of the hallmarks of Neanderthal morphology—a protruding occiput, a large juxtamastoid crest, a suggestion of a suprainiac depression, a maximum breadth low on the parietals, and other characters not mentioned by Santa Luca. [see Plate 83] The stone tools associated with the Biache remains have been described as Levalloisian in type. Perhaps the most remarkable aspect of the Biache site is its lack of organization—there are no hearths or evidence of structures—that it reveals, despite the excellence of its preservation.

The site of Le Lazaret in the south of France, which dates from the same period, is quite different. There some Neanderthal scraps were found at a living site within a cave mouth. Inside the cave, piles of rocks and the distribution of tools and broken animal bones suggest that lean-to shelters may have been rigged up against the cave wall, using posts to which skins were presumably attached. Evidence for a couple of hearths was also reported. The associated stone tool kit has been described as Acheulean with a weak Levalloisian component. Also from this early period is an enigmatic piece of frontal bone from the French site of Fontéchevade, once thought to be evidence for a pre-*sapiens* phase in Europe, but now regarded as too eroded to be of significance. The archaeological context is Tayacian, mostly with crude bifacially flaked chopping tools, although some flakes were apparently produced using prepared-core techniques.

The evidence is slim, then, for the earliest Neanderthal occupation of Europe. But the record picks up somewhat in the last interglacial phase (127,000 to 115,000 years ago), notably with the two skulls from Saccopastore, in Italy. One of these specimens, assumed to be female, is complete with the exception of the brow ridges; the other, more heavily constructed, consists only of the cranial base and

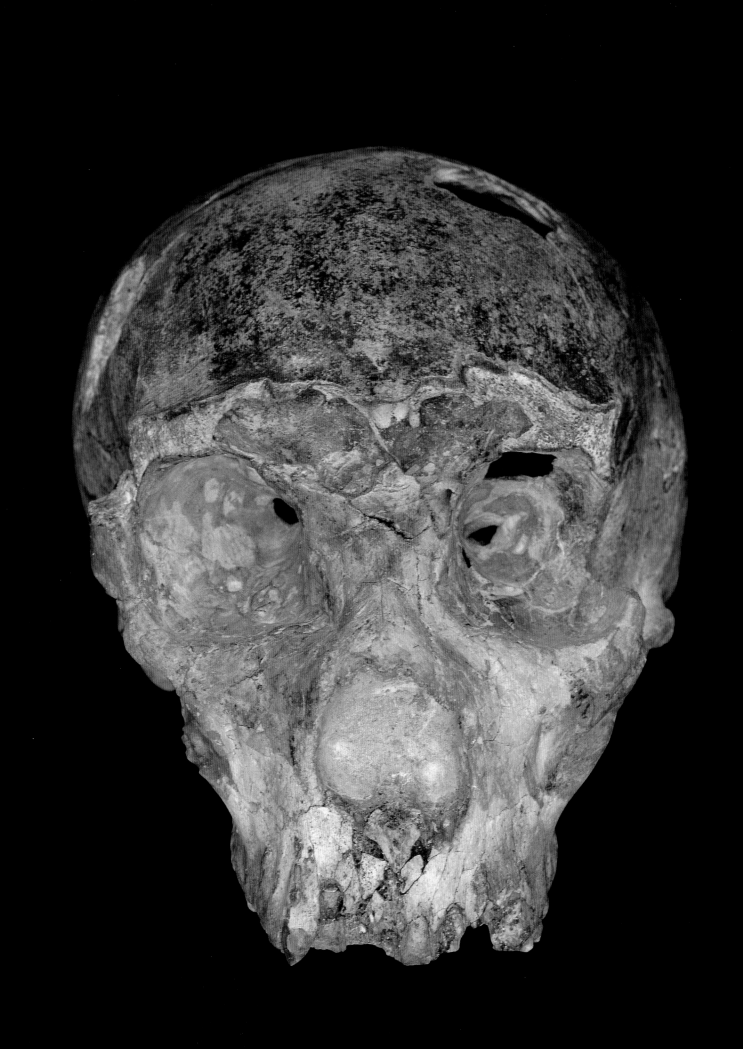

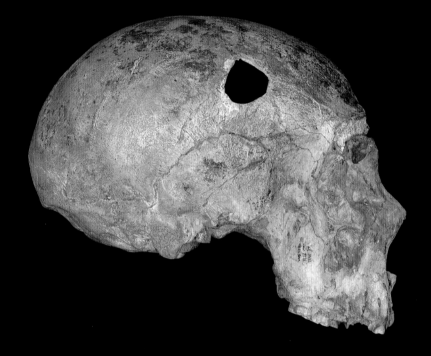

97 and 98
Front and side views of the cranium from Saccopastore, Italy.

Dated to about 120 thousand years ago, this is the best-preserved European Neanderthal skull from the last interglacial. Lightly built, it is assumed to be that of a female.
Courtesy of Museo di Antropologia "G. Sergi" (Dipartimento di Biologia Animale e dell'Uomo), University of Rome "La Sapienza".

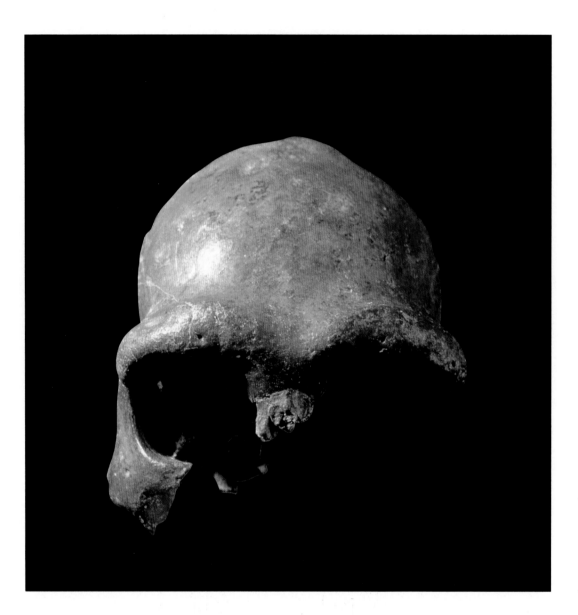

99

Upper face from Zuttiyeh, Israel.

Recovered in 1925 during rather
uncontrolled excavations, this
fragment is at least 125 thousand
years old, and may be twice that.
The relationship of this rather
generalized fossil to later Levantine
humans is uncertain.
*Photograph courtesy of Israel Antiquities
Authority.*

some fragments of the face. [Plates 97 and 98] These fossils are generally similar to later Neanderthal specimens: the more complete individual has a large, pulled-out midface and a complete suite of Neanderthal features of the base and rear of the skull, except for a protruding occipital "bun." Its cranial volume is relatively small, though, at less than 1200 ml. The archaeological association is unambiguously Mousterian, however, as is that of the approximately contemporaneous hominids from the lowest levels at Croatia's Krapina. [see Plate 60] The Krapina specimens, too, lack the robustness of some later "classic" western European Neanderthals, but nonetheless they fall squarely in the Neanderthal camp.

The picture is murkier in the Levant where the last interglacial phase is probably represented by the Zuttiyeh upper face from Israel, whose associated culture has been described as a primitive variant of the Mousterian (which appeared in the Levant about 150,000 years ago). [Plate 99] Although this specimen is not particularly similar to anything attributable to *Homo heidelbergensis*, neither does it preserve any features that would align it specifically with the Neanderthals. Most authorities have considered it to be rather "generalized," and some have thought of it as a potential ancestor of *Homo sapiens*—although this must be looked upon as something of a default judgment. There's no doubt, however, about the affinities of the Tabūn cranium from Mount Carmel, which tentative U-series

and ESR dates suggest is well over 100,000 years old—in which case it is approximately contemporaneous with the Zuttiyeh specimen. [see Plate 70] The Tabūn specimen is about the most lightly built of any reasonably complete Neanderthal cranium known, and is quite rounded at the back; nevertheless, it bears a host of Neanderthal hallmarks, including very large juxtamastoid crests, big mastoid tuberosities, more than a hint of suprainiac depression, and brow ridges which, though thin, are of typically Neanderthal form. The associated industry is firmly Mousterian.

 Neanderthals of the Last Glacial
The heyday of the Neanderthals came in the last glacial, from about 70,000 years ago to the time around 30,000 years ago when the glacial peak was approaching. Neanderthal fossils from this period are abundant in sites ranging from the Atlantic to Uzbekistan, and from northern Germany all the way south to Gibraltar. The associated fauna suggests that the original Neander Valley fossil comes from this time, as do the "classic" (in every sense of the word) skeletons from La Chapelle-aux-Saints and La Ferrassie, together with such other western European notables as the Spy, Guattari, and Le Moustier specimens. [see Plates 53, 54, 59, 61, 63, 68, and 107] Further east, the roster contains the Kebara and Amud skeletons from Israel, the Shanidar group from Iraq, and the child from the far-flung outpost of

100 and 101

The Neanderthal burial from Kebara cave, Israel, close-up (left) and in situ during excavation (below).

This well-preserved 60 thousand years-old male skeleton (lacking only the cranium, the right leg and both feet) is the most robust Neanderthal known. It has been suggested that the cranium was removed as part of some postmortem ritual.

Photographs courtesy of Yoel Rak.

Teshik-Tash in Uzbekistan. [Plates 100 and 101 and see Plates 75, 76, 77, 78, 81, 82, 142, and 143]

The last reasonably complete Neanderthal specimen before these distinctive humans disappear from the record is a 36,000-year-old specimen discovered at Saint-Césaire, in western France, in 1979. [Plate 102] The skull is partial and badly crushed, but it is clearly that of a Neanderthal, with a large nasal orifice in a protruding mid-face, typical brow ridges above capacious rounded orbits, a long, low profile to the braincase, a mastoid crest, and a long, receding lower jaw. Interestingly, the stone tool industry associated with the Saint-Césaire Neanderthal is Châtelperronian—a technology that, as you'll recall, was long regarded as incipiently Upper Paleolithic because blade tools are as common as flake implements in the assemblage. This find seems largely, though not entirely, to have settled the argument over who was responsible for the Châtelperronian industry. How Neanderthals acquired this technology is still debated, though.

Some much less complete Neanderthal remains are considerably younger than those found at Saint-Césaire. Notable among these are fragments from the site of Figueira Brava Cave, in Portugal. These fossils, which date from about 31,000 years ago, were found in an "evolved Mousterian" archaeological context and suggest that the rugged mountains of Iberia may have been the Neanderthals' last redoubt. This possibility is reinforced by strong rumors that Mousterian tools from the site of Zafarraya, in southern Spain, are as young as 27,000 years old and that Neanderthal remains from this site are not much older. [see Plates 1 (frontispiece) and 141]

Thus, the overall picture suggests that the basic constellation of Neanderthal features had become established by the beginning of the last interglacial and possibly before, 150,000 years ago or more. Exactly when and where this morphology originated—and it must have had a distinct geographic origin, doubtless assisted by the fragmentation of populations

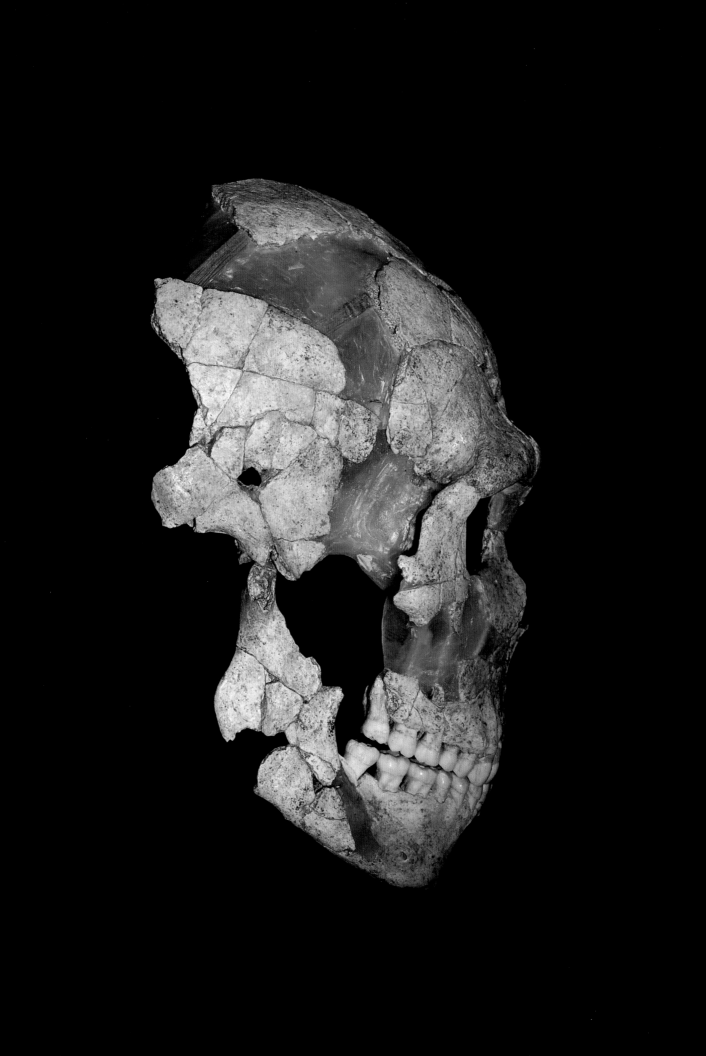

Partial skull from St-Césaire, France.

The burial from St-Césaire is among the most recent Neanderthals known. Dated to 36 thousand years ago, it is associated with a Châtelperronian stone toolkit.
Courtesy of Bernard Vandermeersch.

entailed by the climatic fluctuations of the Middle Pleistocene – is still a matter for speculation. The early Neanderthals tended to have less heavily constructed skulls (though fossils such as those from Saccopastore are at least partial exceptions to this general rule) than the later ones from the last glacial. Even less clear-cut is the pattern, noted in the mid-twentieth century by such paleoanthropologists as Keith, McCown, and Howell – on a rather restricted known sample – of a general trend toward lightness of build toward the east. Skulls such as those from Shanidar and Amud are, in their own way, as robust as those from La Chapelle-aux-Saints and La Ferrassie, which are of about the same age; the specimen from Kebara is reportedly the most heavily built Neanderthal skeleton known. Certainly, there appear to have been minor regional differences in skull structure, as one would anticipate in any widespread mammal species. The appearance of the later Levantine Neanderthal skulls tends, for example, to be somewhat less beetle-browed (for want of a better term) than that of the western European "classics." Even here, however, the small number of complete specimens involved makes it dangerous to generalize. On balance, then, there appears to have been substantial stability in Neanderthal form over the life of the species, despite the expected variability among individuals and an apparent slight tendency over time toward greater robustness.

Aside from the evocative aspects of their relationship to us, this picture of the Neanderthals in time and space makes them appear to be a pretty run-of-the-mill species in the larger scheme of things. As befits our rather hazy knowledge of how species originate in general, *Homo neanderthalensis* made a rather poorly understood debut on Earth. But once this distinctive species was established, it remained recognizably the same over the rest of its tenure even as, true to form, local populations pursued their own adaptive agendas. I've already noted that species seem normally to vary in much the same way in time and space, and it's hard to make an exception of the Neanderthals. Even the much-debated disappearance of these humans is in this larger perspective not much of a mystery, though as its putative authors we are inevitably fascinated by this event. New species of all kinds have regularly replaced each other in the fossil record over the documented history of life; and viewed in this way the disappearance of one more species, albeit a human one, hardly disturbs the larger pattern. We will continue to see this more general pattern reflected as we pursue the ways in which the Neanderthals exploited their environment.

Albeit indirectly, there's perhaps another lesson for us here, too; for just as the disappearance of the Neanderthals was nothing extraordinary, neither was our own appearance on the scene. We may think of ourselves, *Homo sapiens*, as pretty special; but we are certainly not the product of a special process ∎

8

Neanderthal Lifestyles

WE are now at a point in the history of archaeology at which the exuberance of early interpretations of prehistoric life has subsided considerably. Although substantial attention has been paid in recent years to how the evidence of ancient living and activity sites can be construed, there is a general attitude of caution among archaeologists, and a lot of effort has been devoted to the reevaluation of previous interpretations of the lives of our precursors. From early on, for example, it was assumed that the Neanderthals were hunters, subsisting mainly on meat gained by raiding the herds of grazing mammals that populated the Late Pleistocene steppes of western Eurasia in great abundance. By the 1980s, however, an attitude of greater caution prevailed, and it was suggested that the Neanderthals had hunted only the smallest mammals, or that they had been, at least seasonally, scavengers rather than hunters. If this new prudence made for a less dramatic and clear-cut picture of how the Neanderthals lived than we once thought we had, it also offered the advantage of defictionalizing the traditional story. At least as important, it cleared the decks for revised behavioral inferences based on sophisticated new techniques of analysis.

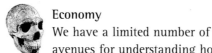

Economy
We have a limited number of avenues for understanding how our vanished precursors—certainly those that existed before the invention of houses and settled agriculture—lived. People who hunt or gather or scavenge for a living do not tend to leave behind a great deal to tell us about their lifeways. Our primary evidence comes from the stone tools our Old Stone Age forebears made and used, and from the animal bones they left behind at living or butchery sites. This sparse evidence is a poor reflection of total lifestyles that must have included many complex behaviors. Even when we take into account what we can learn from the wear on the stone tools about how they were used, or from the materials and reconstructible processes by which such tools were made, or from the proportion of different animal species or animal parts that we find at a site, or from how the tools and bones were scattered around by those who left them, we still don't have a huge amount of evidence. Such is true even for quite elaborate Paleolithic living sites that preserve the remains of ancient fires, say, or putative evidence for rudimentary structures. What, then, can we reasonably infer about how Neanderthals lived? [Plate 103]

Let's look first at the nature of the places where Neanderthals have been found. Generally, sites bearing traces of Neanderthal activity are simple, lacking the structured use of space typical of behaviorally modern humans. Hearths defined by rings of scorched cobbles or scooped-out areas are occasionally found at Neanderthal sites, but evidence for the use of fire comes more commonly in the form of burned bones or deposits of ash scattered randomly, leaving no evidence

103

A Neanderthal group.

Painted in the late 1960s, this
scene of Neanderthal life in the
foothills of the Pyrenees reflects the
understanding of the Neanderthals
then current.
Painting by and © Jay Matternes.

104
Cast of a hole made by a tent peg at Combe-Grenal, France.

At this Neanderthal site, archaeologists excavated a hole apparently made by a tent-peg (probably wooden) that was driven into the ground some 50 thousand years ago. Evidence that Neanderthals at least occasionally rigged up shelters has also been found elsewhere.
Photograph by Alain Roussot.

105
Lenses of ash in the deposits at Kebara, Israel.

In the succession of living floors at the Kebara cave are found numerous ash deposits, sometimes overlapping. These indicate the emplacements of hearths, around which stone litter was cleared away. The hearths are concentrated in the middle of the living area; and this, together with disposal of animal bones and stone chippings toward the rear wall of the cave, seems to indicate some organization of their living space by the Kebara Neanderthals.
Photograph courtesy of Ofer Bar-Yosef.

of any spatial focus of activity. Occasionally, however, it is possible to discern where an individual knapped flint, from the chips scattered around the clear space where he or she knelt. Traces of structures are more or less nonexistent, except maybe for the early site of Le Lazaret, already mentioned, and at most one or two others—though these include Combe-Grenal, discussed below. [Plate 104]

One possible exception to the typically haphazard organization of Neanderthal living places is the Israeli site of Kebara, excavated by the Harvard archaeologist Ofer Bar-Yosef and colleagues, where lenses of ash signal abundant recognizable hearths, concentrated for the most part in the center of the space defined by the broad, high cave entrance. Each new occupation of a cave leaves a fresh layer of debris on the floor, and in the space between occupations, dust blows in and bits of rock fall from the roof. At Kebara, sediments several meters thick accumulated in this way, and numerous successive "living floors" have been identified in this central area where most hearths were found. [Plate 105] Newer hearth areas tended to intrude upon older ones,

making the evidence for each difficult to interpret. Apparently, however, the spaces around the hearths were frequently cleared of naturally occurring stones, and concentrations of rock chips indicate that flints were frequently knapped next to the hearths. Animal bones, by contrast, seem often to have been flung toward the rear of the cave. Thus at Kebara there is some indication of at least rudimentary organization by Neanderthals of their living areas.

A rather different example of structured Neanderthal living space comes from studies undertaken by the Southern Methodist University's iconoclastic Lewis Binford, one of the most fertile minds in archaeology. It was Binford, in the early 1980s, who suggested that Mousterian people had tended to be foragers, in contrast to Upper Paleolithic people, who were collectors. For Binford, the primary distinction is that foraging is an opportunistic process that involves simply roaming around the landscape and making use of any resources encountered, whereas collecting involves the planned use of resources whose whereabouts are known and carefully monitored. He contended that, since collecting among modern hunting and gathering peoples tends to involve specialization within the group—with specialized parties going after particular resources—the sites created by collectors should betray a distinct structure related to those specialized functions, whereas those of foragers should not. The lack of organization in Mousterian sites suggested that they were the work of foragers, beings not capable—or at least not in the habit—of forward planning in the way that we are.

Binford has reportedly since concluded, however, that some type of structure is discernible at the Mousterian site of Combe Grenal, in southwestern France—even if it does not reflect the kind of organization typical of collectors. Living floors at Combe Grenal, he found, were consistently composed of distinct areas. One area, which Binford called the "nest," was typified by ashy deposits where fires had once burned, by very simple tools made of stone available on the spot, and by many splintered marrow bones and cranial fragments from medium-sized mammals. Nearby, one or two dozen feet away, were one or more spots containing more-complex stone tools, notably those known as scrapers, and the ends of marrow bones (sometimes the same individual bones whose middles turned up, smashed, in the nests). Carbonized sediments showed that fires burned in these places, but at a much higher temperature than those that produced the ashy deposits. Intriguingly, the associated tools were made from materials available only at some distance from the site, even miles away. What's more, the type of stone used corresponded to what was available where the animals lived whose bones were found alongside the tools. Tools made from river valley rocks were found with river valley mammals such as pigs, while stone from the neighboring plateau accompanied horses and other plateau animals. Evidently, two very different kinds of economic activity were taking place on each living floor. Binford suggests that the nests were occupied by more-sedentary females, who foraged in the local areas for plant materials and cooked over low flames. The other areas were those of the males, who ranged more widely in search of animal sustenance and who may have returned to the home sites only at intervals. Bones associated with the fleshy parts of mammals were rare in such spots, suggesting that males ate the meat where they caught it and brought home only the marrow bones and heads, which required heat—high heat—to release their maximum fat content. Thus, he claims, Neanderthal males and females led largely separate economic lives—though not completely separate, as the splintered bones in the nests attest.

This picture is a dramatic contrast to the situation among all recent hunter-gatherers, who bring food home to be shared by all. Even if Binford is only partially right, this idea makes it much more difficult for us to comprehend the Neanderthals as living creatures than it seemed to be when modern humans were taken as a model from which the behavior of their precursors could be extrapolated. To put it crudely, it has traditionally been felt that earlier humans did what we (that is to say, those of us who lead hunting-gathering lifestyles) do—only not as well. Thanks to the efforts of Binford and others, it is becoming clear that this approach is no longer valid.

Binford's latest views on the Neanderthals have not yet been articulated in a scientific forum, where his evidence can be examined in detail by his colleagues. Whether or not his Combe Grenal conclusions are ultimately vindicated, however, it is already clear that the only ancient peoples who we can understand in the framework of the way we ourselves see and manipulate the world, are early members of *Homo sapiens*—and behaviorally modern *Homo sapiens* at that. When we look at *Homo neanderthalensis,* we are looking at a creature that possessed another sensibility entirely.

Two other researchers, Mary Stiner and Steven Kuhn, have also looked at the evidence for foraging patterns in European Neanderthals, albeit from a different perspective. On the western coast of Italy, south of Rome, are a number of caves that preserve evidence of Mousterian occupation during two different periods: one from the last interglacial, after about 120,000 years ago, the other from the last glacial, between about 50,000 and 40,000 years ago. The question here was whether any change in subsistence strategies could be detected between the two periods. It turned out that in the earlier time, when cave occupations appear to have been quite brief, animal remains associated with stone tools consisted principally of the cranial remains of older individuals. Stiner and Kuhn thus concluded that scavenging of the remains of animals that had died of natural causes may have been quite important in the diets of the Neanderthals who used the sites.

During the later period, by contrast, animal remains were largely those of individuals in the prime of life, and consisted of bits from all parts of the body. Along with greater numbers of stone tools, this evidence suggested more-prolonged use of the sites, as well as the use of ambush-hunting techniques to procure animal carcasses that were transported entire to the cave. Whether this difference was due to an improvement of techniques over time, or whether it represents a response to changing conditions as the climate cooled, remains anybody's bet, and possible disturbance of the evidence by carnivore activity complicates the picture further. But there seems to be little doubt that during the last glacial, at least, these Italian Neanderthals were systematic hunters of medium-sized herbivores such as red and fallow deer, and it's clear that they varied their strategies to gain sustenance from a changing landscape. Indeed, many authorities would now concede that Neanderthals hunted animals of this size with some regularity, at least under certain conditions, although they would rarely have tackled anything much bigger. Oddly, perhaps, small animal bones are rare at Neanderthal sites, but Binford would argue that while these valuable and easily available resources must have been hunted, they were consumed on the spot rather than being transported to central campsites.

The fact remains, however, that although Neanderthals were at least capable of being effective hunters, their sites lack the complexity associated with Upper Paleolithic localities, and Binford's distinction between foraging and collecting does seem to be an important one. An intriguing sidelight on this question has been cast recently by research in the Levant by Dan Lieberman, of Harvard, and by John Shea, of the State University of New York at Stony Brook. Recall that sites in Israel yielding both Neanderthals and early anatomically modern humans have produced stone tool industries all described as Mousterian. The fact is, though, that the Mousterian was more variable in time and space than is often assumed, and it has recently been proposed that different variants of this culture were associated with the two different human types.

The site that contains key evidence bearing on this issue is Tabūn, where a number of different Mousterian traditions have been recognized. As we saw in Chapter 5, the youngest of these, Tabūn B (about 90,000 to 50,000 years ago), is underlain by Tabūn C levels. The presumed female Neanderthal skull was found in a pit close to the contact between levels B and C. In her excavation report, Dorothy Garrod provisionally assigned the specimen to the Tabūn C sequence, but noted that it might well have been buried in these deposits in Tabūn B times. By contrast, the robust mandible with the chin was found well within level C. [Plate 106] Most characterizations of stone tool industries from other sites in Israel have been based on comparisons with the Tabūn sequence. Of particular significance is the fact that the Neanderthals from Kebara are associated with tools typical of Tabūn B, while the tools made by the moderns from Qafzeh are typical of Tabūn C. Lieberman and Shea have looked carefully at the faunal remains and stone tools from all three of these sites to determine what differences in behavior can be determined for the hominids who left them behind. Among the sophisticated techniques they employed were an analysis of the teeth of some of the mammal remains to determine in what season the animals died, and an examination of wear and breakage on stone tools that reveals how they were used.

Lieberman and Shea started from the notion that two possible subsistence strategies were available to ancient hunter-gatherers in the Levant. One they called the "circulating-mobility" pattern, which involves the regular shifting of campsites as the group moves around its territory, responding to seasonal changes in available resources and to

106
The Tabūn II mandible.

Robust, but possessing a distinct chin as well as a retromolar space, this mandible was found within Level C of the Tabun cave. It is probably over 100 thousand years old.
Photograph courtesy of Israel Antiquities Authority.

107

Bones of the original Neanderthaler, showing heavy build and expansive joint surfaces.

The Neanderthals are remarkable for their very robust bones, with large joint surfaces. These may represent adaptations to a very strenuous way of life.

Photograph by John Reader.

the routine depletion of resources that occurs around any campsite. The other approach they called the "radiating-mobility" strategy, in which a relatively permanent central campsite serves as the base for forays to temporary satellite camps near important resources. Inevitably, depletion of local resources eventually forces foragers to move their base camps, but practitioners of radiating mobility seek to maximize the amount of time they reside at any particular place. In particular, hunting trips become longer and more frequent. In analyzing the tools and animal remains from Tabūn, Qafzeh, and Kebara, Lieberman and Shea found that Neanderthal sites (Kebara and Tabūn B) produced the remains of animals killed

year-round, as well as pointed tools (presumably hafted onto spears) that are impact-damaged as if used in hunting. Conversely, the sites yielding anatomically modern humans (Qafzeh and Tabūn C) had fewer tools with impact damage, while the mammal remains were almost entirely of animals killed in a single season.

These observations suggest that the Neanderthals of Kebara practiced a radiating-mobility subsistence strategy, whereas the moderns of Qafzeh favored the circulating-mobility strategy. Of course, these strategies need not have been mutually exclusive, but a fundamental difference in regularity of occupation at the two sites is implied by other evidence as well. At

108

A Neanderthal male.

This reconstruction, displayed in a diorama at the American Museum of Natural History, reflects the robustness of the Neanderthal physique. The individual is in the act of sharpening a wooden spear; wear on some Mousterian implements indicates that they were used for shaping wood.
Photograph by Dennis Finnin and Craig Chesek.

Kebara, for example, faunal remains are much more copious relative to tools than at Qafzeh. This suggests that incursions by scavengers were much less frequent at the former than at the latter: exactly what you would expect if Kebara had been more consistently occupied by humans than Qafzeh had. Significantly, too, Lieberman and Shea believe that environmental differences between the two sites were not great enough to explain by themselves the difference in occupation strategies. Although these findings, based as they are on a very small sample of sites, are only preliminary, the notion that, despite the general similarity in their technologies, Neanderthals and early modern humans in the Levant exploited their similar environments in different ways is a suggestive one. The interpretation from Kebara is somewhat similar in comparable respects to Binford's from Combe Grenal, and the overall analysis certainly parallels Binford's notion of foraging by Middle Paleolithic humans in contrast to the collecting which he believes to be typical of the Upper Paleolithic.

Nothing in the Lieberman and Shea scenario suggests that the Neanderthals were *necessarily* inferior users of their environment. Although the evidence shows that these humans were not totally lacking in foresight, perhaps we should not make too much of this fact. Every primate is capable of knowing where the resources in its habitat are, and of finding them at the appropriate times. Moreover, other lines of evidence strongly suggest that these archaic humans had a less complex understanding of their environment than we have of ours—or at least that they used their environment in a less complex manner.

Perhaps the most significant of these lines of evidence is the relative lack of organization in and of structures at Neanderthal living sites about which I've already remarked.

In support of their scenario of Neanderthal use of the landscape, Lieberman and Shea adduce a biological aspect of the Neanderthals: their great skeletal robustness. [Plate 107] The load-bearing joints in *Homo neanderthalensis* are large, and the shafts of the long bones are much thicker than is typical of *Homo sapiens*. Bone is responsive to stresses placed on it in life, and it has long been suggested that the heavy build of Neanderthal bones is the result of a particularly strenuous lifestyle. [Plate 108] Lieberman and Shea suggest that a radiating-mobility strategy on the part of the Neanderthals would have involved considerably longer times spent foraging—and hence more stress on the musculoskeletal system—than the more energy-efficient circulating-mobility pattern of the early moderns. As Lieberman and Shea point out, the archaeological evidence does not enable one to determine whether Neanderthal robustness was the result of the choice of foraging strategy, or whether Neanderthals chose this strategy because they were particularly suited for it. But the biological fact that even quite young Neanderthal children show the characteristic heavy build seems to rule out the first possibility. To me, it is the unusually light build of modern humans—which is a new factor in human evolution—rather than the heavier build of the Neanderthals, that requires special explanation.

One aspect of Neanderthal subsistence that we haven't yet explored is the type of group in which the Neanderthals lived and foraged. This is largely a matter for speculation, but in general, Neanderthal sites do not suggest that social groups were big. Particularly if they were practicing radial mobility, groups could not have been very large, for forays from a central base in search of sustenance for an extended group would quickly have become impossibly long. Perhaps ten or a dozen adults at most, plus children of various ages, would have been a likely size for Neanderthal social groups. The Shanidar individual with the withered arm suggests that such groups afforded long-term support for at least some disadvantaged members—though we should remember that this individual also bears skeletal

damage that suggests he may have been stabbed in the back.[see Plate 78]

The ranges of groups operating out of adjacent centers would probably have overlapped somewhat, making it possible to exchange group members and maintain a larger community over wider areas; and the sizes of those ranges would have varied with the richness of the environment. In the Mousterian, unlike the Upper Paleolithic, there is little evidence (whether associated with Neanderthals or with modern types) for contacts and exchanges over long distances. And although the greater ranges of objects in the Upper Paleolithic record makes such activities easier to discern, it's probably significant that the relatively rare nonlocal stone found at Neanderthal sites never came from more than a few miles away.

One final note. Virtually all inferences about Neanderthal subsistence have been based on animal bones, because these preserve relatively well at archaeological sites. Nobody doubts, however, that plant foods were extremely important in the Neanderthal diet, although it is difficult to say anything precise because plant remains are vanishingly rare in the archaeological record. Plant remains hardly ever preserve, although some charred legume seeds have been found in hearths at Kebara, and Binford's "nests" at Combe Grenal apparently contained cattail pollen, suggesting that these plants might have been part of the females' diet (if indeed females were the nests' occupants). Additionally, plant foods may

109
View of the Vézère Valley, southwestern France, near the classic Upper Paleolithic site of La Madeleine.

The lovely limestone valley of the Vézère River, with its wealth of rockshelters and caves, contains the largest concentration of Upper Paleolithic and Mousterian sites known from anywhere in the world. *Photograph by Alain Roussot.*

most often have been consumed where they were found, and thus may never have made their way to the campsites from which we learn about Neanderthal activities.

Technology

For historical reasons, the study of the Mousterian technology that is usually, but not exclusively, associated with the Neanderthals has been centered in France. The name was originally applied only to industries from the Dordogne region's Vézère River valley, but it has since become used as an umbrella term for tool assemblages from widely scattered regions throughout Europe and western Asia, and even from parts of northern Africa. [Plate 109] The result is that a substantial variety both in the kinds of tools in different places and in the precise techniques used to produce them has been disguised—making it especially important to remember that the Mousterian was emphatically not an entirely monolithic culture in time and space.

Even in France a simple classification of Mousterian tool assemblages has proved difficult to develop, and attempts early in the twentieth century to recognize a developmental sequence of the

Mousterian based on diagnostic artifact types rapidly foundered. In the 1950s the French prehistorian François Bordes took a different tack, recognizing four distinctive Mousterian variants principally on the relative frequencies of different tool types. Bordes identified a huge variety of different Mousterian tools (sixty-three different kinds of flake tools and twenty-one handaxe types, to be precise), although later work has suggested that many of these types simply represent different stages in the resharpening of a smaller number of fundamental tool types. [Plate 110] Bordes also factored in the importance of Levalloisian technique, which is much more common in the Mousterian of the Levant than in Europe. Bordes believed that his various tool kits were the work of different ethnic groups of Neanderthals whose technologies remained relatively stable but which replaced each other at varying times and places over the long period of the Mousterian in Europe. His attitude toward the Neanderthals was summed up in the famous statement that they "made beautiful tools stupidly," encapsulating his belief that these people, though highly skilled, possessed a strictly limited capacity for innovation.

The work of Bordes was highly influential and extremely important in imposing order on the chaotic variety of Neanderthal technologies known from France. It was not long, however, before his inferences about why the differences existed were attacked. Lewis and Sally Binford concluded in the 1960s that the different tool kits that Bordes had recognized were not the work of different ethnic groups who had mindlessly handed down unitary technologies over the millennia, but rather reflected different activities in which the groups who made them were engaged. Later researchers have added the caveat that many of the typological distinctions between different Mousterian tool kits may well be due to differences in the local availability of raw materials, which are known to affect the tool types made from them. Add to this the great differences in climate, environment, and available resources that faced the Neanderthals from time to time and from place to place, and it is hardly surprising that Neanderthal tool kits were quite variable over the long period and the vast

Mousterian flint tools from various sites in France.

A selection of typical Mousterian tools is shown here. From left: two scrapers on flakes; point on flake; and two small handaxes.
Photographs by Ian Tattersall.

geographic range in which the Neanderthals lived.

But even if, Bordes to the contrary, the Neanderthals were capable, at least within limits, of adapting their tool kits to changing circumstances, Mousterian technology was still relatively uncomplicated, certainly in comparison to the Upper Paleolithic technologies that succeeded it. The procedures used to produce tools were quite simple, and the vast majority of tools were made using whatever stone was on hand, whether or not it was the best material for the job. No doubt, however, the Neanderthals knew good materials when they saw them, for as a general rule, artifacts made from stone available only at a distance from the site of recovery were intensively reworked to keep them in the best working shape. On the other hand, bone, an abundant resource used to magnificent effect by Upper Paleolithic people, was almost never used by Mousterians to produce tools. Boneworking is tricky and demands of the toolmaker a sophisticated understanding of the material; perhaps the Neanderthals—certainly the average Neanderthal—simply didn't possess this kind of insight.

Although the Neanderthals may not have had such insight themselves, apparently they were nonetheless capable of learning the fruits of it. Some late developments of the Mousterian tradition, from regions as widely spaced as France, Italy, and Central Europe, have been viewed as "transitional" to the Upper Paleolithic. The most significant of these is the Châtelperronian of western France, a short-lived industry that occurred at the end of the Middle Paleolithic (about 36,000 to 32,000 years ago) and in the period following the arrival of Upper Paleolithic peoples in western Europe. At a few sites the Châtelperronian is interlayered with Aurignacian (earliest Upper Paleolithic) levels that presumably reflect occupation by fully modern humans. François Bordes believed that the Châtelperronian derived from one of his Mousterian variants, but others disagreed, because a high proportion of Châtelperronian stone tools were made on blades struck from cylindrical cores. This innovation had been brought into

Europe by invading Upper Paleolithic peoples, although similar techniques were occasionally used in the African Middle Paleolithic.

Careful studies have borne out the views of Bordes, however. The principal similarities of the Châtelperronian do appear to lie with the Mousterian. Other evidence supporting this theory is the discovery of the burial at Saint-Césaire, which for most archaeologists, at least, has settled the Neanderthal identity of the Châtelperronian toolmakers at that site. [see Plate 102] Why, then, this mixture of techniques? One intriguing suggestion that has gained wide acceptance is that the resident Neanderthals picked up from the invading moderns some Upper Paleolithic ways of doing business. Significantly, stone toolmaking is not the only example. At the famous French site of Arcy-sur-Cure, a carved bone pendant, along with pierced animal teeth and the foundations of what was probably a hut, was found in a Châtelperronian layer. [Plate 111] Like blade technology, such phenomena were typical of the Upper Paleolithic and were virtually absent in the Mousterian, but they are believed to have been the work of Neanderthals. Specimens such as those from Arcy-sur-Cure strongly hint at interaction between the Neanderthals of the Châtelperronian and Upper Paleolithic people. The nature of such interaction, however, remains a subject for speculation.

One unusual aspect of the Neanderthals that only presumptively concerns technology is the typically highly worn state of their front teeth. [Plate 112 and see Plates 75 and 76] Even quite young individuals tend to show a degree of wear

111
Carved bone pendant from Arcy-sur-Cure, France.

This is one of the very few decorative items to have been found in a (very late) Châtelperronian context.
Photograph by Alexander Marshack.

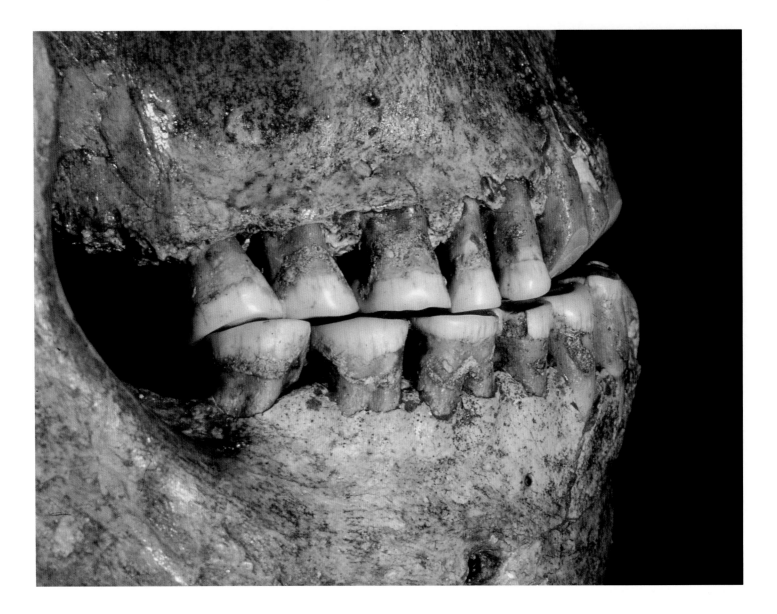

112

Side view of the front teeth of individual 1 from Shanidar, Iraq.

Neanderthals typically exhibit heavy, rounded wear of the front teeth. Seen particularly well here in the aged Shanidar 1, this feature is often well expressed in individuals who died much younger.
Photograph by Erik Trinkaus.

113

Reconstruction of a female Neanderthal.

This reconstruction, part of a diorama at the American Museum of Natural History, shows a young adult female scraping a hide. The worn front teeth of Neanderthals suggest that they were used in hide treatment, and the wear on some Mousterian stone tools indicates hide-working.
Photograph by Dennis Finnin and Craig Chesek.

on their incisors that is quite atypical for modern humans, including Upper Paleolithic people. Where there is considerable wear on human incisors today, it is usually associated with cultures in which the front teeth are used extensively in the preparation of hides, for example by chewing. Whether this explains the state of Neanderthal incisors is anybody's guess, but in the absence of evidence to the contrary, it seems to be the most likely reason. Given the severe climates in which many Neanderthals lived, they must have worn clothing of some kind, and animal hides are the obvious material. [Plate 113] We will never know exactly what such clothing was like, but it seems reasonable to assume that hides were prepared in some way and perhaps

tied on the body with thongs, for even in late Neanderthal times, sewing (as evidenced by eyed bone needles) was a thing of the future.

Symbolism
Modern humans live by symbols—in communication, in aesthetics, and in their explanation to themselves of their internal and external worlds. There is abundant evidence for a similar sensibility among the people of the Upper Paleolithic. Is there any reason to believe that Neanderthals were also symbol-dependent, at least to some degree?

Bear cults and associated bizarre rituals would certainly qualify as symbolic behavior, but we have already seen that

Neanderthal mandible from Regourdou, France.

This lower jaw, probably about 70 thousand years old, bears one of the best-preserved of Neanderthal dentitions. It comes from a site at which probably fictitious evidence of a "bear cult" has been reported. *Photograph by Alain Roussot.*

the early stories of the bear cults of the Drachenloch and other localities such as the French site of Regourdou are not borne out by close examination of the evidence. [Plate 114] Nor are accounts such as Blanc's of ritual beheading and brain eating at Monte Circeo. Indeed, burial of the dead apart, Mousterian sites seem to lack much of anything we might reasonably associate with ritual. Occasionally at a Mousterian site, bones are found that bear traces of incisions that may have been made intentionally, but the patterns they form appear to be largely random (possibly analogous to those made on a cutting-board), with no suggestion of a coherent symbolic system. In a few cases perforated bones and teeth have been reported at Mousterian sites,

and at La Ferrassie a limestone block was found that had had a number of shallow circular depressions pecked into it. But again, symbolic significance is hard to discern. A sinuously engraved plaque, the design of which does appear to be deliberate, has been described recently from the approximately 50,000-year-old Mousterian site of Quneitra in the Golan Heights, but there is no evidence currently available to show which type of human made it.

Invertebrate shells and the odd fossilized mollusk imported into Neanderthal living places hint at some type of aesthetic sensibility, or at least curiosity, for other than a few sharpened shells, such objects were clearly not utilitarian items. And as to their true purpose, hint is all

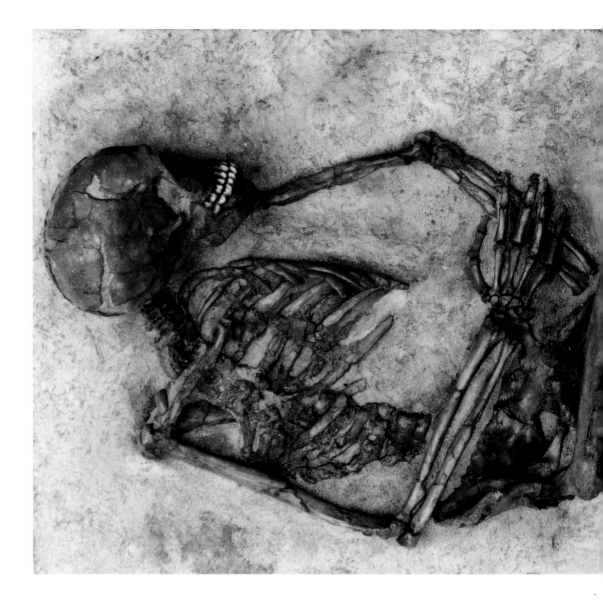

they do. Another possible indication of symbolic behavior includes deposits of pigments—black manganese, red and yellow ochre—at some Mousterian sites. The meaning of such deposits is a matter for debate. Perhaps these pigments were intended for body painting, but they could also have been used for more-mundane tasks, such as preserving hides—though this practice itself would have been quite a sophisticated activity.

The final line of evidence for Neanderthal symbolic behavior is equally tenuous, coming as it does from putative indications of cannibalism—or, to be more precise, of the deliberate defleshing of bodies. (The Neanderthals were not the first to engage in defleshing; the Bodo *Homo heidelbergensis* skull, for instance, appears to have been defleshed.) Early

notions of cannibalism, we've seen, proved unreliable, and this practice is extremely hard to demonstrate in the archaeological record. Cut marks on human bones, by contrast, can show whether a cadaver was deliberately defleshed, and among modern humans this is usually done for reasons other than cannibalism. Such reasons most commonly involve secondary burial, with cleaning of the bones as the first step. Such a practice is in itself an indicator of complex patterns of belief. Whatever the motivations, however, Neanderthal defleshing of the dead was rare indeed—much rarer than burial. A recent review indicates that reliable evidence for this practice comes from only three, or at most four, Neanderthal sites, all in Europe. At these localities, human bones

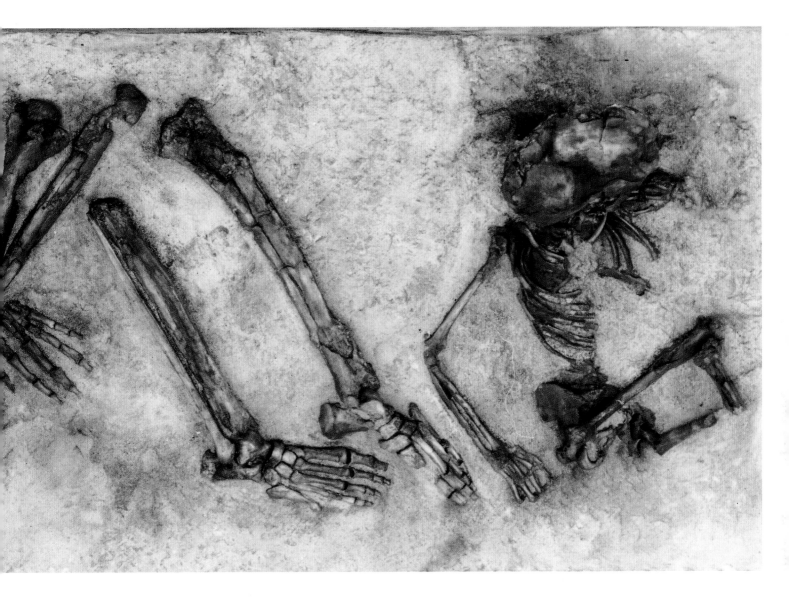

115

Double burial from Jebel Qafzeh, Israel.

At this site a young Mousterian woman was laid to rest over 90 thousand years ago, with an infant, possibly her child, at her feet. The deceased were, however, members of *Homo sapiens*, and this careful burial contrasts with the more casual interment typical of Neanderthals.

(see Plate 74)

Photograph courtesy of Bernard Vandermeersch.

show patterns of dissection that may differ from those betrayed by cut marks on the bones of animals that were presumably consumed. If substantiated, this difference would imply defleshing for a purpose other than consumption. A great deal of work remains to be done before this question is settled, if ever it can be. Meanwhile, these few indications suggest at least a certain behavioral complexity.

The Evidence for Burial

The matter of Neanderthal burial has been debated loud and long. Although some authorities have gone so far as to deny that it ever occurred, it clearly did, at least occasionally. It would be rash to assume, however, that Neanderthal burial had exactly the type of symbolic significance that it holds for

us, with all the implications for ritual and belief in an afterlife that burial and its complex associated behaviors have among modern humans. It may just as well have been simply a way of conveniently disposing of bodies that would otherwise have unpleasantly cluttered living spaces—and attracted hyenas. Or, given the near certainty that the Neanderthals did not see and comprehend the world in the same way that modern humans do, burial might have had a significance to them that we would find hard to imagine from our modern perspective.

Whatever its exact implications, Neanderthal burial is a fact that cannot be ignored. The "Old Man" of La Chapelle-aux-Saints, for example, was interred in a pit filled with earth that distinctly contrasted in color with the sediments around it, and a whole series of burials at La Ferrassie was equally evidently intentional. Other Neanderthal burials in France are well documented; so are several from western Asia, among them those at Amud, Tabūn, and Kebara in Israel, as well as Shanidar in Iraq. [see Plates 59, 63, 70, 75, 76, 77, 81, 82, 100, and 101] The juvenile from Teshik-Tash, in Uzbekistan, was also apparently buried, although the complexity of the burial, reportedly surrounded by the horns of ibex and with a hearth nearby, has been convincingly disputed. (see plates 142 and 143)

The big difference between Neanderthal burials and those of the Upper Paleolithic people who succeeded them comes not in the digging of the graves themselves, but in the items that accompanied the deceased. Upper Paleolithic burials were often quite complex, with richly adorned bodies accompanied by elaborate grave goods. Items interpreted as grave goods in most Mousterian burials, on the other hand, are everyday objects such as stone tools and individual animal bones. Although these might have been intended to equip and sustain the deceased in an afterlife, they were the kinds of things that were naturally lying around in the living and working areas of caves and that might well have found their way into the grave by accident. Indeed, there are few cases in which Mousterian "grave goods" stand up to serious scrutiny. The most famous putative case of this kind is that of the

Shanidar "flower burial." Even here, it is possible that the pollen from spring flowers that was found in the grave was introduced by the activity of burrowing rodents or other factors not related to the burial itself.

The best evidence for Mousterian grave goods comes from burials associated not with Neanderthals, but with anatomically modern humans at Qafzeh and Skhūl. [Plate 115] Animal remains in these graves were found in intimate association with the human skeletons, suggesting that they had been deliberately placed there, as in the case of the lower jaw of a wild boar found "clasped in the hands" of one skeleton at Skhūl. So here's another interesting apparent behavioral difference between Neanderthals and modern humans, albeit both Mousterians, in the Levant. Still, there can be no reasonable doubt that Neanderthals did, from time to time and simply, bury their dead. As far as we know, no archaic humans before them had ever done that. Why Neanderthals only occasionally resorted to burial, most commonly abandoning the cadavers or perhaps, very rarely, defleshing them for purposes of cannibalism and/or secondary burial, remains a mystery.

 Did the Neanderthals Have Language?
Our view of the world is enshrined in our possession of language. Language structures our thought patterns and governs our learning and communication, to such an extent that we have difficulty

imagining humanity in its absence. The Neanderthals, so close in time to us and similar to us in so many ways, must have been capable of quite sophisticated interindividual communication—vocal, gestural, and otherwise. But did they have articulate language, that complex system of syntax, grammar, and object naming that both permits and depends on a high capacity for symbolic reasoning? This question is very difficult to answer because there's no obvious way of testing alternatives through the very limited lines of evidence available to us in the fossil and archaeological records. It is widely felt, however, that language is so intimately tied to our complex and often unfathomable behaviors that it's unlikely that creatures which, like the Neanderthals, behaved significantly differently from us, could have had language in the sense in which we are familiar with it. Put the other way around, it seems improbable that the symboling capacities that are basic to language would ever fail to express themselves in at least some of the complex features that are so conspicuously lacking at Neanderthal sites—and that are present in the Upper Paleolithic.

Language is a function of the brain. Yet recent studies have shown that we cannot hope to read linguistic capabilities from the external contours of this organ, which are all that we have to go on in the fossil record. Sheer brain size won't do it, either, even on a probabilistic basis. But the use of articulate language doesn't depend simply on neural architecture;

it also requires the peripheral structures that produce the sounds associated with speech. In the early 1970s a pioneering study by Ed Crelin, an anatomist at Yale, and the linguistician Phillip Lieberman, of Brown University, ushered in an entirely new approach to the interpretation of speech capacities in fossil humans. Crelin and Lieberman noted that the sounds of speech are generated in the soft structures of the vocal tract, which do not directly preserve in fossils. But the roof of the vocal tract (that is, the base of the skull) is preserved, at least from time to time.

Using the base of the La Chapelle skull (as reconstructed by Marcellin Boule) as a guide, Crelin produced a model of the Neanderthal upper vocal tract, which Lieberman then analyzed in terms of the sounds that it would have been able to produce. [see Plate 63] According to this analysis, the Neanderthal vocal tract would have been unable to produce three of the basic vowel sounds ([a], [i], and [u]) associated with modern human articulate speech. In later years this approach was extended and refined, principally by Jeffrey Laitman of the Mount Sinai School of Medicine in New York, who produced similar reconstructions of a wider range of extinct hominids and compared the vocal tracts of mammals in general. He found that, as in virtually all other mammals, the skull base of *Australopithecus* is flat. In *Homo ergaster*, by contrast, the skull base shows a small degree of downward bending, and the Kabwe *Homo heidelbergensis* skull, even more. The greatest

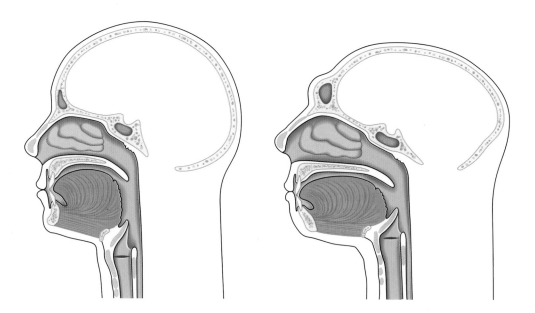

Comparison of the airways in a Neanderthal (left) and a modern human.

These vertical mid-sections through the head and neck of a modern human and a (reconstructed) Neanderthal show the differences in the structure of the upper vocal tract between the two species. Note the long palate and tongue of the Neanderthal, and the higher placement of its larynx.
Illustration by Diana Salles, after sketches by Jeffrey Laitman.

flexion occurs in adult *Homo sapiens*, although in the newborn modern human the primitive flat configuration is retained; the bending develops during the first few years of life.

This flexion of the skull base is the result of an important rearrangement of the upper airways. In the primitive state, the larynx (voice box) is positioned high in the throat and is connected to the oral cavity by a short piece of tubing called the pharynx. In adult modern humans, on the other hand, the larynx is low in the throat, with a much longer pharynx above it. This high, looping pharynx is what is accommodated by the bending of the skull base, and what is manipulated by the muscles of the throat to modulate the vibrations of the air column produced at the larynx. Without this long pharynx, the full range of sounds demanded by articulate speech cannot be produced. The advantage of the low-larynx configuration is thus apparent; the downside is that simultaneous breathing and swallowing

(as required of a suckling newborn) are no longer possible, which introduces the unpleasant possibility of choking to death.

In the human evolutionary trend toward a highly flexed skull base, and thus toward a vocal tract capable of producing articulate speech, the classic Neanderthals of western Europe may be something of an anomaly. Even using a recent reconstruction of the approximately 50,000-year-old skull base from La Chapelle that shows more bending than the original Boule version showed, Laitman found that this specimen was less flexed than the Kabwe skull (probably at least 200,000 years older), apparently reversing the trend. [Plate 116] More studies are needed, though, especially since the earlier (about 120,000-year-old) Neanderthal individual from Saccopastore does show significant flexion. [see Plates 97 and 98] Why does the La Chapelle skull have this strange configuration? One possibility is that the apparently primitive high larynx was a secondary specialization: a way of warming and humidifying the cold, dry air of the last glacial period and thus of protecting the fragile lungs beneath. This function had, in fact, already been suggested as an explanation for the enlarged midface and nasal openings of the Neanderthals (although these features were established by the last interglacial, before the severe cold of the Würm maximum set in). The anomaly remains.

One hope for resolving the issue was that a Neanderthal hyoid bone would be discovered. This free-floating bone is the attachment point for a variety of throat muscles, and the hope was that its structure in Neanderthals would provide additional pointers toward speech abilities. The discovery of a hyoid at Kebara, however, succeeded only in unleashing a heated argument over its significance. [Plate 117] The problem is that, while the morphology of the Kebara hyoid is quite modern, its bony component is only part of the total structure; what the unpreserved cartilaginous component looked like is unknown. All bets are thus off, and at this writing the debate as to whether in life the Kebara hyoid was part of a modern or an archaic type of upper respiratory tract is nowhere near resolution.

What, then, can we conclude about Neanderthal communication? We can make no definitive statements, but two conclusions seem reasonable if necessarily subjective. The first is that the Neanderthals must have had quite a sophisticated form of communication that was probably at least largely vocal. The only requirement of such communication would have been consistency with their way of life, which it is reasonable to suppose did not demand articulate language as we know it. Thus, we arrive at the second conclusion: that the Neanderthals did not communicate as we do—certainly not in exactly the same way. To return to a point made earlier, it seems likely that a creature capable of—and using—modern language and articulate speech would have left more evidence of a complex way of life than we find at Neanderthal archaeological sites. Of course, the early moderns from Skhūl and Qafzeh certainly had the physical apparatus for articulate speech, yet their technology remained resolutely Mousterian, and their sites contain nothing of the material richness that characterizes those from the Upper Paleolithic—whose makers undoubtedly possessed language. What these apparent inconsistencies mean is hazy in the extreme, although they may suggest that potential and performance are not the same thing. In the case of the Neanderthals, however, we are probably on firm ground in excluding ourselves as models for behavior—in communication as in other realms∎

9

The Origin of Modern Humans

IN the last chapter I hinted very heavily that the Upper Paleolithic offers a much richer archaeological record than does the Middle Paleolithic. Everywhere its evidence is found, the Upper Paleolithic is clearly the work of fully modern humans. Contrasting the Upper Paleolithic archaeological record with that of the Mousterian is the best way to comprehend the achievements and limitations of the Neanderthals—and, conversely, to measure ourselves against our closest well-documented relative in nature. Such a comparison is the main aim of this short chapter, but first let's quickly review the biological evidence for the origin of our own kind.

The Evolution of *Homo sapiens*

Earlier in this book I introduced the two currently competing models of modern human origins. One is the "Multiregional Continuity" notion, which is sustained neither by convincing fossil evidence nor by evolutionary theory. If new species arise as geographic isolates of old ones, then we should expect their origins to be associated with particular geographic areas, and probably with limited areas. To which region must we look for fossil evidence of our own origin? The leading alternative choice to the Multiregional model of modern human origins is the "Out of Africa" scenario, which does not pin down the origin particularly closely, but at least confines it to one continent. "Out

of Africa" is still supported in general outline by the mtDNA data, despite the latters' recent vicissitudes. But the main reason for believing that modern humans arose in Africa is quite simply that the earliest fossil evidence comes from that continent, though admittedly the evidence from the Levant (which, because of faunal similarities, might best be viewed effectively as part of Africa) comes in a very close second.

Modern people differ physically from Neanderthals and other archaic humans in a variety of ways. (Of course, all proposed morphological definitions of *Homo sapiens* still need refining, and there's no getting around the problem faced by all paleontologists that species are defined not by morphology but by reproductive isolation.) All modern humans, for instance, contrast with the Neanderthals in having short, high braincases that are more or less rounded at the back and that achieve their maximum width high up. Our faces are small and are tucked in beneath the front of the braincase, below relatively steep foreheads. Rarely do we have anything worthy of the name of brow ridges; when we do have brow ridges, they are small, with two distinct surfaces, and they taper laterally. Our lower jaws are short from back to front, and possess chins. Remarkably, our skeletons lack the robustness of all earlier kinds of humans (although early

118

Sites 1 and 2 of Klasies River Mouth, South Africa.

The Middle Stone Age localities of Klasies River Mouth, some layers of which are dated to as much as 120 thousand years ago, lie beneath the large hollow in the cliff at center.
Photograph by Willard Whitson.

119

Fragmentary pieces of human skulls from Klasies River Mouth, South Africa.

The human fossils from Klasies, some dated to as much as 120 thousand years ago, are generally modern in aspect if variable in robustness. Signs of burning and modes of breakage have elicited the suggestion that these bones are evidence of cannibalistic activities.
Courtesy of the South African Museum.

moderns tended to be more robust than modern populations).

Among the earliest human remains that plausibly fit this description are some from a site close to the southern tip of Africa, the caves at the mouth of the Klasies River. [Plate 118] The oldest of these fossils are dated to well over 100,000 years old, and could easily be as old as 120,000 years. Unfortunately, all the fossils are fragmentary (the University of Stellenbosch's Hilary Deacon, the cave's current excavator, thinks they are the remains of a genuine cannibal feast). [Plate 119] Although the fossils vary a bit in robustness, only the staunchest proponents of the "Multiregional Continuity" viewpoint doubt that the specimens represent modern *Homo sapiens*. The associated stone tools are firmly

Middle Stone Age (Africa's answer to the Middle Paleolithic), although Deacon believes that he can detect at the site significant signs of spatial organization equivalent to that of the Upper Paleolithic. Interestingly, in later levels at Klasies, which are nonetheless of great antiquity (about 70,000 years old), an industry (the Howiesons Poort) appears that shares a good deal with much later cultures (lots of blade tools of imported stone, for instance), before the Middle Stone Age resumes for thousands of years more.

Moving north, the Middle Stone Age site of Border Cave, on South Africa's frontier with Swaziland, has yielded more-complete remains of unquestioned modern humans. [Plate 120] These date from at least 70,000 years ago and may be much older, although poorly controlled early excavation techniques put their

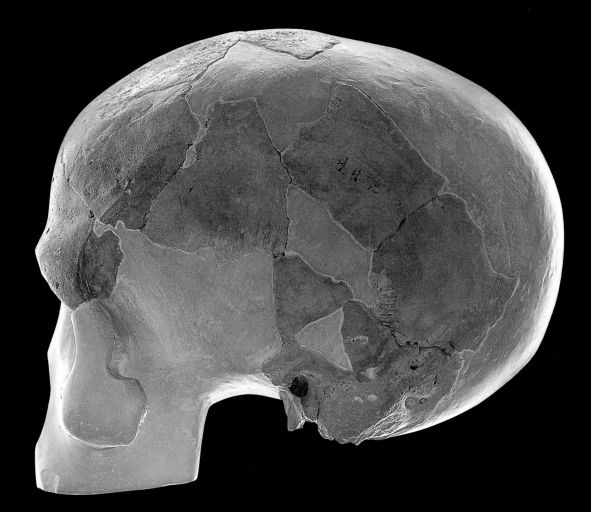

120
Reconstruction of the Border Cave 1 skull, South Africa.

Located on the boundary of South Africa and Swaziland, Border Cave has yielded human fossils that are of distinctively modern aspect. These fossils are older than 70 thousand years (some maybe much older), although poor excavation techniques place their exact ages in doubt.

Photograph by Gerald Newlands.

exact age in some doubt. A more definite date of about 120,000 years ago applies to a cranium from a Middle Stone Age context at Laetoli, in Tanzania, but this specimen is not particularly modern-looking and presumably belonged to an archaic (but morphologically less specialized) population that played a role in Africa equivalent to that of the Neanderthals in Eurasia. [Plate 121] Further north yet, the Omo River basin of Ethiopia has yielded two crania, either or both of which may be as old as 125,000 years. One of these is rather archaic in aspect—low, with ridges above the eyes and an angled rear—but the other appears entirely modern. [Plate 122] Finally, we can conclude this account of the most significant later fossil humans from Africa with a mention of two crania and some fragments from the site of Jebel Irhoud, in Morocco, recently ESR dated to more than (maybe a lot more than) 106,000 years ago. The braincase of the more complete specimen is a bit low, and the face is relatively large, with distinct brow ridges, but otherwise the individual looks modern and has been viewed as a potential ancestor for modern humans. The Jebel Irhoud specimens certainly have no Neanderthal affinities, although the archaeological context is said to be Levalloiso-Mousterian. The second cranium looks more modern in front, but less so in the rear.

Taken together, the suite of African fossils suggests that fully modern humans evolved somewhere on that vast continent

123

"The Walls of China", Lake Mungo, Australia.

These sand dunes surrounding a dried-up lake have yielded lightly-built *Homo sapiens* fossils (the remains of cremations) that date from about 26 thousand years ago.
Photograph by Dragi Markovic; courtesy of Alan Thorne.

(exactly where remains a matter for conjecture) by maybe as early as 120,000 years ago. More-archaic species hung on beside them for some time, much as the Neanderthals did in western Asia. As the fossil record improves, we can hope to gain a clearer picture of the identities and interactions of human species in Africa during this period. Reinforcement of the "Out of Africa" notion can also be found in the archaeological record, for Africa was also home to early developments in stone toolmaking of the kind that later characterized the Upper Paleolithic of Europe and western Asia. Recent finds in Zaire suggest (though this remains extremely controversial) that highly sophisticated boneworking industries may have been in full swing there as early as 60,000 to 80,000 years ago, and ostrich-eggshell beads at a site in Kenya's Rift Valley show that modern human behaviors were established there well over 40,000 years ago.

Geographically, Africa is a logical place of origin for the early moderns of the Levant, and although absence of evidence is not evidence of absence, it may be significant that the African fossil record, sparse as it is, is incomparably better than is the record for central-western Asia, the other geographic possibility. No fossils from western Asia to the east of the Levant bear on modern human origins, whilst in eastern Asia the dates for the earliest modern human fossils are much later than the Levantine ones. Interestingly, though, it now seems that humans had occupied Australia by about 60,000 years ago, and it is assumed that these earliest Australians were modern in behavioral capacity because of the sophisticated craft building and navigational skills required to travel across at least sixty miles of open ocean. [Plate 123]

 The Earliest Modern Europeans
Fully modern humans arrived in Europe rather late, for reasons that are not even incompletely understood. It may be significant, however, that

the earliest penetration of Europe by *Homo sapiens* followed quite closely on the heels of the development of the earliest Upper Paleolithic cultures in the Levant, about 45,000 to 47,000 years ago. If so, the spread of *Homo sapiens* into Europe, at a time when the last glacial was nearing its maximum, may well have been made possible by the technological developments of the Upper Paleolithic. Perhaps the resident Neanderthals of Europe, subject to more severe climatic conditions than those of the Levant, were indeed biologically adapted to cold – and were thus able to outcompete technologically archaic though physically modern *Homo sapiens* in their northwestern redoubt until the advancing technology of the moderns equipped them to invade. Whether or not this was the case, it is now becoming clear that once the moderns succeeded in penetrating Europe, they spread rapidly, for the earliest dates for Upper Paleolithic occupation of Europe come from opposite ends of the subcontinent. Sites in both Bulgaria and Spain have yielded dates of about 40,000 years ago, earlier than any yet obtained for Upper Paleolithic localities in between. [see Plate 139] The traditional supposition has been that moderns simply entered Europe from the east and spread westwards, but the early Spanish date necessitates some rethinking. Perhaps modern people occupied Europe in a pincer movement, via both eastern and western routes, and possibly by others, too. At the moment, the evidence is too sparse to

allow anything more than speculation, particularly since it is not clear where the Aurignacian, the earliest culture of the European Upper Paleolithic, first emerged.

Latecomers though they were, in the period between about 34,000 and 10,000 years ago the early modern Europeans (often known as Cro-Magnons, for the French site at which their remains were first discovered) left us incomparably the best record of cultural and technological innovations of the late Ice Age known from anywhere in the world. [see Plate 59] Since these Upper Paleolithic people occupied the same region of the world as did the Neanderthals, at about the same time and under a similar range of climatic conditions, they provide the most appropriate comparison for the Neanderthals. The rest of this chapter briefly makes that comparison.

 The Upper Paleolithic
As I have already mentioned, a succession of four major cultural periods marks the Upper Paleolithic in western Europe. [see Plate 23] The first of these is the Aurignacian, which appeared about 40,000 years ago and continued to about 28,000 years ago (as always, Upper Paleolithic cultures appeared in different places at somewhat varying times). The Aurignacian is defined by large numbers of finely crafted blades – long, slender flakes – struck from cylindrical cores from which numerous such "blanks" were obtained. These blanks were then reshaped into specialized forms, typical

examples of which include end scrapers
(blades on which one or both ends were
fashioned into a curved scraping surface
by applying pressure with a soft implement—usually bone or antler) and burins
(finely pointed piercing tools). [Plate 124]
A distinctive slender bone point, forked at
the base, was also a characteristic Aurignacian tool. Most excitingly, the Aurignacian was marked by an outburst of
creativity. Art, decoration of objects, symbolism, personal ornamentation, notation,
and music (in the form of wind instruments) all made their first appearance in
the archaeological record in the earliest
Aurignacian of the Franco-German region
(although glimmers of similarly or even
more ancient artistic expression are just
now beginning to emerge from elsewhere,
notably Australia and Africa).

The Aurignacian was followed by the
Gravettian industry in the millennia
between about 28,000 and 22,000 to
18,000 years ago. The Gravettian is characterized by smaller and narrower blades,
often pointed and "backed" (blunted
along one edge), along with pointed bone
awls and blunter "punches." Early in the

Gravettian delicate eyed bone needles also made their first appearance. [Plate 125] Such industries persisted longer over most of Europe than in southwestern France and Spain, where the period between about 22,000 and 18,000 years ago saw the separate flourishing of the Solutrean industry, characterized by ovate and astonishingly finely worked "laurel-leaf" blades, some of which were so thin and delicate that it is hard to imagine they were put to any practical use. [Plate 126] Finally, between about 18,000 years ago (the height of the last glacial) and the end of the Upper Paleolithic (about 10,000 years ago), when the present interglacial had already begun, we find the Magdalenian industry, dominated by the sophisticated working of bone and antler and an abundance of "microliths," tiny stone tools that were presumably hafted into handles. [Plate 127] Each of these industries contains many variants, indicating a much greater pace of technological innovation than had ever been witnessed before. Each culture also produced its own particular art forms, which we will look at in a moment.

Contrasts between the Mousterian and the Upper Paleolithic

If ever there was a great leap forward in human cultural history, it was the one that occurred between the Middle Paleolithic (roughly

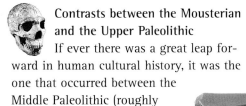

200,000 to 30,000 years ago in Europe) and the Upper Paleolithic (about 40,000 to 10,000 years ago in the same region). This leap was so great that it is impossible to avoid the conclusion that entirely different sensibilities and capacities were involved. Let's look at some of the behavioral differences between humans of the Middle and Upper Paleolithic periods that the archaeological record suggests.

In the realm of stoneworking technology we find, as we've seen, that stone tools made from long, slender blades predominate. Middle Paleolithic technology often produced more than one usable flake tool from a single core, but the cylindrical cores of the Upper Paleolithic, rotated as each new blade was produced, yielded many more utensils per pound of material. This technique may have been introduced to cope with circumstances in which good primary materials— notably flint and chert— were rare, although it proved highly successful even where excellent raw materials were abundant. Wherever they lived, however, Upper Paleolithic toolmakers were much more choosy about the kinds of stone they worked with than their

Middle Paleolithic predecessors had been. Upper Paleolithic stone tools are also much easier to categorize (and into many more categories) than Middle Paleolithic ones, suggesting that the final form of each specialized type of tool existed as a highly specific image in the minds of Upper Paleolithic toolmakers. By contrast, Middle Paleolithic craftsmen may simply have been using tested techniques to produce a particular attribute, such as a point or a broad scraping surface.

From the very beginning, Upper Paleolithic people used a wide variety of materials for their tools. Some Middle Paleolithic stone tools show characteristic types of polish that indicate they were used to work wood. Bone and antler, however, both abundantly available, were hardly ever used – and never for specialized implements. In the Upper Paleolithic, on the other hand, bone, antler, and ivory were widely carved and polished into a huge variety of useful and decorative forms, including the eyed needles already mentioned, which announce the advent of tailored clothing. [see Plate 125] The ways in which such materials were worked betray a profound understanding of the special properties of each substance. Utilitarian items were decorated with geometric and representational designs, as were plaques that had no obvious functional use.

One of the starkest contrasts between the industries of the Middle Paleolithic and those of the Upper Paleolithic is the enormous variety in space and time seen among the latter. We have seen that Mousterian industries were not as static and unvarying as was sometimes thought, but the variety among them pales in the face of that evident in the Upper Paleolithic. Sometimes it seems as if the Upper Paleolithic people of each valley were developing their own technological expressions with a restless spirit of innovation, industry succeeding industry at an accelerating rate. No one doubts that all Upper Paleolithic peoples possessed language in the same way that we do; and who knows, maybe it was the invention of modern articulate language, with all that this suggests, that somehow turned anatomically modern Middle Paleolithic people into the first bearers of Upper Paleolithic culture. It has even been proposed that the regional diversification of Upper Paleolithic technology was paralleled by the development of different languages, or at least of regional dialects.

In the Upper Paleolithic, burial of the dead became a regular cultural feature and was often elaborate, strongly suggesting that interment was accompanied by ceremony and ritual. Grave goods – suggesting belief in an afterlife – were often buried with the deceased and included bodily ornaments, carvings, and stone tools of various kinds. At the Russian site of Sungir, dating from about 28,000 years ago, an adult male and two children were very elaborately buried wearing clothing onto which literally thousands of mammoth-ivory beads had been sewn. [Plates 128 and 129] The

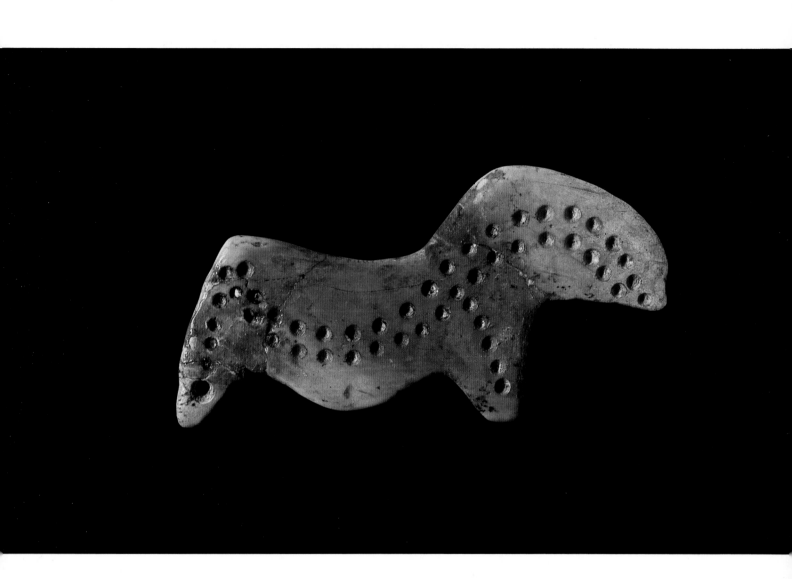

128

The "spotted horse" from Sungir, Russia.

This small pendant of colored and perforated mammoth ivory is of late Aurignacian age (about 28 thousand years ago), and shows a very early use of cut outline (10 thousand years earlier than in western Europe). The Sungir site has also produced the most elaborate Upper Paleolithic burials yet discovered.
Photograph by Randall White.

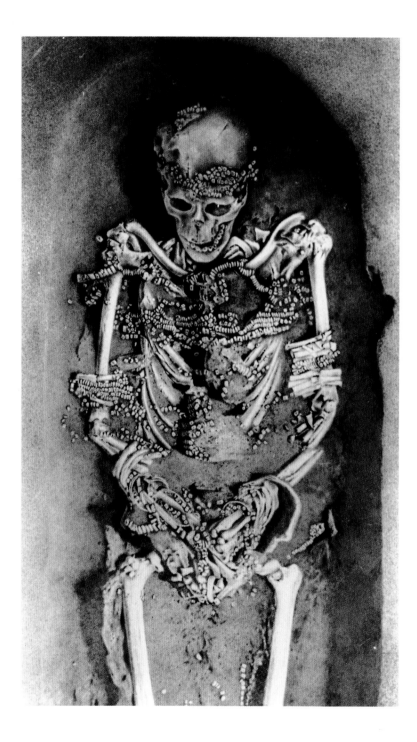

129 *left*
The male burial at Sungir, near Vladimir, Russia.

This 60-year-old individual, who lived some 28 thousand years ago, was buried in garments, presumably of leather, onto which was sewn hundreds of mammoth-tusk beads. He was also wearing mammoth-tusk bracelets and pendants and necklaces of shell and animal teeth. Two juveniles in a neighboring grave were equally richly dressed and adorned.
Courtesy Novosti/Science Photo Library.

130
Magdalenian lamp in limestone, from Gabillou, France.

In the center of this piece of limestone, which shows signs of scorching, a shallow depression was hacked or ground. In this depression a lump of animal fat burned through a vegetal (probably juniper) wick.
Photograph by Alain Roussot.

131

Cobbled shelter floor from the site of Cerisier, France.

At this Magdalenian open-air site the outlines of a hut, some 13 feet wide and 16 long, are seen in this careful arrangement of river cobbles. Such stones are absent from the surrounding area.
Photograph by Jean Gaussen.

decoration of these garments must have involved at least as many thousand hours of labor, and their wearers must have enjoyed high status in their society—which in turn hints at some division of labor. Multiple burials such as that at Sungir were not unusual, with veritable graveyards at some sites. Graves were sometimes covered with rock slabs, possibly to discourage exhumation by scavengers.

Both *Homo neanderthalensis* and *Homo sapiens* used fire. The people of the Upper Paleolithic, however, used it in much more efficient ways than ever before. They dug pits and built complex hearths—much more elaborate than any the Neanderthals had made—to contain it and clearly knew a lot about how to maximize the heat produced and how to employ that heat to best advantage. Uses for fire multiplied; water, for example, seems to have been heated by dropping hot stones into skin-lined pits. Such was the pace of innovation that it was not long before kilns were introduced, such as those built 26,000 years ago at Dolni

Věstonice in Moravia, to fire clay figurines at 800 degrees Fahrenheit. For the first time we also find lamps in which light came from burning animal fat through wicks made from juniper twigs and similar fibrous materials. [Plate 130] Along with this more sophisticated control of fire we find the remains of substantial living structures at some Upper Paleolithic sites, most commonly cobble pavements that presumably served as the foundations for shelters made from wood and animal skins. [Plate 131] These two factors together may explain how early modern people managed to colonize some of the harshest habitats of northeastern Europe, which the "cold-adapted" Neanderthals had been unable to penetrate.

Upper Paleolithic people were without a doubt skilled hunters of all kinds of game. They possessed a subtle and intimate understanding of the environments they inhabited, as well as an efficient arsenal of hunting equipment, which came to include such innovations as spear throwers and barbed harpoons, and at the very end of the last glaciation, bows and arrows. The bones of many more species of animals are found at Upper Paleolithic sites than at Neanderthal localities. Bird and fish bones, for example, start appearing at Cro-Magnon sites where before they had been virtually absent from the archaeological record. These people also appear to have exploited the migratory movements of game to the maximum possible advantage. Thus, Upper Paleolithic sites are often found close to places where migrating herds would have forded rivers. Storage of food was an extension of this strategy; for example, pits dug into the permafrost at sites in the Ukraine were natural "freezers" that allowed the storage of meat, so that it could be consumed long after the reindeer herds it came from had moved away. At such sites archaeologists have excavated the remains of large huts constructed from many tons of mammoth bones, presumably sledged in from the surrounding tundra. There was a clear organization of space at living sites, with different areas reserved for different activities. Some sites had specialized functions, however, among them the "workshops" where huge numbers of stone tools and the chips flaked off in making them have been found.

Another aspect of Upper Paleolithic living sites is their great variation in size, implying variation in the kinds and sizes of social groups. The fact that many larger Upper Paleolithic sites are found near places which would have had an abundance of seasonal resources—spawning

fish or migrating reindeer, for example—suggests that small bands may have ranged widely when resources were rarer or more scattered, coming together in seasons and at places where the resources were available to support larger groups. Social networks were not merely local, however; they were maintained over wide areas, as indicated by the frequent transport of materials over long—sometimes vast—distances. Baltic amber, for example, has been found at sites in southern Europe, and Mediterranean seashells have turned up in Ukraine. Exactly how these artifacts were transported remains obscure, but objects could not have traveled these enormous distances without a continuous trading network of some kind.

Examples such as these make the point clear: compared to any of their predecessors, the people of the Upper Paleolithic (and their equivalents elsewhere) were unprecedentedly complex, inventive, and creative, with a subtle understanding of the world around them. We don't know exactly how or why these remarkable capacities were acquired. Did the Mousterian moderns of the Levant have them latently, simply not exploiting them, or was some extraordinary neural wiring subsequently acquired, independent of outward physical change, that permitted the developments we see in the Upper Paleolithic? But although the means are unclear, the result is quite evident. The people of the Upper Paleolithic were us, and can be understood as such; the Neanderthals were not, and cannot.

132
Horse carved in mammoth ivory, from Vogelherd, Germany.

Carved about 32 thousand years ago, this tiny (less than 2 inches long) and elegant sculpture is perhaps the earliest work of art known, and was worn as a pendant. Its graceful lines express the essence of the horse, rather than literally rendering the stocky proportions of late Pleistocene horses.
Photograph by Alexander Marshack.

133

Aurignacian engraved bone plaque from Abri Blanchard, France.

Dating to about 32 thousand years ago, this incised and pitted plaque was evidently used for a symbolic purpose. The prehistorian Alexander Marshack has interpreted it as a lunar calendar.

Photograph by Alexander Marshack.

 Ice Age Art

Before we finish discussing the accomplishments of the Cro-Magnons, we should look briefly at their most remarkable attainment: their art. From the beginning, the invading moderns brought with them to Europe an aesthetic sense and achievement that rivals anything since. The earliest art, in other words, was not crude art. For example, early Aurignacian levels at the site of Vogelherd in Germany, about 32,000 years old, have produced a series of figurines of remarkable delicacy, most of them carved from mammoth ivory. The most famous of them is a tiny horse, whose flowing lines are not by any means a literal rendition of the chunky Pleistocene horses that roamed the European steppes. [Plate 132] Instead, they express the graceful essence of the horse, with a certain element of abstraction that is characteristic of art throughout the latest Ice Age. The Vogelherd horse is polished from years of use, and was possibly worn as a pendant. Other extraordinary

objects from the beginning of the Aurignacian include, from the southwestern French site of Abri Blanchard (about 32,000 years old), an engraved plaque with complex notations that have been interpreted as a lunar calendar and certainly represent a symbolic system of some kind. [Plate 133] From the Pyrenean site of Isturitz comes a bone flute of similar age, with complex sound capabilities. [Plate 134] Art, notation, music: what better evidence of a fully human sensibility?

Other art forms emerged in the succeeding Gravettian period. This ran from about 28,000 to 18,000 years ago in the west, but certain "Epigravettian" variants of this tradition lingered to the end of the Ice Age in sites from Italy to Siberia. The most famous Gravettian art forms are the remarkable female representations found at sites from western France to Siberia. [Plate 135] Some of these (usually carved or molded in three dimensions but sometimes engraved) are quite slender, but typically they show exaggerated breasts, buttocks, and bellies, lack features of the

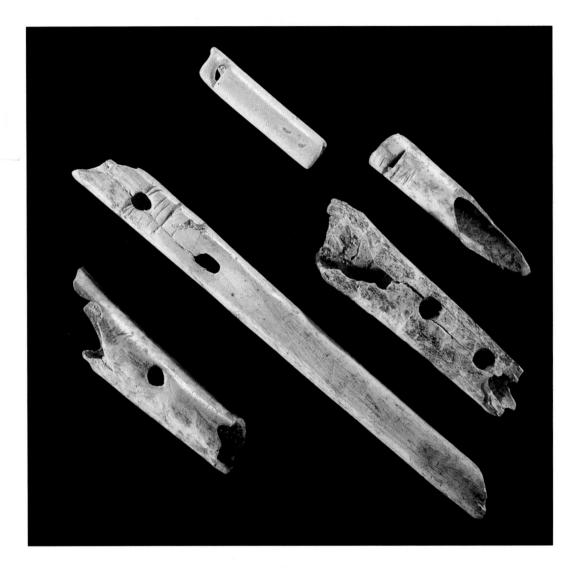

134

**Paleolithic bone flutes
and whistles.**

Musical instruments such as this
appear at the very beginning of the
Upper Paleolithic in France, at least
32 thousand years ago. They are
among the most striking indicators
of a new sensibility among the
people of the Upper Paleolithic.
The examples shown here are from
various French sites ranging in age
from Gravettian to Magdalenian.
Photograph by Alain Roussot.

135
**"Woman with Horn" from
Laussel, France.**

Sculpted and engraved on a
limestone block, and originaly
painted in red, this Gravettian figure
is typical of female representations
of the period in omitting facial
detail and the feet, while
emphasizing the breasts and
abdomen.
Photograph by Alain Roussot.

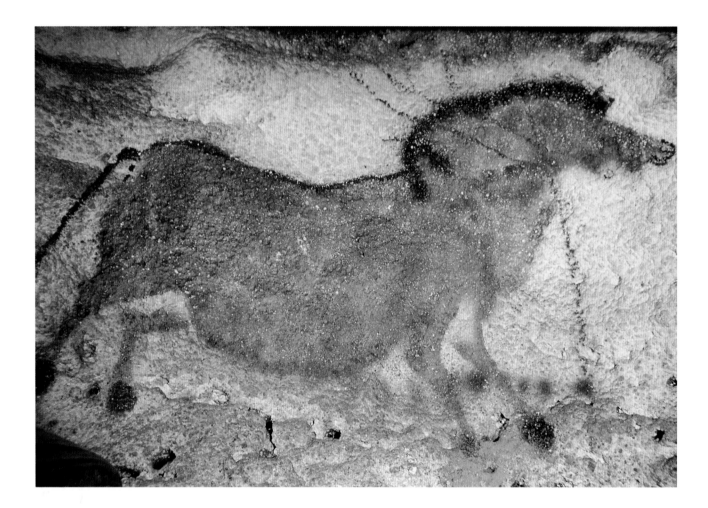

136
**The "Chinese Horse" from
Lascaux, France.**

Painted about 17 thousand years
ago, this startling image is only one
of dozens of large polychrome
paintings that cascade across the
walls of this Magdalenian cave.
Photograph by Jean Vertut.

Section of painted cave wall at Niaux, France.

The bold monochrome animal drawings in the "Salon Noir" at Niaux include some of the most powerful images in Ice Age art. Stylized yet animated, those seen here include bison and ibex.
Photograph by Jean Vertut.

face, and have relatively de-emphasized limbs. Traditionally they have been interpreted as fertility symbols, but we should bear in mind that fertility is rarely an issue among hunting-gathering people. Such people frequently move, and children are so encumbering under these circumstances that hunter-gatherer women often maximize the time between offspring by greatly prolonging breast-feeding. Only with labor-intensive settled agriculture does fecundity assume an economic importance. Technically, perhaps the most remarkable products of the Gravettian are the molded and kiln-fired human female and animal figurines from the Moravian site of Dolni Věstonice. Other Gravettian forms include deeply incised engravings of animals on large rock slabs and some wall art inside caves.

The Solutrean is a highly localized culture, which occupied the period from about 22,000 to 18,000 years ago in western France and parts of Spain. Solutrean creativity was directed most strikingly at the production of extraordinarily finely worked flint tools. However, sites of this culture have also produced boldly carved animal figures in high

relief, and some cave art can also be attributed to this period. The apogee of Ice Age art, though, was achieved during the Magdalenian (about 18,000 to 10,000 years ago), in which an astonishing profusion of everyday objects was decorated by engraving, both of realistic animal figures and of geometric symbols. The delicacy of much Magdalenian carving is truly astonishing, revealing an acute observation of nature on the part of the artist, to such an extent that it is sometimes possible to detect in which season of the year an animal is depicted. The Magdalenian produced the greatest masterpieces of cave art, including the unforgettable polychrome images of Lascaux (17,000 years old) and Font de Gaume and Altamira (15,000 years old), the extraordinary line images of Niaux (15,000 years old) and Rouffignac (13,000 years old), the astonishing clay sculptures of a pair of bison found almost a mile underground at the Tuc d'Audoubert (maybe 14,000 years old), and the newly discovered Grotte Chauvet (an astonishing 30,000 years old). [Plates 136, 137, and 138] The intricate associations in Magdalenian cave art between different

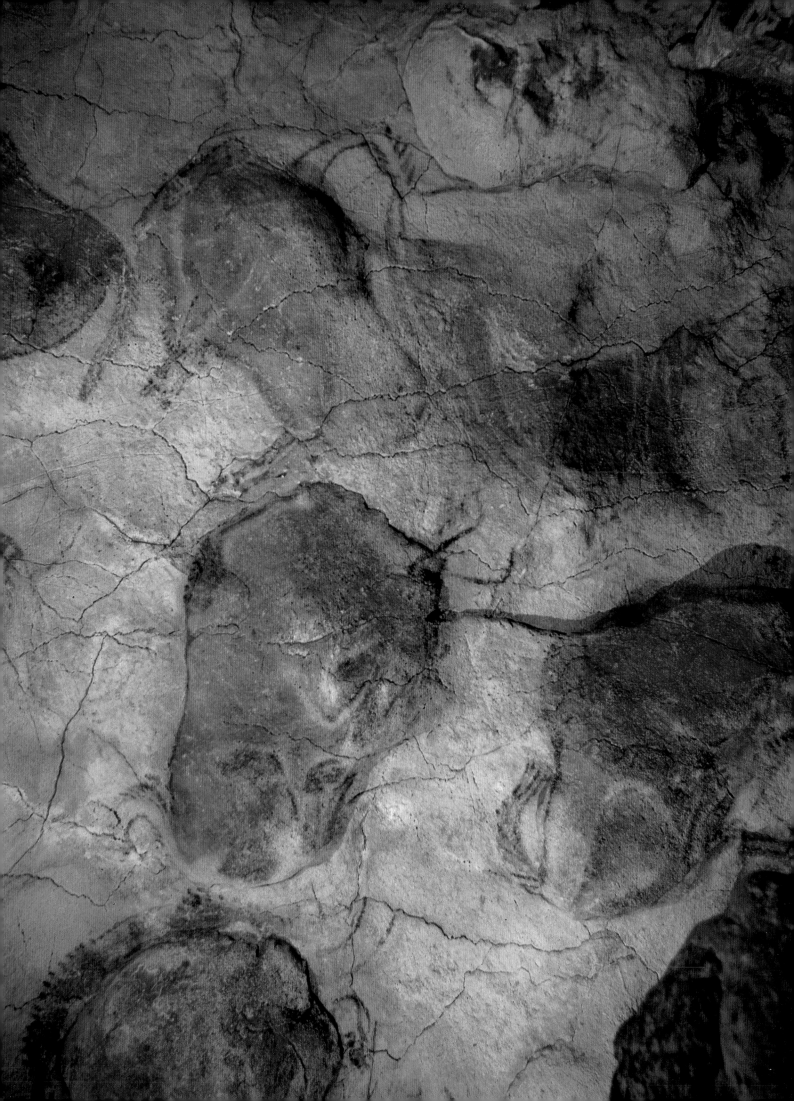

Section of painted cave ceiling at Altamira, Spain.

Created some 15 thousand years ago, a multitude of vibrant polychrome images crowds the low ceiling of a recess in the Altamira cave, the first cave art site to be discovered. Most of the images seen here are of bison.

Photograph by Jean Vertut.

animal species, and between these and apparently highly regularized sets of abstract symbols, hint at an enormously complex body of belief, story, and myth. But why Magdalenian artists should, at the cost of such discomfort and personal risk, have penetrated these dark and dangerous recesses of Earth by the light of guttering fat-burning lamps to create images to which they might never have returned remains a mystery. There's no question, though, that this phenomenon reflects a profound urge, perhaps spiritual, of the kind that any modern human can understand.

Nonetheless, this art also had an economic basis, for its execution could have been possible only in societies that were running a considerable economic surplus. At some sites, literally hundreds of engraved implements and plaques have been found, requiring, like the clothing from Sungir, many hundreds of hours to make. Magdalenian artists obviously had plenty of time on their hands, either because they were being supported by other members of their groups, or because they did not have to spend all their time in the basic business of making a living. This time was available at least partly because of the great richness of the environment in which they lived. Cave art, along with most of the sites where an abundance of carved and decorated objects have been found, is concentrated in areas of France and Spain that were particularly favored by nature. The varied and sheltered topography of these

regions was home to a wide variety of animal species, and in particular, the open steppe and tundra environment supported great herds of medium-sized and large-bodied mammals. For humans as clever as the Magdalenians, making a living in such a habitat would not have been an enormously time-consuming business.

The fact that at least in certain areas cold times were not hard times probably had a lot to do with the occurrence of this great era of Ice Age art around the climax of the last glacial period. The problems started after the climate began to warm up, after about 14,000 years ago. As the warming progressed and the ice sheets retreated, forest moved in where open steppes had been before. The great animal herds moved north, and many of the larger mammals became extinct. The Magdalenians discovered that life was much harder hunting red deer and wild boar in the forests than it had been ambushing reindeer crossing rivers in the open, and by about 10,000 years ago their materially rich way of life began to give way to the simpler cultural expressions of the "Epipaleolithic" period. Thus ended the most sophisticated development of ancient hunting and gathering lifeways yet recorded. Ironically, though, analogous environmental changes to the south and east were simultaneously spurring the innovations that led, fatefully, to the adoption of settled agriculture: the most fundamental revolution of all in human economic existence■

10

The Last Neanderthal

BY little less than 30,000 years ago the Neanderthals had disappeared from the fossil record, after a tenure of 150,000 years or more in a vast region that stretched from the Atlantic to Uzbekistan. What happened to them? They had led hard lives, certainly: virtually none of the Neanderthal fossils known is that of an individual who survived beyond the age of about forty years, and few made it past thirty-five. Degenerative joint disease was common among these people, and many Neanderthal bones show evidence of injury. Yet the Neanderthals had successfully occupied a large area of the world over a long period in which climates fluctuated wildly, and their way of life was evidently flexible enough to cope with changing environmental conditions. Their abrupt demise must thus have been due to an entirely new factor. And that factor, almost certainly, was us. I have, of course, already noted that the extinction of species has been a normal and frequent occurrence throughout biological history, and that our own emergence and evolution took place through unexceptional processes. Nonetheless, the ways in which our complex behaviors contrast with those of the Neanderthals serve to underline the fact that with the arrival of behaviorally modern *Homo sapiens* the world faced and entirely new phenomenon: one from whose impact it is still reeling, and of which the Neanderthals were among the first to bear the brunt.

We have seen that Neanderthals and *Homo sapiens* shared the Levant for an extended period, possibly about 60,000 years or even more. We don't know whether Neanderthals and moderns ever coexisted side by side in the region; the paucity of sites during this long time and the uncertainties of dating make possible arguments both pro and con. One popular idea is that Neanderthals occupied the Levant in cooler phases, during which modern humans withdrew south toward the kinder climates of Africa; when the climate warmed up, the latter moved back in and the Neanderthals retreated northward. Indirect support for this notion comes in the form of modern human body proportions, which suggest a heat-shedding habitus for *Homo sapiens*, in contrast to the heat-conserving proportions of the Neanderthals. But although the fossil record does suggest an African origin for modern humans, and the initial modern penetration of the Levant presumably came from this quarter, our body proportions could be a simple matter of heritage rather than one of specific adaptation to warm climate. This is especially so given modern humans' long-standing mastery of fire and the near certainty that clothing was available to mitigate the effects of cold climate.

What is clear, however, is that during Mousterian times, despite possible differences in economic strategies, neither Levantine group was able to outcompete the other in any definitive way. Neanderthals and moderns may have come and gone in the Levant, but both continued to exist somewhere. There is no convincing

Sclayn · 38 kyr

Geissenklösterle · 36 kyr

St-Césaire · 36 kyr

Combe Grenal · 39 kyr

El Castillo · 40 kyr

L'Arbreda · Moust. 40 kyr
U.Pal. 39 kyr

Bacho Kiro · 43 kyr

Figueira Brava · 30 kyr

Zafarraya · 27 kyr

139

Latest Neanderthal and earliest *Homo sapiens* sites in Europe.

This map of major well-dated sites shows the closeness in time of the last documented *Homo neanderthalensis*/Mousterian and earliest *Homo sapiens*/Upper Paleolithic occupants of Europe. *Illustration by Diana Salles.*

biological evidence in the region for intermixing of Neanderthal and modern morphologies—and if *Homo neanderthalensis* and *Homo sapiens* were indeed different species, as the anatomical distinctions between them so strongly suggest, they could not have interbred successfully, certainly not over the long term. The two groups thus appear to have been in some sense separate but equal during most of the latest Pleistocene. Only with the arrival of Upper Paleolithic technologies in the Levant do we see the final exit of the Neanderthals. The Upper Paleolithic was fully established in this region by about 45,000 years ago, and the latest Neanderthal date comes from Amud, about 40,000 years ago. This general coincidence in time appears to be significant, although the Levantine record is much sparser than one would like.

The record is much denser in Europe, with dozens of sites both of Neanderthals and of Cro-Magnons. And it is made that

much better by the fact that the first modern people to enter the subcontinent brought Upper Paleolithic technology with them. The Neanderthals, for their part, remained steadfastly Mousterian, with the minor exception of such short-lived "transitional" industries as the Châtelperronian. If we assign Upper Paleolithic sites lacking human fossils to *Homo sapiens*, and Mousterian ones to *Homo neanderthalensis*, the record becomes little short of excellent. We've seen that the earliest evidence of Aurignacian occupation of Europe dates to about 40,000 years ago both in the far west of Europe (in Spain) and in the east (in Bulgaria). The Mousterian declines rapidly after that time, although final dates come in quite late, about 30,000 years ago or even less. [Plate 139] *Homo sapiens* and *Homo neanderthalensis* thus overlapped in Europe for at least 10,000 years, but it's probably more significant that at individual sites the shift between

140

Excavations at l'Arbreda, Spain.

At this Spanish cave, a continuous archaeological sequence documents an abrupt change from Mousterian to Upper Paleolithic occupation between about 40 and 39 thousand years ago.

Photograph by Julià Maroto; courtesy of James Bischoff.

Mousterian and Aurignacian appears to have been abrupt. This pattern starts right at the beginning. At Spain's L'Arbreda Cave, for example, dates for the latest Mousterian industry average 40,400 years ago, and for the earliest Aurignacian 38,500 years ago. [Plate 140] These dates are part of a continuous, uninterrupted record, for the sediments yielding them are homogeneous and show no sedimentary break between levels. What's more, the artifact assemblages show no evidence of cultural intermixing.

Biologically, the evidence for intermixing isn't much better. Advocates of "Multiregional Continuity" have claimed that a few crania from Aurignacian strata in eastern Europe show some Neanderthal-like features—for example, a bit of occipital protrusion, or heavy brows. Thus, they claim, these specimens provide putative evidence of interbreeding between Neanderthals and moderns. This is, however, really no more than a fall-back position from the notion, now total-ly discredited by precise dating (among other things), that Neanderthals gave rise directly to modern Europeans. One ingenious theory supporting the idea that today's Europeans possess at least some "Neanderthal genes" has been the proposition that the "transition" from Neanderthal to modern morphology was essentially a process in which skeletal robustness was reduced. On the assumption that robustness is a function of use (as to some degree it is, especially in the postcranial skeleton), it is thus proposed that Upper Paleolithic cultural innovations reduced demands on the masticatory apparatus. This reduced need would in turn have lightened the build of the face, and such reduction, together with interbreeding among Neanderthals and moderns, would have hastened the rapid and total disappearance of Neanderthal morphology. This smacks heavily of special pleading, however. First, the argument depends on the mistaken assumption that Neanderthals and moderns are variants of the same species. Second, it assumes that at least many of the structural differences between the skulls of Neanderthals and moderns are reflections of use rather than of heritage. Given the scale and the nature of those differences, both assumptions are totally implausible.

What is certain is that there was some kind of interaction between the resident Neanderthals of Europe and the invading moderns. The nature of that interaction is particularly difficult to discern because in the absence of convincing evidence for biological hybridization, all the evidence we can bring to bear on the question is indirect. Contact, we can safely say, was not generally prolonged; the pattern of short-term replacement of the Mousterian by the Upper Paleolithic is too consistent for it to have been otherwise. But if, as by now is widely if not universally accepted, the Châtelperronian was a product of the adoption of Upper Paleolithic technologies by Mousterians, rather than an indigenous development by the latter, there must have been some cultural contact, direct or indirect, between Neanderthals and Cro-Magnons. What's more, that contact cannot have been uniquely destructive; for if it had been, the Châtelperronian would never have developed as a distinctive industry. Nonetheless, it's notable that Châtelperronian sites were much more scattered than the Mousterian ones that preceded them (only a handful are known, over a 4,000-year period), suggesting that Neanderthal populations thinned out considerably during Châtelperronian times.

Exactly what form contact between Neanderthals and Cro-Magnons took thus remains obscure. Maybe the moderns trickled slowly into the areas where the Châtelperronian developed—in which case, occasional interactions between individuals could have been sufficient to transfer some technology. On the one hand, it's quite easy to imagine this happening because the high consistency and craftsmanship of the Mousterian suggests strongly that Neanderthals learned easily by imitation. On the other hand, though, envisioning exactly how beings who differed enormously in their cognitive capacities would have communicated and interacted is difficult. Perhaps it's not too far-fetched to imagine that only the cleverest Neanderthals could have managed such contacts successfully and passed their newfound knowledge on to others. Or maybe, as my colleague Niles Eldredge suggested only half in jest, an exceptionally gifted Neanderthal stumbled upon the remains of an abandoned Cro-Magnon campsite, recognized the utility of the unfamiliar blade tools and cores lying around, and figured out how to make them. Irrespective of how the idea of making blade tools and bone ornaments was acquired, though, it's clear that its subsequent spread among the Neanderthals would have been a natural development.

Whatever the nature of those early contacts between Neanderthals and Cro-Magnons, they were clearly not enough to dislodge the former from their homeland immediately. But dislodged they eventually were. Within about 10,000 years of the first arrival of the Aurignacians in Europe, the Neanderthals were gone. Europe, of course, is a big place with many inaccessible mountain fastnesses, and it is highly improbable that a single wave of Aurignacians swept away the Neanderthals before it from east to west. [Plate 141] Indeed, the interlayering of Châtelperronian and Aurignacian levels at a couple French sites argues strongly that this was not the case. The complex local geography and the low population levels of hunting-gathering peoples would have combined to make the complete takeover of the subcontinent by *Homo sapiens* a gradual and fragmented process. To what extent the Neanderthals themselves impeded that process is not known. Did they resist the invaders

directly? Were their hunting and gathering practices efficient enough to make them effective competitors for ecological space, at least for a while? Did short-term environmental changes cause the balance to shift from one to the other for at least a few millennia? Was there, as some paleoanthropologists still think, a process of peaceful assimilation, the local Neanderthal genes eventually becoming "swamped" by those of the invaders?

We will never know for certain what happened. All we can say with assurance is that in the end, the moderns won out. It may be that despite their species difference, the Neanderthals and moderns were similar enough externally to have elicited the occasional attempt to interbreed—or perhaps more likely, the urge to ravish. It's vanishingly unlikely, however, that peaceful assimilation was an overall option, with groups of the two kinds of humans exchanging members when they met and going their separate ways, or joining forces. More likely, perhaps, if intermixing is to be considered at all, is a scenario of well-equipped and cunning *Homo sapiens* descending on Neanderthal groups, killing the males—through strategy and guile, certainly not through strength—and abducting the females. Yet it's highly improbable that viable offspring could have been produced by the resulting unions; Neanderthal females would hardly have been of much reproductive value to the invaders.

Whatever the details, in view of the ways that invading *Homo sapiens* have tended to treat resident members of their own as well as other species throughout recorded history, encounters between *Homo neanderthalensis* and *Homo sapiens* probably were not often happy ones. Today when we think of the Cro-Magnons we tend to focus on their more admirable achievements, particularly the ethereal art of such sites as Lascaux, Altamira, and Font de Gaume. Like us, however, the Cro-Magnons must have had a darker side. Their arrival in Europe heralded the extinction of a large variety of mammal species. Those that have survived until now are those that managed to adapt to this remarkable new phenomenon on the landscape. The Neanderthals, it seems, could not—which is not surprising, for it is hard to imagine two species so similar, if at the same time so different, sharing the same habitat for long. To return to the two scenarios proposed at the beginning of this book, it may be that the Last Neanderthal suffered the unhappier fate, or at least something not too unlike it.

One last cautionary note. It is the winners who write history, and this is the story of the Neanderthals written by a member of *Homo sapiens*, for an audience of *Homo sapiens*. In the evolutionary game the Neanderthals were ultimately "losers"—as, in the narrow sense of extinction, all species, like all individuals, must eventually be. But the Neanderthals were highly successful for a long time, longer certainly than we have yet been, and they occupied a unique place in nature. Evolution is not a straight-line process, each successive species bringing its lineage closer to some goal, preordained or otherwise. There are many ways of playing the evolutionary game, and the Neanderthals' strategy simply differed from ours. We may certainly look upon the Neanderthals as a mirror to reflect our own species' position among the almost infinite variety of living things, but it is profoundly misleading to see them simply as an inferior version of ourselves■

141

The Neanderthals' last redoubt?

Dating to as recently as 27 thousand years ago, the southern Spanish cave of Zafarraya (in the cliff at upper left) is—by 3,000 years—the latest known site yielding Mousterian tools, as well as Neanderthal fossils only slightly older.
Photograph by Fernando Ramirez Rozzi.

cave

Postscript

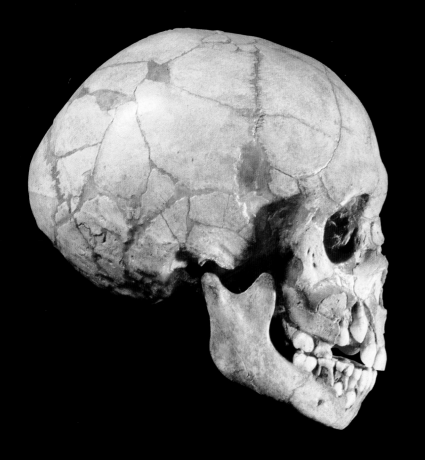

142 and 143

Adolescent cranium and cave site, Teshik–Tash, Uzbekistan.

Cranium of a nine-year old boy, discovered in 1938. [left] This youth was reportedly buried in a circle of ibex horns, although the elaborateness of his burial has been disputed. Situated high in the Bajsun-Tau mountain range south of Samarkand, Teshik-Tash is the Neanderthals' most easterly known outpost. [below] From the topmost of five Mousterian levels at the site, this skeleton is probably around 50 thousand years old, give or take a large margin of error.

Skull: Photograph by Andrei Maurer, courtesy of the Institute and Museum of Anthropology, Moscow State University.
Teshik-Tash cave: Courtesy of the Institute and Museum of Anthropology, Moscow State University.

cave

Further Reading

There is a vast literature on the Neanderthals, mostly buried in technical journals. Here I list many of the recent major books that bear on the subjects treated in this volume. Most of them contain detailed bibliographies that will serve as introductions to the rest of the primary literature.

Bahn, Paul and Jean Vertut. 1988. *Images of the Ice Age*. New York: Facts on File.

Bräuer, Günter and Fred Smith (eds.). 1992. *Continuity or Replacement: Controversies in* Homo sapiens *Evolution*. Rotterdam: A. A. Balkema.

Burenhult, Goran (ed.). 1993. *The First Humans: Human Origins and History to* 10,000 *B.C.* San Francisco: HarperCollins.

Day, Michael. 1986. *Guide to Fossil Man*. 4th edition. Chicago: University of Chicago Press.

Eldredge, Niles. 1991. *Fossils: The Evolution and Extinction of Species*. New York: Harry N. Abrams.

Eldredge, Niles. 1995. *Dominion*. New York: Henry Holt.

Gamble, Clive. 1986. *The Palaeolithic Settlement of Europe*. Cambridge: Cambridge University Press.

Gowlett, John. 1984. *Ascent to Civilization: The Archaeology of Early Man*. New York: Alfred A. Knopf.

Johanson, Donald, Lenora Johanson, and Blake Edgar. 1994. *Ancestors: In Search of Human Origins*. New York: Villard.

Klein, Richard. 1989. *The Human Career: Human Biological and Cultural Origins*. Chicago: University of Chicago Press.

Leakey, Richard and Roger Lewin. 1992. *Origins Reconsidered: In Search of What Makes Us Human*. New York: Doubleday.

Lewin, Roger. 1987. *Bones of Contention*. New York: Simon and Schuster.

Lewin, Roger. 1993. *The Origin of Modern Humans*. New York: Scientific American Library.

Mellars, Paul and Christopher Stringer. 1989. *The Human Revolution: Behavioural and Biological Perspectives on the Origins of Modern Humans*. Edinburgh: Edinburgh University Press.

Otte, Marcel (ed.). 1988. *L'Homme de Neandertal*. 8 volumes. Liège: Eraul.

Reader, John. 1988. *Missing Links: The Hunt for Earliest Man*. 2nd edition. London: Penguin Books.

Schick, Kathy and Nicholas Toth. 1993. *Making Silent Stones Speak*. New York: Simon and Schuster.

Smith, Fred and Frank Spencer. 1984. *The Origins of Modern Humans: A World Survey of the Fossil Evidence*. New York: Alan R. Liss.

Stringer, Christopher and Clive Gamble. 1993. *In Search of the Neanderthals: Solving the Puzzle of Human Origins*. London: Thames and Hudson.

Tattersall, Ian. 1993. *The Human Odyssey: Four Million Years of Human Evolution*. New York: Simon and Schuster.

Tattersall, Ian. 1995. *The Fossil Trail: How We Know What We Think We Know about Human Evolution*. New York: Oxford University Press.

Tattersall, Ian, Eric Delson, and John van Couvering (eds.). 1988. *Encyclopedia of Human Evolution and Prehistory*. New York: Garland Publishing.

Trinkaus, Erik (ed.). 1989. *The Emergence of Modern Humans: Biocultural Adaptations in the Later Pleistocene*. Cambridge: Cambridge University Press.

Trinkaus, Erik and Pat Shipman. 1992. *The Neandertals: Changing the Image of Mankind*. New York: Alfred A. Knopf.

White, Randall. 1986. *Dark Caves, Bright Visions: Life in Ice Age Europe*. New York: American Museum of Natural History/W. W. Norton.

Wymer, John. 1982. *The Palaeolithic Age*. New York: St. Martin's Press.

Olduvai Hominids *5*, *7*, *9*, 51, 52, 57, *62*, 64
Omo River 51, 177
Oppenoorth, W.F.F. 97
"Out of Africa" hypothesis 115, 174, 178
Oxygen-isotope analysis 121
　dating 120

Paleolithic 34-35, 82
　Lower 36, 83, 130
　Middle 36, 37, *71*, 83, 134, 184
　Upper *35*, 36-37, *71*, 83, 92, 106, 111, 116, 127, 153, 158, 179, 184, 199, 200
Paleontology 23, 24
Paranthropus aethiopicus 51, *71*
Paranthropus boisei 51-52, 56, 61, *71*
Paranthropus robustus 46-49, *71*
Pathology 77-78
Peking Man 24, *59*, 60, 97, 101, 104
Penck, Albrecht 83-84, 120
Petralona fossil 67, 131
Pharynx 172
Phyletic gradualism 25
Piltdown 93-94, 97, 106
Pithecanthropus 60, 86, 87, 92
Pleistocene epoch 37, 83, 120, 122
　climates of 120-123
　Late 37, 123
　Middle 37, 87
Pliocene epoch 37
Pontnewydd 84
Population thinking 23-24
Potassium-argon dating 33, 51
Predators 30
Primates, Order 18, *19*
Pubic ramus, superior 15
Punctuated equilibria 24-25

Qafzeh fossils 116, 154, 156, 157, 170, 173

Radiating-mobility 156-157
Radiocarbon dating 32-33, 111, 120
Rak, Yoel 15
Regourdou *167*
Reilingen 132
Relative dating 31
Reproductive isolation 26-27
Resources, seasonal 189
Rhodesian Man. *See* Kabwe
Riss glacial period *83*
Riss-Würm interglacial period *83*, 87, 101, 107
Ritual 167
Rivaux 84
Rock, sedimentary 31-32
Rock shelters 31
Rouffignac 195

Saccopastore fossil 139, *141*, 147, 172
　site 101, 107
Saint-Acheul 62
Saint-Césaire fossil 113, 145, *146*, 162
　site 199
Santa Luca, Albert 116, 139
Scavenging 30-31, 63, 148
Schaaffhausen, Herman 74, *76*, 77, 84, 86
Schick, Kathy 54
Schindewolf, Otto 27
Schmerling, Philippe-Charles *78*

Schoetensack, Otto 88, 92
Schulz, Adolph 111
Schwalbe, Gustav 84
Sclayn *199*
Sea level 123
Shanidar fossils 107, 108, *110*, *111*, 143, 147, 158, *164*
　site 170
Shea, John 154, 156
Sima de los Huesos. *See* Atapuerca
Simpson, George Gaylord 22-23
Single Origin hypothesis *114*
Single species hypothesis 114
Sipka 84
Skhūl fossils *103*, 113, 116, 170, 173
Smith, Grafton Elliot 93-94
Soft hammer technique 64
Solecki, Ralph 107
Solo River 101
Solutrean *35*, 37, 82, 183, 195
Specialization, anatomical and behavioral 38
Speciation 26-29
　allopatric *26*, *28*
Species 10, 20, 24, 26-29
Speech, articulate 171-173
Sphenomandibular ligament 13
Spy fossils 81, 86, 116, 143
Stasis 26, 29
Steinheim fossil *71*, 97, *99*, 116, 132, 134
　site 107
Sterkfontein site 44
　stone tools at 57
Stiner, Mary 153
Stone Age 82
　Late *35*
　Middle *35*, *175*
　New. *See* Neolithic
　Old. *See* Paleolithic
Straus, W.L. 111
Stringer, Chris 128
Subspecies 26
Sungir 184, *185*, *186*, *187*, 197
Suprainiac depression *6*, *12*
Supramastoid tuberosity *116*
Susman, Randy 41
Swanscombe fossil *71*, 97, 116, 132, *133*
　site 107
Swartkrans fossils 46, *47*, 48
　site 46, *48-49*
Symbolism, early 165-169
Synthesis, evolutionary 21-24, 106

Tabūn fossils *102*, 103, 113, 116, 143, 154, *155*, 156
　site 170
Taung 44, 46, 97
Tautavel. *See* Arago site
Tayacian *35*, 130, 139
Temporal muscles 12
Terra Amata 72
Teshik-Tash 145, 170, 205
Thermoluminescence (TL) dating 33
Thermoregulation 42-44
　hairlessness and 43
　upright posture and 43
Thomsen, C.J. 82
Tools, Acheulean 62
　mental template and 62
　Oldowan *54*

platform preparation and 63
prepared core 73
See also Mousterian, Upper Paleolithic
Trends, evolutionary 28
Trinkaus, Erik 108, 111
Tuc d'Audoubert 195
Turkana boy 60-*61*
Turkana, East 55-*56*, 60, 114
　Lake 60
　West *61*

Uranium-series (U-series) dating 34, 143

Vandermeersch, Bernard 119
Verteszöllös 132
Vézère River valley 82, 89, 159
Virchow, Rudolf 77-78, 84, 86, 92
Vogelherd *190*, 191

Wallace, Alfred Russel 18-*20*
Weidenreich, Franz 101, 104, 113-114
Wheeler, Pete 42
White, Tim 40
Wilson, Allan 115
Woodward, Arthur Smith 92-94
Worsaae, J.J.A. 82
Wright, Sewall 22
Würm glacial period *83*, 107

Zafarraya fossils 145
　site *199*, *203*
Zhoukoudian 59, 60, 101, 104
"Zinjanthropus" 51-52
Zuttiyeh fossil *142*, 143
　site *104*